OUTDOOR
ADVENTURE
GUIDES

BACKPACKING
& HIKING

By Jason Stevenson

ALPHA

Publisher Mike Sanders
Senior Acquisitions Editor Janette Lynn
Art Director/Book Designer William Thomas
Compositor Ayanna Lacey
Proofreader Monica Stone
Indexer Celia McCoy

To my father, who first took me camping.
And to my children, for whom the adventure continues.

First American Edition, 2020
Published in the United States by DK Publishing
6081 E. 82nd Street, Indianapolis, Indiana 46250

Published in the United States by Dorling Kindersley Limited

A catalog record for this book
is available from the Library of Congress.
ISBN 978-1-465-49264-7
Library of Congress Catalog Number: 2019950697

DK books are available at special discounts when purchased in bulk for sales promotions, premiums, fund-raising, or educational use. For details, contact: DK Publishing Special Markets,
1450 Broadway, Suite 801, New York, NY 10018
SpecialSales@dk.com

Printed and bound in the United States of America

All images © Dorling Kindersley Limited
For further information see: www.dkimages.com

Reprinted and updated from *The Complete Idiot's Guide® to Backpacking & Hiking*

A WORLD OF IDEAS:
SEE ALL THERE IS TO KNOW

www.dk.com

CONTENTS

PART 3 **LIVING ON THE TRAIL**   193

APPENDIXES

Introduction

Pick any hiking trail in any part of the country on a summer weekend afternoon, and you'll find people of every size, shape, age, and ability. You might spot a middle-age couple speeding along at three miles per hour, effortlessly carrying on a conversation as they clamber over logs and sprint up switchbacks. Behind them is a troop of kids, moving slowly as they search the forest floor for nature's shiniest pebbles and smoothest sticks as several fleece-wearing parents and zigzagging dogs herd them forward. And finally there might be a former athlete trying to reclaim the vigor of his younger days as he huffs and puffs to reach the top of the next hill. When he gets there, he stops and enjoys the view as he catches his breath and prepares for the next climb.

Despite their different styles, speeds, and motivations, everyone on that trail is breathing fresh air, getting great exercise, and experiencing the simple beauty of the natural world. Each of them is part of a growing community, an outdoor nation that seeks a powerful, individual release far away from the digital racket of the paved world.

If you're picking up this book, you probably want to be with those hikers on the trail. You're planning your own adventurous goals and looking to join the outdoor nation. And you easily can, because this club doesn't have any membership restrictions or requirements. (Although buying this book will help.) When you're on a trail, you can hike at your own pace—by yourself or in a group—and over any distance you choose. You can camp in a tent, in a cabin, or snug inside an RV or trailer. You can drive to your local conservancy or fly across the country to visit one of America's breathtaking national parks. You often hear the phrase, "It's so easy that your grandmother could do it," to describe something simple to accomplish. Well, lots of grandmothers are avid hikers and active members of the outdoor nation. If they can do it, then so can you.

The key to getting off the couch is to discover what motivates you to get outside and then indulge it. Are you looking for a fresh and more exciting way to exercise? Do you want your kids to grow up with the same appreciation for nature and wide-open spaces you did? Do you love to hear the crunch of leaves and pine needles under your boots? Are you looking to get in better shape without joining another gym? The possibilities of what you can find outside are as endless as what you might be searching for. And when you're out there, surrounded by nature, you'll discover that abstract distractions like office politics and undone chores evaporate as you focus on the nitty-gritty of your physical needs. How can I light this fire? Will this rock support my weight? Where is the easiest place to cross this stream?

The first step is always the hardest. Far more people imagine themselves hiking and camping than those who actually kick up dust along a trail. This book will get you over the initial planning and logistical bumps, but it's going to take something more—something that develops inside of you—to make it to the top of a peak or the end of a trail.

If you really want to hike and camp more, the real question you need to ask yourself is this: When Saturday afternoon rolls around, where do you want to be?

I hope you'll be on a trail. And if you meet me there, I'll be the one huffing and puffing.

How This Book Is Organized
The outdoor skills crammed into this book are divided into four parts, which are grouped by common themes. That way, if you've got a pressing need in one of these areas, you'll know exactly where to flip to:

Part 1, The Great Outdoors at Your Feet, puts you on the right path with a progression of skills that starts with day-hiking, proceeds to overnight camping, and concludes with backpacking. You'll learn how to boost your fitness level, where to find local trails and hiking partners, and how to navigate and keep from becoming lost.

Part 2, Gearing Up, will be your how-to manual on buying and using essential camping and hiking equipment like footwear, rain jackets, and backpacks. Plus, I explain how to navigate a gear shop, where to find reliable product reviews, and how you can save money with smart shopping.

Part 3, Living on the Trail, covers all your basic needs for food, shelter, and water, including how to plan and cook meals, which tent to buy, and how filtering water makes it safe to drink. And because hiking and camping can be a messy business, I'll explain how you can stay as clean as possible.

Part 4, Surviving the Outdoors, delivers realistic advice on how to respond when problems arise. Find out what to do if you get lost, sprain an ankle, or stumble upon a black bear. And when trails get steeper and tougher, you'll learn how to scramble out of danger, as well as how to boost the adventure level of your hikes.

Extras

There's an old saying that intelligence tells you that it's going to rain, but wisdom reminds you to carry an umbrella. It teaches that just because you recognize a fact doesn't mean you know how to react to it. This book is designed to boost both your intelligence *and* wisdom about backpacking and hiking. To make the advice more practical, I've sprinkled two types of sidebars through every chapter to call your attention to particular points that will boost your trail smarts.

Trail Tips Knowing dozens of shortcuts separates the hiking pros from the amateurs. These expert-tested strategies will give you a jump-start on learning them.

Safety Check Save time or prevent a serious injury by paying attention to these important health and danger warnings.

Acknowledgements

First I'd like to thank my perceptive editors at Penguin Random House/Alpha Books, Brandon Buechley, Janette Lynn, and Rick Kughen for their patient and sharp-eyed handling of this new edition made much better by their skillful efforts.

I appreciate the assistance of Nathan Gehlert and Shannon Davis, two long-time friends and fellow outdoor enthusiasts, whose trail-tested advice and suggestions underlie many of the updates in this edition.

I'm indebted to the outdoor community that has encouraged and taught me to love hiking and camping, from my Boy Scout days in Ohio with Troop #333, to memorable treks in the White Mountains with the Appalachian Mountain Club, to the long roster of writers and editors at *Outside* and *Backpacker* magazines who shaped my passion into a career.

To my parents, Jim and Steffi, who shouldered more than their burden by shuttling my brother and me to countless troop meetings, campouts, and summer camps while encouraging us to always leave things better than we found them.

Lastly, my wife Jackie was my entire world when I wrote the first edition of this book. Since then, we have grown our family to include two boys, Calvin and Mitchell, two dogs, and added the spectacular backcountry of our new home in Utah to explore. She knows the real stories behind much of the advice described in this book. Yet, she still says, "Sure, let's go, but remember to bring the right map this time," whenever I propose a new hike. I'm thankful for her support, and look forward to many more exciting seasons of outdoor adventure.

Trademarks

PART 1

THE GREAT OUTDOORS AT YOUR FEET

Whether you spent some of your childhood weekends hiking and camping or you're just getting into the game now—a great adventure awaits you. Exploring the outdoors is a lifelong affair that can begin whenever you feel the urge. These initial six chapters will provide the foundation to get you started. First, we'll answer the crucial questions: What gear do I need? Where should I go? Who can I hike with? Soon, you'll not only know the basics, but you'll also have the tools to teach yourself new skills and raise your hiking goals to the next level.

CHAPTER 1

GET STARTED: TRIP PLANNING AND DAY-HIKING

Okay, it's settled. You're ready to hike! An afternoon of crisp, fresh air and incredible views awaits you. Quickly now, grab a pack, load your car, and head out the door. You're bound for the wide-open trail.

But wait a second.

You've forgotten to ask yourself a few critical questions. Where are you going? How long will you be gone? And most importantly—why are you going? I know you want to jump in your car and drive off to experience the wonders of nature. But like any new pursuit, there are a couple of details worth considering first.

Day-Hiking vs. Backpacking

Before you lace up your hiking shoes, you need to know the distinction between *day-hiking* and *backpacking*—two terms you'll see a lot in this book. Both terms refer to related, but slightly different, approaches to hiking.

A day-hike is exactly what it sounds like—a walk that you start and finish within a single day without staying overnight along the trail. Instead of sleeping in a tent, you'll spend the night in your own bed, at a motel, or at a previously established campsite. As a result, day-hikers don't need to carry a tent or a sleeping bag to set up camp. The length of a day-hike can vary widely: from 3 easy miles on a Saturday afternoon to a tough 20-mile dawn-to-dusk trek.

A backpacking trip lasts longer than one day and requires shouldering a larger pack and camping out overnight—or for several nights—in a tent, cabin, or lean-to shelter. Unlike day-hikers, backpackers carry tents, sleeping bags, and all the gear they need to cook meals, sleep outside, and get up the next morning to hike again. Backpacking trips can involve a single overnight or continue for many days and even weeks. The distinctive characteristic of backpacking—and what makes the activity so attractive to many participants—is that backpackers are entirely self-sufficient. They carry everything they need to survive in the outdoors.

New hikers should start with day-hikes first. These shorter adventures give you a chance to test your gear, learn from other hikers, and put some miles on your legs and gear. Just like you shouldn't take a brand-new car on a 5,000-mile road trip, you shouldn't attempt a 50-mile hike the first time you venture into the woods.

As you gain more experience on day-hikes, you can add overnight camping and backpacking to your outdoor skill set. Not everyone needs to follow this sequence, but you'll probably enjoy each trip more if you don't push yourself too fast. Overnight camping and backpacking not only require new skills, but they also require special equipment that enable you to support yourself on the trail. Day-hiking, on the other hand, requires only a sturdy pair of boots or trail shoes, a small backpack, water bottles, snacks, and some basic navigation and survival gear.

Where to Go

It's late on Thursday afternoon and the weekend is fast approaching. You want to plan a day-hike, but you don't know where to go. The main factor you'll want to consider is time. Not only should you determine how much time you have for a hike, but you also should decide how long you want to travel to reach a *trailhead* where you can begin your hike. A trailhead is a starting point for a trail and is usually located near a road, campground, or parking lot. Most trailheads have specific names and provide informational signs and maps. Some require hikers to register or pay parking fees. Obviously, the longer you spend driving in a car, the less time you'll have to hike. That's why it's best to begin with hikes closer to home.

Hikes Near You

Chances are the nearest walking path to your front door isn't very adventurous. It might be a sidewalk or cinder track populated by dog-walkers and parents pushing strollers—not exactly an escape from civilization. But once you start looking for better trails, you'll be surprised at how many there are, even if you live in a place not known for outdoor amenities. There are literally hundreds of potential trails within a few hours' drive of any city or town in the United States. Consider these local trails your home base—the routes where you can recharge, get exercise, or break in new gear.

Most of these nearby trails are in parks and recreational areas like these locations:

◊ City, county, and state parks

◊ Rail-trails and river walks

◊ Wildlife refuges and conservation areas

◊ Lakeshores and seashores

◊ National forests and Bureau of Land Management areas

◊ National parks or national monuments

Your hometown might not have all these hiking trail hotspots within close driving distance, but there should be a few.

Finding Local Trails

The fastest and easiest way to find local places to hike is to type "trail" into your smartphone's map app. This quick approach avoids the extra steps of downloading apps or signing into the websites we'll discuss next. Because the map's initial results will likely include city parks, zoom out to scan for nonurban hiking options. Some trails will have online reviews and detailed information, while others might just be a pin on your phone's map.

Look for search results located in the green-shaded areas on the map (recreation areas), and write down the names of trails or trailheads that appeal to you. Now you have a list of potential trails to research on the web, in guidebooks, or by seeking expert advice.

You can also ask for hiking suggestions from people in your area who know this information as part of their jobs or hobbies. Often, the best local trails are discovered by word-of-mouth tips, including some little-known routes that never show up in online search results or guidebooks.

Knowing the names of local recreation areas ahead of time— either by searching online or using a local map or road atlas— will help you focus your questions about trails. For example, asking someone, "Where can I go hiking in Pisgah National Forest?" will get you better results than a general question like, "Where can I go hiking in North Carolina?" If you want in-person trail advice, seek out the following sources:

◊ City or county parks and recreation departments

◊ Park rangers and guides

◊ Staff at local outdoor gear and apparel shops

◊ Your public library

◊ Local hiking our outing clubs

If you want to devote more time and resources to finding local trails, check out websites and apps that list trails close to your city or zip code. The entry for each trail often includes useful information about mileage, terrain, elevation profiles, reviews, and even coordinates to download as a route to your GPS device or smartphone.

 Trail Tips Modern smartphones contain GPS chips that can pinpoint your location even when you're outside cell phone coverage. This means your smartphone can mimic a GPS device—especially if you download navigation apps like Gaia GPS, AllTrails, or ViewRanger that let you track your route on detailed topo maps you download before a hike.

*GPS-based apps can deliver accurate
backcountry maps and trail details straight
to your smartphone.*

Many websites and apps employ an easy-to-use Google Maps–
based search tool that enables you to zoom in on a map to locate
the trail and scan the surrounding landscape. The websites in
the following table offer a national database of hiking trails
that is frequently updated and expanded, along with the ability
to sync hikes to user-friendly smartphone apps. Note that some
apps require paid subscriptions to download trail maps for
offline usage—like when you're on the trail.

Find a Local Trail Online	App	Find Trails	Download Offline Maps	Trail Reviews
backpacker. com/trips (*Backpacker* magazine)	ViewRanger	Free	Yes	No
alltrails.com	AllTrails	Free	Subscription	Yes
hikingproject. com	Hiking Project	Free	Yes	Yes
gaiagps.com	Gaia GPS	Free	Subscription	Yes

If you prefer a more hands-on approach to finding local hiking trails, you can purchase a local guidebook. Check your local library or bookstore for a guide focused on your area. You might find an independent work produced by a local hiker or club, or you might find a book that is part of a national series. Three of the most popular hiking series are *50 Hikes,* published by Countryman Press; *Hiking Guides*, published by Falcon Guides; and *100 Classic Hikes,* published by Mountaineers Books (see Resources). All three of these publishers hire writers who are local experts in the states and regions they cover. Most guidebooks will indicate trailheads, provide maps of the routes, and include a narrative description of the trails' highlights and challenges, giving you the chance to preview a hike before venturing out the door.

Another popular route-planning option is the *Trails Illustrated* map series from National Geographic. You can find detailed trail maps for most national parks and popular recreation areas in every state. (Utah alone has 32 maps.) But keep in mind that these maps don't provide important details such as mileage, elevation gain, or difficulty level that you can learn from a trail guide.

 Safety Check If information about a trail in a guidebook or on a website is more than 3 years old, check the internet or contact the local park or agency to find out if any details have changed.

Destination Day-Hikes

Occasionally, you might want to hike a trail farther from home. You might be traveling for business, visiting friends in another state, or on vacation.

First, you'll need to find out where the trails are located. You can use the same websites and apps I mentioned previously, except you probably won't be as familiar with the area. If you're hiking in a new place, pay special attention to trail descriptions and reviews for important details on parking, water access, and weather, such as if afternoon thunderstorms are a daily occurrence during the summer.

National parks are often a major attraction if you're visiting from out of town. If you think that national park trails are only reserved for burly backpackers, you're wrong. Park staff and planners create recreational opportunities to appeal to all types of visitors—including day-hikers. You can find detailed information on all 419 national park properties using the search map at the National Park Service's website, nps.gov/findapark. All national park websites have suggested trails and itineraries for day-hikers under the "Things to Do" menu.

Second, you'll need to figure out how to reach the trailhead. This is easy if you have access to a car, but if you're dependent on public transportation, don't give up! Lots of major cities—including New York, Boston, and San Francisco—have many trails that you can access by bus, shuttle, train, or tram. You'll need to check a guidebook or call the rangers at the specific park to find out if and how you can get to a trailhead by public transport—but it's definitely doable.

Here are eight major cities that feature easy access to nearby trails—and where those trails are located:

◊ **Boston, MA** Harbor Islands National Recreation Area, Cape Cod National Seashore

◊ **Washington, D.C.** Creek Park, C&O Canal National Historical Park

◊ **Denver, CO** Red Rocks, White Ranch Park

◊ **Phoenix, AZ** Phoenix Mountains Preserve

- ◊ **Las Vegas, NV** Red Rock Canyon National Conservation Area, Zion National Park (UT)
- ◊ **Seattle, WA** Olympic National Park
- ◊ **Salt Lake City, UT** City Creek Canyon, Big Cottonwood Canyon, Little Cottonwood Canyon
- ◊ **San Francisco/Oakland, CA** Lands End, Marin Headlands, Redwood Regional Park, San Francisco Bay Trail

Despite the extra preparation involved, you should take advantage of any opportunity to hike in a new place—especially if the terrain, wildlife, and climate are completely different from what you normally experience.

Types of Trails

Most parks and recreation areas contain networks of trails that intersect and overlap with each other. While these trail systems can make maps confusing, they also give hikers more flexibility when planning hikes. For instance, you can combine several short trails into a longer route. Trails often are distinguished by periodic *blazes,* which are paint stripes or buttons placed on tree trunks or posts several hundred feet apart. These blazes can help you tell the trails apart and alert you when you've started hiking on a new trail. Each trail is identified by a unique blaze to help hikers stay on the correct route.

Out-and-Backs vs. Loop Trails

There are two main types of trails: out-and-backs and loops. Loop trails circle back to their original starting point, while out-and-back trails require hikers to walk the same ground twice. This repetition is why out-and-back routes are considered to be less-attractive options than loop hikes. However, out-and-back trails are occasionally the only way to reach a scenic view, a waterfall, or a mountain summit. Sometimes, you can link several out-and-back trails to create a loop and return by a different trail to your starting point. When calculating the distance of an out-and-back trail, remember to double the mileage because you'll need to hike the return leg, too.

Safety Check Wrong turns are the number one cause of lost hikers. Because faster and slower hikers in groups tend to separate along the trail, always stop and wait at a trail junction for the entire group to arrive before continuing.

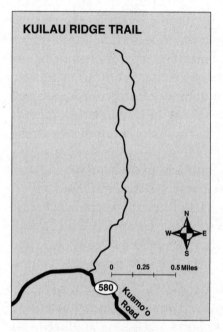

An out-and-back trail requires you to cover the same ground twice.

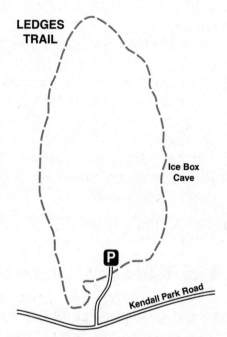

A loop trail returns you to your starting point.

Flat Terrain vs. Elevation Gain

Besides the number of miles, a trail's difficulty is determined by how much it goes up and down in elevation. Some trails can be flat, while others can climb and descend hundreds of vertical feet over the course of several miles. The steepest trail sections often require hikers to use their hands and feet to scramble up ledges or over boulders.

Because it takes longer to hike uphill, add an extra hour to your total hike time for each 1,000-foot gain in elevation on a trail. And while going downhill is less tiring than going up, it can be just as time-consuming for many hikers because of uncertain footing.

Trails that climb hills and mountains are designed with *switchbacks* to reduce the overall gradient. Switchbacks are zigzagging paths that reduce the slope of steep trails to make them easier to climb. Never cut across switchbacks to save time. Ignoring switchbacks accelerates slope erosion and encourages other hikers to do the same, causing more damage to the trail. You should always check to see how much elevation a trail gains and loses. It's also much harder to climb at higher elevations—especially above 6,000 feet—where the oxygen content of the air is noticeably lower. Despite the challenge, gaining elevation on a steep trail brings rewards like scenic views, exotic wildlife, and mountain summits. Most trails gain and lose a couple hundred feet, but the elevation gain over the 2,178-mile Appalachian Trail, which goes from Springer Mountain in Georgia to Katahdin in Maine, is 510,000 vertical feet—the equivalent of climbing the stairs of the Empire State Building every day for 16 months!

Pick a Goal

Escaping the civilized world is as good as an excuse as any to go hiking. You won't find annoying coworkers, sky-high utility bills, or shrill infomercials on the trail. However, you should also consider what you want to discover, not just what you want to avoid. Focusing on specific goals will guide your planning and give you the motivation to embark on an afternoon of hiking. Here are hints on where and how to experience nature's major attractions.

If you just want to get some fresh air …

◊ Go just about anywhere you won't find cars, trucks, or lawn mowers.
◊ Find a ridgeline trail to catch cooling breezes.
◊ Hike just after a rainstorm.

If you want to watch the wildlife …

◊ Linger near lakes and rivers where animals seek water, and go at dawn or dusk when they are most active.

◊ Stake out the edges of meadows and clearings where animals become visible.

◊ Hike in the fall to see animals competing for mates and in the spring to spot newborns.

If your primary goal is fitness ...

◊ Seek out trails with significant elevation changes.

◊ Pack a pedometer or download a fitness app to record your speed in miles per hour.

◊ Load your pack with extra weight to burn more calories.

◊ Use trekking poles to exercise your arms.

If you want to take photos ...

◊ Shoot at dusk and dawn when low-angled light enhances colors and contrast.

◊ Look for unique shots like reflections on lakes and tree silhouettes.

◊ Move around—don't just stand there—to get a different perspective.

If you want to be near the water ...

◊ Plan a fall or winter hike to a hot spring.

◊ Finish a summer hike at a lake, waterfall, or swimming hole.

◊ Find a trail that follows the bank of a river or stream.

If you want to enjoy a scenic view ...

◊ Seek out bald peaks with fire towers and other prominent lookout points.

◊ Hike exposed ridgelines and check out the summits of hills and mountains.

◊ Plan fall foliage hikes when the colors are most brilliant.

◊ Hike in the late fall or early spring when bare trees allow expansive views.

Hiking for All Seasons

Unlike tennis or baseball, day-hiking is an outdoor activity you can enjoy throughout the year. The trails are always there, even during the winter when snow covers the ground. Plus, hiking the same trail in different seasons can make it seem like a completely new place. While the summer months are most popular for hiking, you should remember that hiking can be enjoyed all 12 months of the year. Here are some of the advantages to every season.

In the spring ...

◊ The landscape turns vibrantly green.

◊ You may spot newborn animals.

◊ The days are warm, and the nights lack humidity.

◊ There are fewer bugs.

◊ There is abundant drinking water. (See Chapter 14 for techniques for making water sources safe to drink.)

In the summer ...

◊ Wildlife is at its most active.

◊ The nights are warmest.

◊ The days are the longest of the year.

◊ Wildflowers bloom.

In the fall ...

◊ There are fewer bugs.

◊ The days and nights are cooler.

◊ You can enjoy changing fall foliage.

◊ There is increased animal activity because of migrations and mating.

◊ The trails are less crowded.

In the winter ...

◊ There are no bugs.

◊ The days and nights are chilly (less sweating!).

◊ There are fewer crowds.

◊ It's easier to spot animal tracks in snow.

◊ There is increased visibility.

◊ You can travel by ski or snowshoe.

Preparing for Bad Weather and Other Challenges

Because no one can control the weather, the best we can do is prepare ourselves for whatever nature flings at us. For hikers, that means checking the weather forecast and bringing the right clothes and equipment. One advantage of day-hikes is that you can easily reschedule your trip around bad weather. But if you can't dodge rain or cold temperatures, keep these tips in mind to stay dry and warm in all conditions:

◊ Pack a waterproof jacket—not an umbrella—if there's even a slight chance of rain (see Chapter 10 for more clothing tips on how to stay dry).

◊ Add clothing layers before you feel chilled, and remove extra layers as soon as you begin to sweat.

◊ Automatically put on more layers to stay warm when you stop for rest breaks.

◊ Wear a hat with a brim to keep rain out of your face.

◊ Protect electronic gear like cell phones, GPS devices, and car keys from getting wet by placing them in plastic bags.

 Trail Tips If bad weather or some other unforeseen disaster threatens to ruin your trip, look on the bright side—at least it will be a memorable hike!

Avoiding Crowds

Besides the weather, the most significant change between the seasons is the number of people you are likely to see on the trail. The most popular months to go hiking are June, July, and August. The least popular months are January and February. Crowding can become a problem, especially if solitude is one of your goals. On Fourth of July weekend, some popular trails can resemble a Los Angeles freeway at rush hour. Here are some tips on how to avoid the crowds:

◊ Hike in the middle of the week and during the fall, winter, or spring.

◊ Find trailheads that are located away from main roads or parking lots.

◊ Hike backward by starting at the traditional ending of a trail.

◊ Ask park rangers which trails receive the least traffic.

Avoiding Bugs

The most unpopular companion on any hike is a swarm of vicious mosquitoes or black flies. Unfortunately, these biters prefer the same isolated backcountry areas frequented by hikers—especially those near water. Black flies lay eggs in cold running water, while mosquitoes do the same in warm, stagnant ponds. Water, in fact, is crucial to their survival. While the best defense against biting bugs is a DEET-based repellent (see Chapter 7), here are several tips to help you plan hikes when bugs are less active:

◊ Bug populations generally peak from late May to June but can vary by species and region.

◊ Black flies are most active in the morning, while mosquitoes swarm at dusk.

◊ Most bugs prefer shade and avoid direct sunlight.

◊ When winds exceed 5 mph, most small bugs can't maintain controlled flight.

◊ Mosquitoes are attracted to fragrances, so use unscented deodorant and hair products or forget them altogether.

◊ Mosquitoes become less active when temperatures drop below 60°F.

SUMMARY

By now, you've learned that day-hiking is the first step to more outdoor adventure, including backpacking. Start hiking on local trails, which you can find using apps on your smartphone, or via guidebooks, maps, and advice from local experts. No matter where you live or play, there are always hiking trails nearby, and good reasons to go hiking in every season of the year.

CHAPTER 2

HIKING FOR ALL AGES AND TYPES

Hiking is a lifelong activity. Even if you were 10 years old the last time you stepped on a trail, you can always return to the woods. At every stage of your life, you can still seek and find different challenges. Your hikes as a fearless teenager will differ from trips you take with your own kids, and neither can compare to the hiking you'll do as an active senior citizen. Here's how to make hiking a part of your life no matter what your age or situation.

Solo Hiking

Hiking can be a social activity, but there's nothing wrong with going for a walk as a party of one. Hiking solo enables you to move at your own pace, take rest breaks when you choose, and alter your route on a whim. It also enables you to experience long stretches of silence and self-reflection that are rare luxuries in our modern world.

The downsides of solo hiking include the lack of conversation, no one to share an amazing view with, and no one to send for help if you get injured—not to mention the challenge of balancing your phone on a rock to take a selfie. For people who seek or enjoy solitude, the alone time won't be a concern, but every hiker should stay safe on solo hikes by following these tips:

◊ Share your hike route and itinerary with a trusted friend or family member.

◊ Estimate the time you expect to be off the trail—add an hour or two—and promise to call your contact by then.

◊ Carry a whistle, mirror, or other signaling device and a cell phone.

◊ Bring a map of the trail and the surrounding area, plus a compass.

◊ Carry enough food and water to last the entire hike—plus a little extra.

◊ Hike cautiously, especially when navigating river crossings and steep trails.

Social Hiking

Let's say you've tried solo hiking and now you want to share the experience with someone else. Good news: going for a walk in the woods is a great way to get to know other people. In fact, *eharmony.com* magazine ranks hiking as a top activity for a first date. That's because hiking creates the opportunity for long conversations, sharing stories, and exercise—and it's cheaper than a dinner at a fancy restaurant. And if the conversation lags, the scenery can fill in the gaps. You can learn how the other person handles adversity and whether he or she shares your interests in the outdoors and physical activity. To get started, you can arrange a hike as a one-on-one date or join a larger group of outdoor enthusiasts. Either way, you're bound to meet some interesting and like-minded people.

Hiking as a Date

To find someone to go hiking with, check out local clubs that organize activities, hold events, and can introduce you to a larger social network. Search for local groups on the internet by typing "social hiking" or "singles hiking" followed by the name of your city or region. Focus on groups that feature large membership rosters and active event calendars. For example, Meetup.com is a popular website with hundreds of city and regional hiking groups in every state.

There are also several national online dating websites and apps devoted to people who enjoy the outdoors—think of them as Match.com for the outdoors crowd. While these websites are nationally based, they might have chapters or members in your area.

Hiking Clubs for Singles

Group Name	Website
Fitness Singles	fitness-singles.com
HikerSingles	hikersingles.com
GoSporty	gosporty.com
OutdoorDuo	outdoorduo.com

If you decide to ask someone to go for a hike with you, be sure to follow this advice to make sure the event goes as smoothly as possible:

◊ Pick a trail that is nearby and fairly popular so you won't be the only ones there.

◊ Make it an easy day-hike, not a forced march up a mountain; discuss the mileage and difficulty level beforehand.

◊ Download or bring maps. Getting lost doesn't make a good first impression.

◊ When choosing between looking good and being comfortable, opt for comfort. You'll look better if you're comfortable.

◊ Keep the pace slow enough to maintain a steady conversation. That's the point of the hike anyway, right?

◊ Pick a spot for lunch and bring something special to eat. (See Chapter 13 for ideas.)

◊ Plan to stop for post-hike refreshment once you get off the trail. You've probably earned an ice cream cone.

Joining a Hiking Group

Maybe you're not looking for a date; maybe you're just looking for someone—or a group of people—to join you on a hike. You're in luck! Lots of people enjoy hiking but don't want it to be a solo experience. If you organize a weekend day-hike, you shouldn't have trouble attracting friends to join you. You could also join a local hiking club and participate in its regular activities.

Joining a Hiking Club

Back in 2003, I lived in Boston, Massachusetts, without a car, and I still went backpacking every month in New Hampshire's White Mountain National Forest—150 miles to the north. How did I do it? It was easy. I carpooled with members of the Boston chapter of the Appalachian Mountain Club (AMC)—an outdoor recreation and conservation organization with chapters throughout the Northeast. Not only did the AMC provide me with a ride to the trailhead, but it also introduced me to a half-dozen interesting people with whom I could share the hike.

The AMC is an example of regional hiking clubs that exist all over the United States and in other countries. These clubs organize hikes and other activities, loan equipment, and train leaders. Often there is a small annual fee to become a member, which enables you to register for trips. Here's a list of the largest regional hiking clubs in the country and where they are based.

Regional Hiking Associations

Name/Region	Website
Adirondack Mountain Club, New York	adk.org
Appalachian Mountain Club, New England, Mid-Atlantic	outdoors.org
Colorado Mountain Club, Colorado	cmc.org
Florida Trail Association, Florida	floridatrail.org
Green Mountain Club, Vermont	greenmountainclub.org
The Mountaineers, Pacific Northwest	mountaineers.org

Name/Region	Website
NY-NJ Trail Conference, New York and New Jersey	nynjtc.org
Potomac Appalachian Trail Club, Virginia	patc.net
Sierra Club, National	sierraclub.org
Wasatch Mountain Club, Utah	wasatchmountainclub.org

If you don't see your state or region on the list above, you can search for hiking clubs in your state by checking the comprehensive list maintained by the Hiking Project at hikingproject.com/directory/clubs, or you can look for local hiking groups on meetup.com.

Hiking in Groups

Whether you are an organizer, a participant, or just roped into going along, you shouldn't pass up a chance to hit a trail with family members, friends, coworkers, or one of the groups described previously. Not only do you get to spend time together, but you get to share experiences and get some exercise, too.

Hiking in groups, however, presents different challenges than hiking alone or as a couple. First, groups tend to hike much slower than individuals. Even if a group spreads out along the trail—which always happens—you'll still only be as fast as your slowest member. Plus, rest breaks for groups are always longer. To account for this natural slowdown, add an extra 10 minutes for every mile when calculating the time needed to complete the hike. If one member of a group is consistently slower than the rest, help them out by distributing some of the gear in his or her pack to faster hikers.

Second, a member of a group will occasionally succumb to *summit fever* without considering the risks to their safety or the well-being of the group. Summit fever is a hiking term that refers to someone who selfishly focuses on a goal—like climbing to the summit of a mountain in bad weather or diminishing daylight, despite serious risks to themselves and others. This person might want to continue the hike even when everyone else thinks it's time to turn around. The group leader should be on guard to prevent one person's summit fever from endangering the rest.

Third, most national parks restrict the size of groups to between eight and ten hikers to reduce trail erosion, congestion, and noise. If you have a large group, check with park rangers for size limits before you show up at the trailhead to hike. Groups of hikers should also follow these rules to stay together and safe on the trail:

◊ Every group of more than three hikers should designate a leader to make decisions and resolve disputes.

◊ Because slower and faster hikers tend to separate, you should stop and wait for the entire group to catch up at all trail junctions, turns, or confusing sections.

 Safety Check Splitting up a group—either accidentally or intentionally—is a major factor in hikers becoming lost. Make every attempt to stay together; however, if you do divide up, make sure each group includes experienced hikers and a map of the trail.

◊ Designate an experienced hiker as a sweeper—the last hiker in the group—to keep any slower hikers from falling too far behind.

◊ Give every participant a copy of the trail map in case someone gets separated.

◊ Agree on a rally point—like the trailhead parking lot—in case anyone gets lost.

Hiking as a Couple: Pleasures and Pitfalls

Picture this scene: You're miles from civilization, enjoying a sunny day on the trail, and walking beside you is the love of your life. Couples of all ages can enjoy hiking as a chance to spend uninterrupted time together. Friction, however, is never far from the surface. I'm not referring to the friction that causes blisters, but rather the disagreements and tension that can lead to arguments along the trail. To make sure the honeymoon lasts beyond the first mile, here's how to avoid tripping up as a couple:

◊ Before the hike, use a gear list to plan ahead and address common problems like blisters, rain, sunburn, bugs, pack weight, and fatigue. (See Equipment Checklists.)

◊ Ensure that both of you have the proper water bottles, socks, and footwear to enjoy the hike.

◊ If only one person carries the map or GPS-enabled device, both should consult it when making decisions about navigation and route changes.

◊ Navigate difficult terrain like river crossings and ledges together. The more experienced hiker shouldn't rush ahead.

◊ When camping, divide up chores, such as cooking and setting up the tent.

◊ Recognize that things that are easy for you might be more difficult for your partner—and vice versa.

◊ Adjust your goals if you can't complete the entire hike as planned. The most important goal is to spend time together.

Hiking with Children

Just because you have kids—or plan to have them—doesn't mean your hiking days are over. In fact, bringing the little ones along can transform your relationship to the outdoors. Here's what you can expect at every age.

Infants (6 Months to 2 Years)

You'll be carrying kids this small, so your daily mileage is limited by how heavy they are and how far you want to haul them. Still, you can hike longer distances now compared to the next few stages. Keep infants shielded from the sun with hats and visors—just like during a stroller ride. On cold days, make sure their feet, hands, and heads stay warm and that footwear doesn't slip off. Bring a blanket or mat to let crawlers get down on the ground during rest breaks. Baby slings, front carriers, or kid-carrier backpacks are the essential pieces of gear for this stage of parenthood.

Toddlers (3 to 5 Years)
Your days of long hikes are temporarily on hold. Toddlers are too big to carry but too small and distracted to walk more than a mile or so at a time. Still, their curiosity about the outside world means that every hike is a (slow) nature walk. Encourage their exploration; this will keep them moving and hopefully delay the eventual meltdowns. Plan hikes to lakes, beaches, and other interesting features, but beware of cliffs, fast-moving rivers, and drop-offs.

Preteens (6 to 12 Years)
Kids this age can hike more miles, but they also demand a payoff for their efforts. Pick exciting destinations to keep them motivated along the way. To ward off whining, give them tasks like reading the map, taking compass bearings, or collecting drinking water. Even if they act bored, kids this age want to be involved. Consider bribing them with their own gear that can grow with them, like hydration bladders to slip into their backpacks or adjustable headlamps.

Teenagers (13+ Years)
Older children want to be self-sufficient, so give them more freedom; for example, have them scout ahead of the group, plan meals, or build campfires. They enjoy being outdoors but might not want to share the experience with their parents. One trick is to let them invite a friend. Kids this age generally desire and need their own equipment like a backpack, tent, or trekking poles. (See Chapter 11 for pack measuring guidelines.) Be sure to let them pick out their own gear, such as LED headlamps or waterproof jackets—in addition to hand-me-downs from your prior hiking days.

Kid-Specific Gear
Every parent knows that having kids means accumulating more stuff. The same is true for hiking. Infants might be the smallest kids, but they require the most equipment. You can actually

bring your teeny newborn hiking with a baby sling or a front carrier with an infant insert. These form-fitting carriers can be worn by men and women, and the best models allow infants to face outward or inward, can be worn on your front or your back, and have plenty of breathable mesh to keep you cool. BabyBjörn and Ergobaby make a wide variety of infant carriers adapted for hiking. For toddlers, you'll need to purchase a kid-carrier backpack—an external frame pack with a padded seat for a child and plenty of storage space for water, snacks, and other vitals. Pack makers Osprey, Kelty, and Deuter offer several styles of carriers for between $150 and $300. You also can find them cheaper at secondhand shops and classified-ad websites.

Elementary school–age kids and preteens can carry a small amount of gear—mainly snacks and water—in their school backpacks or waist packs. Don't bother purchasing high-quality backpacks or hiking boots for kids until they reach their teenage years. They can hike in tennis shoes as long as there isn't any snow or serious mud on the trail.

Hiking with kids also requires adjusting your first aid kit to address their potential emergencies. Here are six extra items you should add to your kit:

◊ Calamine lotion or antihistamine cream to soothe bug bites

◊ Extra adhesive bandages

◊ Kid-safe bug repellent (less than 30 percent DEET or another ingredient)

◊ Children's acetaminophen or similar pain reliever

◊ Antibacterial baby wipes

◊ Tweezers to remove splinters and thorns

Motivating Kids to Hike

Tearing a child away from the magnetic pull of video games and *Paw Patrol* reruns isn't easy. Some kids will jump at the chance to go for a hike, while others (and probably the majority) will require bribery. Don't give up too easily. By exposing your kids to outdoor adventure, you're showing them how to achieve a healthy and active lifestyle.

Keeping kids focused during the hike is another challenge. If they don't feel like part of the group or aren't motivated to reach a goal, they'll do their best to make the rest of the trip miserable for others, too. To prevent pint-size meltdowns, try these techniques:

◊ Give kids an inexpensive digital camera or old phone to document the hike.

◊ Reward good behavior by giving candy at rest breaks.

◊ Play games like "I Spy" and make up riddles.

◊ Let kids invent their own games using what they can find nearby.

◊ Give kids a map, GPS, or smartphone with a GPS app and ask them to track your progress and mileage.

◊ When camping, ask them to gather wood to build a campfire.

◊ Participate in the Junior Ranger programs offered at every national park for the chance to collect individualized pins for each park.

◊ Teach your kids a lifelong appreciation for low-impact hiking and Leave No Trace principles by leaving plants and animals alone. (See Chapter 15.)

Hiking with Dogs

If your dog could talk, he would ask to go hiking every weekend. Dogs need exercise, and hiking is a great way to tire them out. However, dogs also have the potential to introduce chaos to a hike, so to prevent your outing from becoming a leash-pulling, wildlife-chasing disaster, keep these tips in mind.

Where Dogs Are Allowed

Sadly, dogs and other pets are not allowed on hiking trails in most national parks, with the major exceptions being Shenandoah, Cuyahoga Valley, Acadia, and Great Sand Dunes parks, and trails above the rim at the Grand Canyon. Even though pets are banned from trails, they are allowed in most parking areas, campgrounds, and other public areas. State and county parks are generally more welcoming of dogs on trails and in campgrounds, but check the park policies before showing up, especially if you plan to hike. Dogs are permitted on trails in national forests and Bureau of Land Management (BLM) properties but might be restricted around swimming areas and lakes and inside buildings. Most beaches also prohibit dogs, which makes it tough for Fido to learn to surf.

If you're looking for parks and trails to take your dog, check out the *Best Hikes with Dogs* guidebook series published by Mountaineers Books. (See Resources.) These books, written by local hikers, highlight dog-friendly parks and trails from San Francisco to South Carolina.

Food and Water

Imagine if your tongue, fingers, and toes were the only parts of your body that could sweat. That's the reality for dogs, which makes keeping them hydrated a priority. Let your dog drink whenever you do—or every 15 to 30 minutes depending on the terrain and temperature. Dogs will slurp water from streams and puddles (and it's almost impossible to prevent them), but they are just as susceptible to intestinal parasites as people. Keep them away from foul, slimy water sources and from places where other hikers are pumping water. If standing water is scarce, bring extra water bottles for your pooch and a small dish or foldable dog bowl to help them slurp it up.

Just like you need snacks during a hike, dogs need extra fuel, too. For day-hikes, pack dog treats to reward good behavior. On longer hikes, pack your dog's regular food in a resealable plastic container that you can store along with your own food away from scavengers.

If you want your pooch to share some of the load, have them carry their own food and water in a dog pack. Pack makers Ruffwear, Mountainsmith, and Kurgo sell dog packs that attach to a harness and cinch around a dog's midsection. Keep the pack's weight below one third of your dog's total poundage.

Safety Check Dogs are magnets for deer ticks, which can carry Lyme disease, especially in the Northeast and Upper Midwest. At the end of the day or the hike, check your dog—and yourself—for any unwelcome sesame seed-sized parasites and carefully remove them with tweezers. (See Chapter 18 for more on removing ticks.)

Health and Safety

The adage that a dog will walk three miles for every mile a person walks is true—and nowhere is it more evident than on a trail. Start with shorter, easier hikes at first to ensure your dog is conditioned enough to cover several miles on a trail. Keep puppies at home until they are at least five months old and have their shots. As you hike, watch for warning signs like limping, stumbling, or wheezing, which indicate your dog might be in trouble.

Almost every park and recreation area requires dogs to be on a 6-foot or shorter leash at all times. While this rule is often ignored—especially beyond the trailhead parking lot—it's designed to protect dogs, other hikers, and wildlife. Unless your dog is voice controlled—meaning that it will stop chasing a rabbit and return to your side when you call its name—keep it on a leash, or at least keep a leash cinched around your waist for quick retrieval. When camping, you can pack a 20- to 30-foot lead or rope to give your dog more freedom to move.

Hiking for Life: Older Hikers

Hiking isn't just a young person's game. My unscientific survey of hikers I've met on the Appalachian Trail shows that about half of them are between the ages of 40 and 65. In fact, retirees are the most visible demographic who visit parks and trails. The reason is clear: hiking is an excellent way to achieve lifelong fitness and health. This trend will likely continue as retiring baby boomers trade in their commutes and cubicles for hiking and camping.

Still, older hikers are more likely to experience health challenges like dodgy knees, achy backs, and weaker hearts. These limitations might mean that senior hikers need to dial back the number of miles they did in their 20s and 30s, but it doesn't mean they should hang up their boots. Consider Emma Gatewood—better known as "Grandma Gatewood." At age 67, she hiked the entire 2,178-mile Appalachian Trail, and then hiked it three more times over the next decade. But because everyone can't hike like that grandma, it's wise to take some precautions.

 Trail Tips The two primary causes of trail fatigue are carrying too much weight and hiking too fast. If you can't keep up, share some of your load with others and schedule more breaks.

First, hikers over the age of 50—as well as hikers who are overweight, are recovering from an illness or injury, or have a family history of heart disease or other heart problems—should consult a doctor and pass a cardiac stress test before training for a hike or undertaking any strenuous physical activity. This also applies to older people who are returning to the trail after a long hiatus.

Once you're cleared and ready to hike, simple pretrip training and preparation can help older hikers avoid problems on the trail:

◊ Maintain your bone density (and prevent osteoporosis) by eating plenty of calcium and vitamin D from dairy products and leafy green vegetables like spinach, broccoli, and kale.

◊ Regular walking, stretching, swimming, or weight training will keep crucial joints in motion and reduce bouts of stiffness and pain.

◊ Strengthen your heart by fortifying your diet with more omega-3 fatty acids found in nuts, vegetables, and fish.

◊ Maintain leg strength—especially your quads and hamstrings—by climbing stairs and doing leg exercises.

Many hikers often find certain trail conditions—like steps and river crossings—more challenging as they grow older. Instead of avoiding your favorite trails or risking injury, try these strategies to adjust your hiking style so that you can press forward:

◊ Reduce your pack weight by acquiring lighter gear and removing extraneous items.

◊ Stick to a slow and steady pace, such as 1 mph, to prevent fatigue and injuries.

◊ Cushion your feet with well-padded socks and thicker insoles.

◊ Use trekking poles to protect your knees while going up and down.

◊ Stay in a cabin or lean-to instead of packing a tent.

◊ Take ibuprofen before and after a hike to reduce pain and inflammation in muscles and joints.

Hikers with Disabilities

Just because someone has a disability—whether it's blindness, diabetes, or the inability to use their legs—doesn't mean that hiking trails are off-limits to them. Many parks and recreation areas are expanding disabled people's access to trails, viewpoints, and campgrounds. For instance, Denali, Zion, and Rocky Mountain National Parks have installed paved trails accessible to scooters, wheelchairs, and walkers. For a list of accessible trails, search for "wheelchair friendly" or "accessible hikes" on the websites and apps mentioned at the beginning of this chapter.

Hikers with diabetes don't need to stay home, either, but they do need to watch their water intake, blood sugar levels, and feet, which are more prone to blisters. The body burns more blood glucose during exercise, at higher altitudes, and in colder temperatures. Diabetic hikers need to stay hydrated, plan plenty of breaks, and bring snacks like apple juice and raisins that will quickly restore their blood sugar levels. Many hikers pack glucose tablets, which offer a standard dose of sugar to bring the blood glucose level back to normal. While pets are prohibited on most national park trails, service animals are the one exception. These animals are allowed everywhere, including trails and buildings. Most parks require hikers using service dogs to register at the ranger's office before beginning a trip.

SUMMARY

You can hike alone or make it a social activity with people you know already, or as a way to meet new friends. Try Meetup.com or social media to find informal hiking groups, while most major cities have established organizations. Use gear, activities, and goals to motivate kids to hike, and know you're boosting their fitness and appreciation for nature. Dogs don't need any encouragement to hit the trail, but remember to keep them on-leash. Finally, don't let age or ability level stop you from hiking; just find a new way to make hiking work for you.

CHAPTER 3

CAMPING OVERNIGHT

Day-hiking is loads of fun, but if the sun begins to set while you're still on the trail, you could end up like Cinderella at the prince's ball—racing to finish the final miles before the last light is gone.

What if you didn't need to rush? What if you could stay and enjoy the vivid sunset, the starry sky, and a roaring campfire?

If any of those options sound appealing, then you're ready for the next step in outdoor adventure—camping overnight. Just like hiking, camping enables you to dial in the right balance of comfort and adventure. For instance, car-campers drive up to a campsite, park their cars, unload their gear, and set up a tent, a trailer, or an RV. Backpackers, on the other hand, hike into the woods to pitch a tent at a campsite far from any roads or cars. No matter how you camp, you can enjoy spending the night outdoors.

Spending the Night Outside

Tell a friend you're going camping and you might hear: "Good luck. I could never sleep on the cold, hard ground." Little do they realize that no one—except the most hardcore Civil War reenactors—still lie down on the bare ground. Between you and the ground will be sleeping bags, ground pads, air mattresses, or cots—all of which are engineered to make camping both warmer and more comfortable.

The biggest fear most people have about camping is abandoning their familiar beds. Without a plush mattress, sheets, and blankets, they worry sleeping will be too cold, bumpy, and rough. It's true that changes to your nighttime routine can disrupt your ability to sleep. The key is to make camping as relaxing, comfortable, and fun as possible. Here are some comfort-focused tips to help first-time campers enjoy a restful night:

◊ Pack a comfortable travel pillow.

◊ Go to bed with a full stomach but not with a full bladder.

◊ Don't try to fall asleep immediately; drift off by reading a book or a magazine or by telling stories.

◊ Bring earplugs to drown out crickets or another camper's snoring.

◊ Bring warm clothes for sleeping; long underwear or sweatshirts and pants work best. (See Chapter 10 for more advice on sleeping apparel.)

If you're still unsure or you're worried that young children might get cranky or homesick, start by pitching a tent in your backyard. While not especially adventurous, backyard camping is an excellent introduction to the car-camping and backpacking experiences I'll describe next.

Types of Campgrounds

The familiar scenes of picnic tables, fire pits, and pine trees make all campgrounds look the same at first glance, but there are as many types of campgrounds as there are kinds of campers. From the kid-friendly activities of private campgrounds, to the seclusion of a shady glen in a national forest, or to a rocky shelf perched on the edge of a canyon, you can find the ideal overnight spot to make your outdoor adventure complete. The secret is matching your desires to the right type of campground.

Private Campgrounds

National chains like KOA and Yogi Bear's Jellystone Park, along with thousands of independent operators, make up the world of private campgrounds. While these campgrounds exist everywhere—KOA operates 485 sites in 46 states and Canada—they are often clustered near the entrances to national parks and other popular recreation areas.

Campers seeking an outdoor experience surrounded by nature won't find it at these densely packed and noisy establishments. They cater more to families seeking an inexpensive, action-filled vacation. Plus, RVs, pop-up campers, and trailers always outnumber regular tents. Some private campgrounds are also recasting themselves as budget amusement parks—complete with water parks, roller coasters, miniature golf, and dirt-bike tracks.

Still, private campgrounds provide a predictable, affordable, and enjoyable outdoor experience to millions of campers each year, at nightly rates below what you'll pay for a motel room. Also, a private campground can be a campsite of last resort if all the tent sites inside a park are filled. Most establishments also welcome pets and provide space for dozens of activities ranging from biking to fishing to shooting sports. Because they are so popular, you should reserve spots at private campgrounds weeks or months ahead of time, especially for summer weekends and holidays.

Public Campgrounds: State and Local Parks

The pristine forests, lakes, and rivers that make state and county parks so attractive also appeal to campers looking for an escape. These publicly owned campgrounds are often smaller than private establishments, and campsites are clustered to preserve more open space for hiking, viewing wildlife, and other outdoor activities.

Tents are the most common form of shelter at public campgrounds, although most places can accommodate RVs and trailers with larger parking spaces. Not all public campgrounds have electrical and water hookups for RVs, so it's best to check ahead of time. Individual campsites often include picnic tables and fire pits, while several sites will share access to potable (i.e., drinkable) water, basic toilets, and sometimes hot-water showers. Dogs and other pets are permitted at state and local parks and nearby trails more often than at national parks and recreation areas.

Most campers who seek out public campgrounds are looking for a traditional outdoor experience involving a place to pitch a tent and sit around a campfire, as well as nearby access to hiking, boating, or fishing. But you won't find amusement park rides or miniature golf at these public campgrounds, which is a factor that keeps their cost and noise levels lower.

Public Campgrounds: National Parks and Forests

Campgrounds located inside national parks and forests offer an authentic and low-frills overnight camping experience that is closer to the main attractions than private campgrounds outside the park or forest boundaries. These public campgrounds can also run the gamut from super luxurious to super primitive. At Grand Canyon National Park, for instance, car-campers and RV drivers can stay overnight at Mather Campground, a sprawling tent and camper village with a full-size grocery store and hot showers located a few hundred yards from the south rim of the canyon. But for backpackers who descend a trail to the Colorado River at the canyon's bottom, their backcountry camping options might include sandy beaches and rock slabs where they might be the only people for miles around.

Whether you camp on the canyon's rim or at the bottom, all campgrounds inside national park boundaries require permits and have a fee. Be sure to check with individual parks prior to booking your trip. Look up campground details for each national park on its website, all of which can be accessed through the National Park Service (NPS) website, nps.gov/findapark. We'll discuss tips on how to reserve national park campsites later in this chapter.

 Trail Tips If your first-choice campground at a national park is completely booked, ask about campsites in nearby national forests and state parks that often surround national park properties.

National forest campgrounds are generally smaller, less developed, and less crowded than those at national parks. These campgrounds are often located at lakes, reservoirs, or trailheads, or along hiking trails and are designed for a mix of car-campers, backpackers, and RVs and trailers. You can find a list of national forests by state at the U.S. Forest Service website, fs.usda.gov, under the "Visit Us" menu. But be warned: the low-tech websites for national forests are notoriously difficult to navigate.

Finding a Campground

Your campground is your home in the outdoors. Because it's the place where you will start and end each day, you want it to be both comfortable and convenient. Like buying a home, finding the ideal campsite is all about location and amenities.

A family looking for a weeklong vacation of fishing and boating should set up camp on the sandy shore of a lake, while a hiker hoping to finish the last 30 miles of a local trail network should pitch his or her tent near a junction of several trails. With the variety of campgrounds out there, you shouldn't pick the first place you come across; you should search for one that matches your needs. Start by making a list of the campground amenities that you want and those you don't want. For instance, if you're looking for nature, avoid campgrounds that advertise themselves as amusement parks. If you want calm evenings, find out about the campsite's evening quiet hours. Also, you should be sure to get answers to the following questions as you research different campgrounds:

◊ Ask about amenities like showers, hot water, and activities fees. Guidebooks and websites aren't always up to date.

◊ Ask whether the campground can accommodate your favorite outdoor activities like boating, swimming, hiking, and fishing.

◊ Make sure parking spaces and turnarounds for RVs or trailers are large enough to accommodate your vehicle.

◊ Find out which campsites are shaded by trees and which ones are out in the open.

 Trail Tips Because space, shade, and privacy can vary among sites at the same campground, drive around before you choose a site, or use the satellite view in Google Maps to scout the best location if you are booking online ahead of time.

Map and Internet Searches

The easiest place to find a campground is on a map. Most private, state, and local campgrounds are marked on road maps by the universal triangle symbol that resembles a tent. Some maps also provide symbols that indicate the amenities offered by campgrounds—like RV hookups, hiking trails, and showers. If you're using a map, write down the names of several promising campgrounds near your destination, look up their contact details on the internet, and call for more information.

To search a wider area, the website reserveamerica.com provides a map-based database of 4,000 mostly private and some public campgrounds. This easy-to-use and powerful website lets you target your search for campgrounds that have RV sites, cabins, tents, or group sites, and it enables you to check specific dates for prices and availability. Reserveamerica.com also provides the name, location, and some details for campgrounds it doesn't manage, such as sites inside national parks and forests, but it doesn't allow you to make reservations at these locations.

If you know you only want to stay inside a national park, national forest, or other public-lands area, you can search for public campgrounds at recreation.gov. This website contains information on 100,000 reservable locations and provides important details like the number of sites, available amenities like drinkable water and flushable toilets, driving directions, and a calendar of which sites are available to reserve. Note that you can easily search campgrounds at recreation.gov, but you must create a free account to make a reservation on the website.

Already know which park or recreation area is your destination? You can bypass the map or website search process and go directly to the location's website to select a date and site.

Campsite Ratings

Not all campgrounds are created equal. To avoid staying at the camping equivalent of the Roach Motel, check online reviews and ratings. The following four websites collect user feedback and reviews about campgrounds on key aspects like cleanliness, facilities, and amenities. These sites can help you find a high-scoring place to park your trailer or pitch your tent:

◊ **Google Reviews (google.com)** Any Google search for the name of a specific campground will likely return reviews that are posted on Google, and they're usually brief and lacking details on amenities. This is a good place to start.

◊ **The Dyrt (thedyrt.com)** This website contains in-depth reviews of thousands of tent sites and car-camping locations, along with helpful lists of amenities and access points.

◊ **Campground Reviews (campgroundreviews.com)** Focused on RV and trailer accommodations, this website has reviews of private and RV campgrounds as well as state and national parks.

◊ **TripAdvisor (tripadvisor.com)** Find reviews of campgrounds near Paris, Tennessee, and many other popular and obscure recreation areas using this comprehensive website driven by detailed user comments and descriptions.

Reserving a Campsite

You can make reservations at private, state, and local campgrounds by calling the location directly, or make your selection and payment online. Many private campgrounds can be reserved at reserveamerica.com or through the location's individual website. You can also reserve "walk-up" sites in person, but your options might be limited during the busy summer months and holiday weekends.

For campsites at national parks and forests—which are managed by the federal government or a hired contractor—look for the "Plan Your Visit" and "Camping" menus on the national park or forest websites. This leads to more information about available campgrounds, seasons of operation, site maps, and how to reserve a spot over the phone, or online at recreation.gov. Most campsites can also be reserved over the phone. Whether you book through a website or over the phone, you can head off problems by keeping these tips in mind:

◊ Because campgrounds at national parks and forests are located closer to major attractions and sites, they are the first choice for many campers. Plan ahead.

◊ Be aware that most campgrounds require two-night minimum stays on weekends, and many have limits on people and parked cars.

◊ To lock in a popular campground where reservations open up 6 to 12 months ahead of time, set a calendar reminder on the first date you can reserve a future spot.

◊ Weekends fill up much faster than weekday slots.

◊ When reserving a specific campsite, consult a map of the campground to select the ideal site with regard to shade, traffic, noise, and proximity to open space.

◊ Ask campground officials about important factors like toilets, water, quiet hours, and local wildlife.

◊ Sometimes, larger groups can book two side-by-side campsites.

Ways to Camp Overnight

At the end of the day, your thoughts are going to turn to where you'll sleep that night. While a tent is the classic outdoor shelter, other available options range from luxurious to primitive. For the most comfort, go with RVs, campers, and pop-up trailers, which are welcome at most public and private campgrounds. For a more rugged outdoor experience, you can spend the night in a cabin, lean-to, or tent. In this section, we'll cover all the available options, starting with the most lavish.

RVs and Campers

Traditionalists might thumb their noses at RVs, but these homes on wheels are a smart way to travel, especially on long road trips. Most established campgrounds, including most national parks, have RV hookups and designated spots for trailers.

Even if you've never considered an RV, it could be the right solution for your upcoming road trip. For instance, renting an RV could be the solution for a Yellowstone National Park vacation that both grandparents and grandkids could enjoy. That's why RV rentals are a common choice among visitors to western states like Colorado, Utah, Arizona, and California. You can rent an RV for about the same price as a single hotel room, and they can sleep from three to seven passengers, depending on their size. To rent an RV, go to the website cruiseamerica.com. You can also locate RV-compatible campgrounds at the website gorving.com, and check recent reviews on campgroundreviews. com and campendium.com.

Cabins, Yurts, Huts, and Lean-Tos

In between RVs and tents on the comfort scale are cabins and other permanent structures. Cabins can be rented at many private campgrounds, though often at a higher price than a tent site. They are better for families with small children, large groups who want to stay in one location, and anyone who desires a "four walls and a roof" approach to camping.

Cabins—sometimes called *huts*—are overnight options in state and national parks and recreation areas. In fact, cabins are an ideal place to stay during fall or winter hiking trips when snow and frigid temperatures can make tent camping less appealing. Some sites include yurts, which are large, circular canvas tents with solid floors and plenty of living space for beds, couches, and tables. In certain popular hiking areas, mainly New Hampshire's White Mountains, California's Sierra Nevada range, and Colorado's Rocky Mountains, you can arrange to stay at a different hut each night during multiday backpacking trips. Not only can you save weight by leaving your tent at home, but you'll spend each night inside a cozy cabin.

A lean-to is a three-walled structure—usually made from wooden planks, logs, or stones—with the fourth side open to the elements. They often have a small porch and overhanging roof. Also called *Adirondack shelters*, lean-tos are popular campsites on long-distance trails in the eastern United States. These established campsites often feature fire pits, picnic tables, and a nearby water source. Some lean-tos require advance booking, but most work on a first-come, first-served basis, with preference given to *thru-hikers*. A thru-hiker is a backpacker in the process of hiking a long-distance footpath like the 2,178-mile Appalachian Trail. Veteran thru-hikers are hardcore backpacking machines who can knock off 20 miles a day on the trail.

Car-Camping

Just like it sounds, you drive up to a campsite, unload the car, and set up camp—usually by pitching a tent. Car-camping is what most people think of when they imagine an outdoor outing, and these are the most common spots at public and private campgrounds. As a result, almost all public and private campgrounds are set up to accommodate car-campers, with each site providing a picnic table, fire pits or grills, and designated tent spaces. Unlike backpacking, you don't need to carry your gear, so you can pack it in duffel bags, coolers, and shopping bags. These campgrounds often have toilet facilities and sometimes hot-water showers as well as access to potable water for drinking and cooking.

Because they aren't meant to be carried long distances, car-camping tents tend to be more spacious and heavier than backpacking tents. The largest car-camping tents are big enough to walk around in and can feature multiple rooms, windows, and porches—all under a roof of waterproof fabric. (For advice on how to choose the right tent, see Chapter 12.)

 Trail Tips When car-camping, bring more gear and food than you think you'll need. You can store any extras in the car—and unlike backpackers, you don't need to lug it around on your back.

The big advantage to car-camping is that it enables you to pack extra gear that you wouldn't be able to carry on a backpacking trip like two-burner propane cooking stoves, thick inflatable ground pads, a cooler, chairs, and sporting equipment.

Boondock Camping

What do you call RV or car-camping when you're not at an official campground? The answer is boondock camping. With a 4WD car, truck, or SUV, you can drive on unpaved roads to access remote and unofficial campgrounds that aren't on any recreational map. These are sites with no caretaker, no picnic tables, no bathrooms, and—especially in the western United States—no available water. Most of these sites are located inside national forests or on the millions of acres owned by the Bureau of Land Management (BLM), which also means they are most common in the West. Camping at a boondock site often requires strong navigation skills, a 4WD vehicle, and enough experience to pack water, fuel, and all the gear you'll need. Websites like thedyrt.com and campendium.com list some boondock sites, but the best locations are shared via word of mouth between camping enthusiasts. A prime example of a boondock site is the Wedge Overlook located on BLM land in Utah's San Rafael Swell.

Backcountry Camping

At the opposite end of the luxury spectrum from a sleek RV is a *backcountry* campsite—an overnight spot that is much closer to nature than to modern civilization. Sometimes described as *wilderness camping,* backcountry describes remote regions that are only accessible by walking trails, making them an adventurous place to hike and camp. Located at meadows, lakes, viewpoints, or river crossings miles down a trail from the nearest vehicle access, these primitive campsites are designed for adventurous campers and backpackers willing to give up some of the comforts of a more established campground. Commonly found in national parks and forests, backcountry campsites provide an open, flat space to pitch a tent, a water source, and occasionally a latrine, but they don't provide any of the amenities like showers, a general store, or garbage containers.

When situated near trailheads, backcountry campsites can be used as starting points for backpacking trips or mountain climbs, or they can be used as a base camp for a series of day-hikes. Remote sites—which are often located along trails—can only be reached by backpackers carrying in all their camping gear.

The primary shelter option at backcountry campsites is a lightweight and portable tent. (See Chapter 12 for more on tent options.) Some campsites also feature wooden platforms, which lift tents several inches off the ground to provide better insulation in cold weather and more protection from rain and mud. Most background campsites are first-come, first-serve, but popular sites must be booked months ahead of time, and some are determined by a lottery.

Choosing the Best Campsite

The importance of location not only refers to how close your campground is to lakes, forests, and trails but also where your individual campsite is located within the campground. Choose the wrong spot and you could wake up to a procession of late-arriving cars shining their headlights through your tent, the constant slamming of a latrine door, or a sea of mud in your kitchen area after a rainstorm. Here are some tips for choosing the optimal spot to pitch your tent or park your trailer in your "camping neighborhood":

◊ The quietest campsites are on cul-de-sacs and farthest from the entrance.

◊ A campsite with an eastern or southern exposure will warm more quickly on chilly mornings.

◊ Choose a spot near the water source—but not immediately next to it—to avoid the noise of constant traffic. The same goes for bathrooms, showers, trash bins, RV dump stations, and other public facilities.

◊ Closely spaced trees can provide shade from the afternoon sun, and they provide convenient anchors for clotheslines and hammocks.

◊ Avoid mud by choosing a site covered in grass or bark chips, and choose the highest well-drained ground.

◊ Campsites with strong breezes and steady sunshine will attract fewer mosquitoes.

Arranging a Campsite

Your campsite will be your home away from home for as long as you are enjoying the outdoors. It needs to serve as your kitchen, bedroom, recreation center, and attic. Setting it up correctly requires smart and efficient organization.

The Sleeping Area

The first decision you'll need to make is where to sleep. RVs and trailers can't stray from designated parking spaces, but you'll have more freedom if you use a tent. If your campsite has several obviously flat spots, you should use them. Pitching your tent in a previously used site reduces the negative impact to soil and vegetation. Once you've picked a spot, here are some guidelines to keep in mind as you assemble your shelter:

◊ To avoid drifting smoke and embers, make sure your tent isn't downwind from the grill or fire ring.

◊ Orient your tent so that the smallest cross-section—usually the front or rear—faces into the wind.

◊ When pitching a tent on a slope, position your sleeping bag so that your head is higher than your feet.

◊ Look up to make sure no dead or dangling branches—called *widowmakers*—are lurking above your tent.

◊ Orient your tent so that the door faces away from other campsites.

◊ Pitch your tent over a bed of pine needles for the best insulation and comfort.

◊ Don't place tent ropes, stakes, and guy lines near busy walking areas.

Once your tent is set up and your sleeping bags unrolled, the next step is to set up the rest of your camp, including your kitchen, eating, and storage areas.

 Trail Tips   Pitching a plastic tarp or shade shelter over your cooking and dining area will protect you and your meals from sun and rain.

The Cooking Area

The majority of time you spend in camp will be around your fire or stove, cooking and eating meals, so you might as well make your outdoor kitchen as comfortable as possible.

If your campsite has a picnic table, move it upwind of the fire to keep wood smoke away from your sitting area. Car-campers should position their folding chairs in the same location. Backpackers can reposition flat rocks and logs for impromptu seats around a fire pit or cooking area. Set up gas stoves on the edge of a picnic table or on flat rocks, and shield the burners from the wind as much as possible.

Here are some other tips to keep your camp kitchen in good order:

◊ Set up your kitchen on dry ground—bark chips are best—that can absorb lots of foot traffic without generating dust or mud.

◊ Position your cooking area at least 30 feet away and downwind from your sleeping area to keep food smells from permeating your tent.

◊ Pick a spot near the fire ring to store damp kindling and firewood so the heat dries it out.

◊ Set up a trash bag suspended from a tree branch near the picnic table or main kitchen area.

◊ Store coolers under a shady tree or a picnic table to better preserve food.

 Safety Check   Some campgrounds prohibit campers from bringing in their own firewood because of the threat from invasive species and diseases. Gather wood from nearby areas, or buy firewood at the campground or from an approved local dealer.

Storing Your Gear

Keeping your gear well organized at a campsite ensures two things: you can find what you need, and you won't lose what you own.

After a couple of days of meals, outdoor activities, and fun, a campsite—especially for car-campers—can look like a junk bomb exploded right over your tent. Backpackers usually have an easier time simply because they don't carry enough stuff to make a mess. To keep your campsite from getting out of control, follow these organizational tips to store and safeguard your gear:

◊ Use nearby tree branches to hang clotheslines or hammocks and to keep gear off the ground.

◊ Discourage raccoons, skunks, and mice from raiding your camp by locking all food and trash in the trunk of your car any time you leave. See Chapter 18 for advice in bear country.

◊ Clean up your campsite before sundown to avoid losing items—or tripping over them in the dark.

◊ Pack plenty of durable plastic bags to haul away trash.

◊ Make sure your tent and belongings are protected against rain and high winds any time you leave camp.

SUMMARY

Camping overnight boosts the adventure level of your trip, while also requiring more gear and careful planning to find and reserve a campsite with the right amenities (water, toilets, showers, RV hookups) at the correct destination. Because locations can fill up fast, planning ahead is key, especially at national parks. If you're sleeping in a tent, you can make choices to maximize the comfort, protection, and appeal of your temporary home under the open sky.

CHAPTER 4

BACKPACKING BASICS

There aren't many human activities today that are entirely self-powered. Backpacking, however, is a throwback to the old days when everything that we did depended on muscle power, stamina, and ingenuity. For our ancestors, of course, hauling a pack wasn't a sport—it was transportation. And thanks to a growing network of trails, lightweight tents, and accurate GPS signals, we can continue this exploration today as backpackers. Except unlike the Lewis and Clark expedition, we're more likely to shoot a deer with a digital camera instead of a muzzle-loading rifle.

Carrying It All on Your Back

Choosing to backpack rather than day-hike amps up the adventure level of any trip. After a day or two on the trail, you will forget about email, cell phones, and appointments. Instead, you'll be thinking about what you need to do during the next hour, day, and night. After all, with backpacking, there is no 4WD car, convenience store, or motel to fall back on. These limitations make backpacking a much more complex endeavor than day-hiking.

These are just a few of the major challenges that differentiate backpacking from day-hiking:

◊ Carrying enough food and water for the duration of the hike

◊ Finding and setting up a campsite

◊ Navigating trail turns and junctions

◊ Remembering to pack all the essential gear

At first, those new hurdles might seem daunting, especially if you've never backpacked before. But they aren't insurmountable, especially if you follow the step-by-step approach I outline in the next few chapters. First, however, you need to find a backpacking trail to explore.

Trails for the Long Haul

Trails designed for backpacking are generally longer than day-hiking trails, but there's no firm distinction between the two. Even if a single day-hiking trail isn't long enough for backpacking, hikers can combine several trails into a route appropriate for a multiday trip. As long as a trail or a park allows overnight camping, you can backpack there.

 Trail Tips Although long-distance footpaths like the Appalachian and Pacific Crest Trails traverse hundreds of miles through multiple states, you can often find guidebooks for sections of the trails in specific states. (See Chapter 20 for more about long-distance trails.)

Certain trails, however, are set up specifically for backpackers. These trails often provide designated campsites or shelters spaced a day's hike apart. They also might have fewer access points like trailheads and road crossings, making it more difficult for day-hikers to get on or off the trail.

Locating a backpacking trail requires the same tools as finding day-hikes. The key differences are that you're looking for longer routes and the ability to camp overnight. Most trail descriptions—whether on the internet or in a guidebook—should give you details on the total mileage, elevation gain, places to pitch a tent, and water sources.

Start on the Web

The internet remains a key resource for locating backpacking trails and downloading crucial information like daily mileage and difficulty ratings. Backpacking-focused websites provide detailed information about campsites, water sources, and trail conditions. Some sites also allow hikers to download topographical maps and GPS routes for the trail. Trail descriptions might be written by website staff or contributed by hikers who recently hiked the trail. (To learn more about backpacking trail websites, see Chapter 1.)

Check Out National Parks and Forests

The wide open spaces of our national parks support vast networks of backpacking trails. Consider the 700 miles of hiking paths within Montana's Glacier National Park as one example. Even urban parks, like northeast Ohio's Cuyahoga Valley, allow backpacking and camping. Because most national park visitors rarely stroll away from their parked cars or buses, backpackers often have the run of the place.

Most park websites suggest multiday backpacking trips under the "Plan Your Visit" menu. In many parks, pitching a tent outside established campsites is called *backcountry camping* and is managed by a separate office with its own rules, fees, and permits. Don't be discouraged by the warnings about backcountry camping plastered on national park websites. These cautions are designed to keep unprepared people out of the backcountry, which, because you're reading this book, doesn't include you. Find websites for every national park and monument at nps.gov/findapark.

Backpackers are also welcome at national forests, which are found in 41 states and contain nearly 200 million acres of land crisscrossed by numerous trails. Although national forest websites aren't as user-friendly as the national park sites, prospective backpackers can learn about trails, download maps, and find contact information for ranger districts. To find a forest near you, check the national forest database under the "Visit Us" menu at fs.usda.gov.

In the western United States, the Bureau of Land Management (BLM) manages most of the public lands. Less developed and with fewer amenities like designated campsites, water sources, and pit toilets, BLM land is the "wild west" for backpacking and hiking. Trails can be poorly marked and rarely patrolled by rangers, making a good map and strong navigation skills (see Chapter 6) a prerequisite before venturing there. Despite these challenges, backpacking on BLM land guarantees solitude, incredible scenery, and the freedom to camp where you like. Find destinations at blm.gov under the "Visit" menu.

Hit the Books

To pull off a backpacking trip, you're going to need detailed trail descriptions, accurate maps, and smart hiking advice. Backpacking guidebooks can provide all this information in one convenient place. These books tend to describe trails in smaller geographic areas, such as a specific park or a popular recreation area in a particular state. So, if you plan to hike extensively in a single region or state, consider buying a guidebook to plan your future trips.

Ask Around, Then Do Your Homework

Surfers on Hawaii's North Shore get in brawls to protect the location of secret surfing spots, but that's not how backpackers operate. Every experienced hiker has their own list of the best backpacking routes, and most are willing to share their locations with other trekkers. So ask away, focusing on these local experts:

◊ Friends and colleagues who are active hikers and backpackers

◊ Park rangers and guides

◊ Local outdoor gear and apparel shops

◊ Local hiking clubs

If you seek trail suggestions from others, be sure to tell them your skill and experience level first. Dangerous scrambles on exposed ledges and river crossings might be easy for them but too risky for you. The same goes for the difficult rating that guidebooks often assign to backpacking trips. Trips described as "strenuous" or "difficult" aren't for beginners.

After your inquiries uncover some promising leads, do your own research on the internet and in guidebooks to learn more about the trail. If you set out on a backpacking trip guided only by the word-of-mouth advice of a friend, you may end up lost or injured.

Planning Overnight Trips

Once you've picked a trail—or at least know the general area where you want to hike—the next step is to plan your trip. You need to decide where to start, where to camp, and how many miles to cover each day.

Planning a trip isn't as thrilling as actually walking down a trail with a pack on your back. However, without some pretrip organization, you might find yourself with no place to pitch a tent at night. Researching destinations and making decisions about where to hike can be fun all by itself.

As you begin the process, keep these route-planning principles in mind:

◊ If you're new to backpacking, hike with an experienced friend or in a group.

◊ Avoid planning too many miles for the first or last days of a trip.

◊ Factor elevation gain and loss into your mileage. Going up and down will slow your pace.

◊ If the trail goes above 6,000–7,000 feet of elevation, add more time to account for acclimatization.

◊ Keep mileage low on days with significant elevation gains and losses.

Where to Begin

Choosing where to start your hike involves more than just picking a place to park your car. Trailheads are like entrance and exit ramps to a trail, and choosing where you begin and end a hike can adjust the mileage of your trip. If the trailhead suggested by the guidebook or trail description is inconvenient to you or doesn't make sense with your itinerary, review a map and select better options.

 Safety Check Some trailheads attract "snatch-and-grab" thieves who target hikers' cars. Lock all valuables in the glove compartment or the trunk and leave nothing visible that might tempt a break-in. Check online reviews or ask park rangers about theft problems at trailhead parking lots you plan to use.

One common trip-planning problem is that the first night's campsite is located too far from the designated trailhead—meaning that you would be setting up your tent in the dark. This often happens on Friday afternoons when you leave work for a weekend backpacking trip. Bypass this dilemma by starting your trip from another trailhead that puts you closer to the campsite or car-camping at the trailhead to get a fresh and early start the next morning.

Judging Distance and Terrain

How many miles do you think you can hike in a day? Five, ten, maybe fifteen? Not only does it depend on your physical fitness and how much weight you're carrying, but it also depends on the terrain. I'll explain how to get in shape in Chapter 5, and I'll talk about reducing your pack weight in Chapter 11. Here, I'll focus on how to evaluate a trail.

Most guidebooks and online trip reports assign trails a difficulty rating, either a numbered scale or descriptive words like "strenuous," "moderate," or "easy." Of course, as I mentioned, a trail that's easy for a veteran hiker like the guidebook author might be more difficult for you. Your best strategy is to know your hiking strengths and weaknesses and be conservative in your expectations.

 Trail Tips   You can preview rivers, mountains, lakes, and trails using the "terrain" setting on Google Maps, or do a 3D "flyover" of your route using free software from Google Earth (earth.google.com).

Most backpackers travel at an average speed between 1 and 2 mph, including rest breaks. More experienced hikers can move at 2 to 3 mph, but you've got to be really trucking to go that fast. Beginning backpackers should limit themselves to trails rated as "easy" or "moderate" and cover between 6 to 9 miles per day, or about 5 to 7 hours of hiking. As you become more experienced, you can increase both the difficulty and mileage of the trails you hike.

When deciding how many miles you want to hike each day, try to leave some wiggle room in case you fall behind schedule. Arrange an easy hiking day after a period with long mileage or serious elevation gain to help you regain your strength. On longer, multiday trips, build in dedicated rest days.

Preparing for Hiking's Ups and Downs

Besides distance, the most important factor in a trail's difficulty is the elevation change. This aspect is normally measured in feet gained (and sometimes lost) over the course of the trail. While both ascents and descents can slow down hikers, the climbs are usually more tiring and deserve closer attention when planning a trip.

Guidebooks, maps, and online reports will often describe a trail's rise and fall with a note like "1,670 feet total elevation gain" or provide a separate elevation profile map. Some trail descriptions also provide warnings about particularly steep sections of trail. For instance, you might read, "As the trail approaches the ridgeline, it gains 750 feet in a half-mile." That means in this section, the trail rises 1 vertical foot for every 3.5 horizontal feet—the equivalent of a 16 percent grade. Although that might sound moderate, a 16 percent grade is actually quite steep.

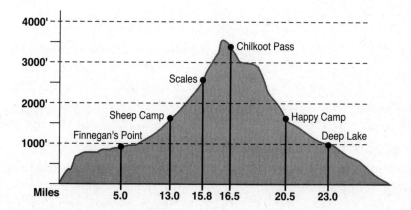

When calculating the effect of elevation on trip time, backpackers should add an hour for every 1,000 feet of elevation gain. Beginner hikers should add a little more time, while veteran or extremely fit hikers can knock it back a bit. Consult the following table to see how long it might take you to complete an 8-mile hike based on your experience level and the trail's elevation gain.

How Long It Takes to Hike 8 Miles

Hiker Level	Speed (MPH)	Elevation Gain (Feet)	Time (Hours)
Beginner	1–1½	+500	6–8½
		+1,000	6½–9
		+1,500	7–9½
Intermediate	1½–2	+500	4½–6
		+1,000	5–6½
		+1,500	5½–7
Experienced	3+	+500	3
		+1,000	3½
		+1,500	4½

Calling a Halt

"Packs off!" is a welcome announcement for backpackers. It means it's time for a rest break. There are no set rules on when to take a breather on the trail. Some hikers prefer to schedule regular breaks—such as every half hour—while others call for breaks before or after a tough section of trail or in a cool and shady spot. If you plan to take a short break, it's best to keep your pack on. Removing your pack can add five minutes to a break.

While planning your hike, you should select a general location for each day's lunch stop, but you don't need to designate a specific spot. Riverbanks or lakeshores are always popular, as are scenic views and places that shade out the noontime sun. Picking a spot near a water source is a smart idea because you can drink your bottles dry and then refill them for the rest of the day.

 Trail Tips You'll stay warmer and reduce muscle stiffness if you take frequent, shorter breaks rather than fewer, longer breaks—especially on cold or windy days.

Leaving in a Hurry

A long-dead German field marshal famously said, "No plan survives contact with the enemy." The same is true for backpacking. There's always a chance you'll need to adjust your trip because of unforeseen circumstances like an injury, bad weather, or a major equipment failure.

You should have a contingency plan in case you need to abandon your planned route and get back to civilization. This isn't normally a problem for day-hikers who can easily backtrack to their cars. But for backpackers who may find themselves deep in the woods or mountains, the closest exit point might not be the way they came in. If you're backpacking, you should select a *bail-out route* for each day you're on the trail. A bail-out route is a quick way to exit the trail to reach a town, road, or other connection to civilization and emergency services. It mainly involves bringing maps and being aware of the region surrounding your trail and knowing how your trail connects to neighboring trails and roads.

Keeping Your Canteen Full

An empty canteen or hydration bladder is one experience you don't want to have. It happened to me in the middle of a fire-blackened forest on the Continental Divide Trail in Montana, setting off a grueling 4-mile hike to the nearest water source. That's why packing enough water—and ensuring you can find more along the trail—is a top priority for backpackers. Carrying all the water you need for a multiday trip isn't feasible for most hikers because of the weight involved. Instead, you're going to need to find water sources along the trail to refill your bottles and bladders. You can read about the various techniques for making backcountry water sources safe enough to drink in Chapter 14.

Trail Tips Some water sources are seasonal and can be dry at certain times of the year. Forest fires, rockslides, and vandalism can also stop water from flowing. Check with rangers for the most updated information on water availability.

Online trip reports and guidebook descriptions will indicate the location of water sources and how clean or reliable they are. They will also mention if the trail or campsite lacks water and will caution you to increase your water-carrying capacity for the trip or for a specific day of hiking.

A Place to Pitch Your Tent

At the end of each day on the trail, a backpacker needs to find a place to set up a tent, cook a meal, and rest until morning. Unlike car-camping, a backpacker's campsite is just a temporary stop. There's no reason to get too comfortable because you'll need to pack it all up the next morning and get moving again. As a result, backpackers should treat campsites as short-term stopovers.

Backcountry campsites can range from established campgrounds with tent sites or cabins to a bare spot in the middle of the woods that no one—except perhaps a black bear—has ever slept on before. On most trails, these campsites are spaced 4 to 8 miles apart—the distance that most people can expect to cover in a day's walk. You'll often find that a trail has more campsites than you'll need—and for that reason, you should pick spots that are appropriate for the number of miles you plan to cover each day. In addition, all backpackers (and day-hikers, too) are expected to pack out their trash and food waste, following the principles of the Leave No Trace ethic. Learn more about what Leave No Trace means in Chapter 15.

Established Campsites

The easiest place to make an overnight stop is a designated backcountry campsite that is marked on a trail map and located near a water source. In addition to flat spaces to pitch a tent, some of these campsites also feature latrines and picnic tables. Others have poles or tall trees to hang bear bags to protect your food and trash from animals. (See Chapter 18.) During popular hiking months, some of these established campsites will have caretakers who are tasked with collecting fees, writing permits, and managing the area. Overnight camping fees range from $6 to $20 per tent, depending on the spot and the agency in charge of the campsite.

Camping in the Middle of Nowhere

Occasionally, you won't be able to find an established campsite for one of your nights on the trail. This can happen when campsites are full, are spaced too far apart or too close together, or just aren't where you need one. In those cases, you'll need to pitch your tent at the best spot that you can find along the trail—a prospect known as backcountry or wilderness camping.

You can use a detailed topographical map to select a general area to camp and then choose the specific campsite when you reach the area. Don't pick the first spot you come across that looks adequate. Instead, evaluate potential campsites with these criteria:

◊ Check local rules to make sure that backcountry camping is allowed.

◊ Locate a nearby and reliable water source.

◊ Note the terrain—valleys and ravines will generally be colder than level ground.

◊ Find a flat space large enough to pitch a tent.

◊ Use trees and rocks to shield your tent from excessive heat, cold, rain, or wind.

◊ Pick a site that isn't close to other campers.

National parks, national forests, and other public land managers often establish limits on where backpackers can stay overnight along the trail. Some land agencies also charge nominal fees for camping permits during popular hiking seasons. Although backcountry camping regulations differ among agencies and locations, they all generally follow these guidelines:

◊ Pitch your tent at least 200 feet from any river, lake, or other water source.

◊ Make sure backcountry sites are several hundred feet away from shelters or other designated camping areas. No ground fires. All cooking must be done with stoves.

◊ Bury all human waste in a 6-inch-deep hole at least 200 feet from water or trails.

◊ Carry a camping permit if required.

Dotting All the I's

Once you've chosen a route, a trailhead, and where to camp each night, only a few minor details remain. Some of these tasks, such as trail reservations and permits, shouldn't be put off to the last minute. In fact, the availability of permits for a particular campsite or trail could determine when and where you can hike.

Prehike Paperwork

Enjoying the freedom of the trail doesn't mean you're completely free from rules and regulations. If you're backpacking and plan to camp overnight, park rangers and managers want to know who you are, where you plan to go, and when you expect to leave the trail. This information benefits your safety and ensures that trails and campgrounds don't become overcrowded.

The permit process for every park and trail is different. Some agencies require permits to hike, while others require them only to camp overnight. Some permits are free, while others can cost between $6 and $20 per day and may fluctuate in cost depending on the season. Other agencies, like national forests, charge a general recreation fee and ask backpackers to record their names, destinations, trip durations, and vehicle details in the trailhead register before hiking. In some parks, backpackers are required to carry an official permit tag attached to their pack or tent. Because there is so much variation among different recreational sites, it's best to visit the websites for specific national parks or national forests or call the ranger office to learn how to make reservations ahead of time.

Press "5" to Reserve a Backcountry Campsite

Unlike car-camping sites, backcountry campsites in national parks aren't listed on the National Park Service (NPS) reservation website, recreation.gov. Instead, backpackers must contact the park office in charge of backcountry permits to apply for permits. If you plan to hike a popular trail or spend the night at a sought-after campsite, you should reserve your spot as far ahead of time as you can. Snagging a tent site at the Bright Angel Campground inside the Grand Canyon can be like trying to get a hotel room in a city that's hosting the Super Bowl. Most sites also set aside a certain percentage of backpacking permits for daily walk-ins on a first-come, first-served basis. However, if you're set on hiking a particular trail, it's best to research your options and make your reservation early. For less-traveled trails and campsites and during nonpeak seasons, you can generally pick up permits at park or forest visitors' centers or ranger offices just prior to your hike.

Reserving backcountry permits at popular national parks like Yellowstone, Zion, Yosemite, and the Grand Canyon can be especially complicated and can require calling and sending emails and faxes up to a year in advance for the most coveted trails and campsites.

Car Spotting

No, this isn't a game to spot exotic license plates from North Dakota or Alaska. Car spotting is a technique that enables hikers to travel a one-way trail without being stranded at the end. It's always easier to hike loop trails that return to your initial trailhead, but sometimes you can't, especially when you're traversing canyons or mountain ranges.

If you have at least two cars and two drivers, you can shuttle one car to the end of the trail, then drive back to your start point in the second car to begin the hike. When you reach the end of the trail, you drive the shuttle car back to the beginning of the trail to retrieve the first car.

The Final Countdown

Because the margin for error for backpackers is a lot slimmer than for day-hikers or car-campers, you need to make sure every detail is complete before you head out the door. Unlike car-camping, backpacking offers little allowance for overpacking because you need to carry it all on your back. However, it's always a good idea to bring extra gear in your car in case you decide to make last-minute substitutions before you hit the trail.

 Trail Tips　Pack your gear using a checklist to reduce the chance that you'll forget something essential—like a headlamp, tent poles, or a butane lighter. Review a complete gear checklist in Equipment Checklists.

Sunny with a Good Chance of Fun

Before you start packing, you should know what kind of weather to expect on the trail. Because most newspaper and TV weather reports focus on places where people live and work—not where they hike—you need to find forecasts for more remote areas. For instance, backpackers often hike at higher elevations where temperatures can be 15°F to 20°F lower than in valleys.

The best forecast source for hikers is the National Weather Service website, weather.gov. Using the Google Maps–based "Detailed Point Forecast" tool, you can click your mouse to retrieve a 5-day weather forecast for a specific spot that includes its latitude and longitude coordinates and elevation. Instead of preparing for your hike using the forecast for Denver, Colorado, you can find out how cold it will be at 12,760 feet at the Boulder Field on the slope of Longs Peak in the Colorado Rockies.

 Safety Check　From May to October, forest fires flare up across the country to blacken the terrain, close trails, and fill the sky with smoke. Find out if fires will affect your backpacking plans by checking the U.S. Forest Service website, fsapps.nwcg.gov.

Spread the News

Hansel and Gretel dropped pebbles and breadcrumbs to make sure they could find their way back home, but hikers are better served by leaving information with trusted friends and family members about where they plan to hike and when they will return.

The person you choose as your safety contact should be responsible enough to alert park rangers or local police if you don't return or phone them on time. Every year, dozens of lost hikers are rescued because they left their route information with a friend who initiated a search-and-rescue mission when they failed to turn up on time.

Here is a list of the information you should give this person:

◊ Your planned route, including start and end trailheads and campsites

◊ The date and time you expect to be off the trail, and when you'll call to announce that everything is fine

◊ Your vehicle make, model, and license number and where it will be parked

◊ The number of people in the group

◊ The hiking experience level of the people on the trip

◊ Your cell phone number and cell carrier information (for example, Sprint or Verizon)

The second place to record your route information is the trailhead logbook. Normally stored in small wooden boxes at the start of a trail, these books are meant to record information including your start date, number of people in a group, intended route and campsites, and expected date of completion. These logs enable park rangers to quickly determine if anyone is potentially lost or overdue from his or her hike. If no logbook is present at the trailhead, you can leave the same information in a note on your car dashboard, making sure that it's visible to a search-and-rescue ranger looking through the windshield.

SUMMARY

Nothing says self-reliance like the ability to carry everything you need on your back—and love it. The best backpacking trips start with careful route-planning that factors in terrain, elevation, weather, and water sources as you pick trails and campsites. Remember to check about permits and rules for backcountry camping, especially in state and national parks. Lastly, tell a trusted friend where you're going and when you'll return, so that no one ends up making a movie about your epic tale of survival.

CHAPTER 5

TRAINING YOUR BODY FOR THE TRAIL

These days, we're all trying to lose a few pounds and lower our cholesterol. Who can blame us? You can't open a magazine or click on the TV without being bombarded with dire warnings about epidemics of obesity, hypertension, and diabetes. Even kids aren't safe. Doctors give us all the same advice to improve our health: maintain a balanced diet and get plenty of regular exercise. That's all easier said than done, of course.

But what if your favorite pastime was also your secret weapon to stay in shape? If you like to hike, this can be true. Whether you're in great shape or seeking to regain your old form (and those jeans that no longer fit), hiking can be your route to both looking and feeling better. Trekking a few miles every weekend can give you a stronger heart; leaner, more muscular legs; and go-all-day endurance.

Before you start hiking, you should make sure your body is ready for the challenge. Proper pretrip training will not only make your hike more enjoyable, but it can also protect you against injuries. These benefits apply whether you're a beginner preparing for your first hike or you are a veteran attempting a more ambitious trip. In this chapter, I'll cover a variety of training methods—from the conventional to more creative—to prepare your body for the trail.

First Things First

Did you know that stressing your muscles, including your heart, beyond its limits can put your health at greater risk? To start on the right foot, tell your doctor when you plan to start hiking or begin a new fitness program. They can encourage you and give you advice. You should also ask your doctor for a physical exam before undertaking any intensive training programs or hikes, especially if you're over the age of 40 or have a history of heart or other health problems. Doctors can do a stress test to discover heart conditions or abnormalities. You should also identify and resolve other ailments like flat feet, allergies, or vertigo before you begin to exercise or hike.

Second, before you begin training, you need to establish a fitness baseline. Recording your fitness level before you start an exercise program will help you judge how much you improve. Here are some key numbers to record:

◊ Current weight

◊ Current height

◊ Waist size

◊ Resting heart rate (measure in the morning before you get out of bed)

◊ Maximum heart rate (220 minus your age)

◊ Flexibility (how close you can get to touching your toes)

I'll show you how to raise your heart rate a little later in the chapter.

Basic Training

The easiest way to train for a hike is to add exercise to your everyday routine. If fitness feels like a natural process, you won't even realize that you're working out. The opposite approach, which includes filling a backpack with bags of rice and walking around your neighborhood, will also work, but it might encourage you to quit early. If you make your training fun and useful—like jogging to complete errands— you'll stay with an exercise program longer.

 Trail Tips   Find out how much you walk during the day by clipping an electronic pedometer to your belt or activating the pedometer app on a smartwatch or activity tracker. For most walkers, 2,000 steps equals one mile.

If you want to be a better hiker, your goal should be to condition your body to withstand the physical demands of multiple trail miles. Because all hiking—including backpacking—is just a variation on walking, the best approach is to increase the number of miles you walk each day.

Walking to Fitness

You don't need to sign up for a marathon to get in shape for day-hiking or backpacking, but you do need to spend more time on your feet. Thanks to our car-dependent lifestyle, walking more than 100 yards at a time is a rare event. To increase your daily walking mileage, start by incorporating some of the following activities into your schedule for 20 to 30 minutes a day, three times a week:

◊ Take your dog for a walk instead relying on doggy daycare or driving to a dog park.

◊ Run errands on foot instead of driving.

◊ Take a walk during your lunch break or after dinner.

◊ Opt for the stairs instead of an escalator or elevator.

◊ Turn your lawnmower's self-propelling drive off when you cut the lawn.

◊ Exit the subway or bus one stop early and walk the remaining distance.

◊ Deliberately park far away from the shopping center or grocery store.

To keep your feet happy and blister-free, wear comfortable, well-cushioned shoes on your extended walks. Better yet, wear the trail shoes or boots you plan to wear during your hike to help break them in.

Training from "9 to 5"

Not only do Americans work too hard, we don't move enough while we work. According to a study by the Columbia University Medical Center, office workers who remained sedentary for more than 13 hours a day experienced double the mortality rate of workers who remained inactive for 11.5 hours a day. Moving more can literally save your life. Because we spend so many hours on the job, our exercise time is often squeezed into the early morning or late evening—times of the day when we'd much rather be sleeping.

Desk-bound office workers are most at risk for daytime sloth. Luckily, getting fit on the job isn't as hard as you think. Here are several tips on how to add fresh air and exercise to your daily calendar:

◊ Take a walk after lunch.

◊ Visit the gym during your lunch hour.

◊ Visit a colleague's office instead of calling or emailing with a question.

◊ Walk or bike to work.

◊ Convert your desk into a stand-up desk, or sit on an exercise ball instead of a chair.

◊ Set an hourly alarm on your computer to remind you to stand up and walk around.

◊ Schedule standing or walking meetings instead of sit-down conferences.

If your boss complains, tell them you're being more productive by taking breaks. You can cite recent studies by Cornell University and the University of Florida that show that taking regular breaks actually improves worker efficiency and prevents work-related injuries.

Building a Stronger Hiker

Walking makes you more active, but a focused strength-training program will give you better results. Take baseball Hall of Fame pitcher Nolan Ryan. He credits his major league record 27 seasons of throwing 100 mph fastballs to a focused weightlifting program he discovered early in his career. Hikers, too, can benefit from gym workouts. The right exercises can help you become stronger, faster, and more steady on the trail.

Effective strength training, however, is more than throwing around dumbbells and grunting loudly. In fact, many exercises don't involve iron weights at all; instead, they just rely on the force of gravity acting against your body weight.

When to Start Lifting

You can pursue a training program prior to a hike or while you are actively hiking. However, if you've never been hiking before or you're training for a strenuous trip, you should start at least 4 to 6 weeks before hitting the trail. This gives your body the time to adjust to the new strain on your muscles and bones and to realize some of the benefits. When you start a new strength-training program, keep these rules in mind:

◊ Warm up with 10 minutes of jogging, cycling, or stretching before lifting any weights.

◊ Do a new exercise with light weights first to learn the proper technique and form.

◊ Rest at least 1 minute between exercises.

◊ Avoid jerky motions that could cause injuries.

◊ If you find yourself cheating to finish a lift (you'll know), reduce the weight.

How Much Is Enough?

Beginners should ease into any strength training routine slowly. Start with smaller weights and increase the load as you gain strength, skill, and confidence. If you hang out in a gym long enough, you'll hear people describing exercises in terms of *repetitions* and *sets*. A repetition, also called a *rep*, is a single lift, such as curling a dumbbell, from start to finish. A set is a series of reps followed by a short rest. A person doing curls with a dumbbell might do 4 sets, each with 8 repetitions, for a total of 32 reps.

Many new lifters get caught in the rut of doing 3 sets of 10 repetitions. However, varying your workout routine, such as doing fewer reps with heavier weights or doing more reps with lighter weights, can improve your results. Generally, an exercise should make you feel fatigued with one set left to finish. The last set should be a struggle, but it should be one you can complete safely. Most fitness experts believe that free weights, like dumbbells and barbells, provide better workouts and results than resistance bands and exercise machines that target the same muscles.

How Often?

Resting is an important aspect of strength training. Taking one day off in between workouts gives your stretched-out muscles the chance to repair and regrow themselves. Most gym-goers establish a workout routine that follows a Monday-Wednesday-Friday or Tuesday-Thursday-Saturday schedule. Whatever schedule you pick, just be sure to add a rest day between your workouts.

Training at the Gym

While strength training isn't necessary to become a better hiker, resistance workouts can help you develop specific muscles and joints. However, because hiking requires endurance and flexibility rather than bulk and strength, pumping iron like Arnold Schwarzenegger isn't the way to get in shape. Those muscles won't help you on the trail—unless you need to heave a few boulders out of the path. Instead, you should focus on the muscle groups that propel you down the trail and carry your load—mainly your lower body and back.

Your Lower Body

Your hamstrings, quadriceps, and glutes—the major muscles in your legs—are often the limiting factor in how many miles you can hike. The excuse "my legs gave out" means something. When your leg muscles cramp up or turn to Jell-O, you can't go on. Stronger legs will help you tackle significant elevation gains, a heavy pack load, or long-mileage days. Try these three lower-body exercises to give your legs a lift:

1. **Stair-climber.** Select a fitness program on the computer that mimics the up-and-down terrain you'd encounter on a trail. Place both feet in the stirrups and stand up tall with your hands resting lightly on the handrails. Start with 15-minute sessions and add more time and increase resistance as you progress.

   Advanced: Wear a backpack while on the stair-climber—starting with a 10-pound load.

2. **Walking lunges.** Stand with both feet together, holding a 5- to 10-pound dumbbell in each hand, with your hands at your side. Step forward with your right leg, landing on the heel first. Lower your body by flexing the knee and hip of your extended right leg until the knee of your left leg is hovering just above the floor. Then push up with your front leg—through your heel—to bring both of your feet together and stand upright. Lunge forward with the opposite leg. Do 10 lunges, alternating between opposite legs, and make sure you have enough space ahead of you.

   Advanced: Increase the weight of the dumbbells.

3. **Box jumps.** Stand facing a 12- to 16-inch-tall exercise step or sturdy box that you can jump on. Keep your head facing forward and your torso upright. Place your feet shoulder-width apart. Dip your knees and upper body, drive upward with your arms, and leap from both legs at the same time. Land on the box with both feet. After landing, extend your body upward to full height (don't crouch). Jump down backward from the box and repeat. Do 3 sets of 6 to 10 reps, resting 1 minute between each set.

   Advanced: Increase the height of the box.

Although you can easily do these exercises in a gym, you can also do them in your home. Substitute a regular staircase in place of a stair-climber machine, and substitute milk jugs filled with water for dumbbells.

 Safety Check Stretching your legs and back after a day of hiking helps reduce the aches and pains you might feel the next morning. Try calf stretches and toe touches.

Your Back

Everything is connected to your back. If you've ever pulled it, you know what that means. The muscles in your torso—both in the front and in the back—are your body's central pivot for walking, lifting, scrambling, jumping, and almost every kind of motion. For hikers, these muscles also keep a backpack fixed to your body and help you stay balanced on steep trails. Practicing these three exercises will give your body a strong foundation for all on-trail movements:

1. **Shoulder shrugs.** Holding 5- to 10-pound dumbbells at your sides, stand with your feet shoulder-width apart. Without moving your arms, lift your shoulders toward your ears. Hold, then slowly lower them. Keep your arms straight and rigid, and lift only from your shoulders. Do 3 sets of 10 reps.

   Advanced: Increase the dumbbell weight.

2. **Rowing machine.** Start the motion leaning forward, with your arms straight and your shins vertical. Gradually lean back, first by pushing with your legs, then by pulling with your arms. Keep your elbows close to your body and move from your hips. Finish with your legs straight, your arms bent upward, and the rowing handle at your stomach. Start with 5 minutes and add more time as you get stronger.

   Advanced: Add speed workouts where you row as fast as possible for 2 minutes.

Quadriceps stretch

Calf stretch

Hamstring stretch

Groin stretch

Pelvic stretch

Back stretch

These six stretches, done during and after workouts and runs, target the muscles that hikers use most.

3. **Back extensions.** Lie face down on a mat with your arms folded and your hands under your chin. Keeping your feet and hips on the floor, lift your chin and chest about 3 to 5 inches off the ground. Hold that pose for 10 seconds, then slowly lower them back to the mat. Do five sets of six to eight lifts.

   Advanced: Lie face down on an exercise bench or ball.

Getting Limber

Most people don't consider stretching to be an exercise, but done correctly, it can be just as beneficial as a good run. Stretching your muscles during and after workouts increases flexibility, improves circulation, and relieves stress. Reducing muscle stiffness not only improves your ability to move, but it can also help resist trail injuries like twisted ankles and pulled muscles. In general, it's better to start stretching after you've already warmed up or completed a workout.

Hold all stretches for a count of 10 to 15 seconds and repeat three times before switching to a different stretch. Keep all movements smooth and under control. Bouncing and arching your back to stretch farther could cause pain and injuries.

Train by Video

The two biggest impediments to exercising are 1) finding time and 2) staying motivated. This is why the high-intensity workout videos on YouTube that cram a half dozen exercises into 10 minutes or less of fitness have tallied millions of views. Led by enthusiastic (and super-fit) instructors, these videos move you through a circuit of simple bodyweight exercises like squat jumps, planks, and push-ups designed to be done in your living room. And, there's actual medical research proving that short bursts of intensive training have the same impact as endurance training but in much less time. If this approach appeals to you, search YouTube for "7-minute workout" and focus on the videos with the most views.

Getting a Move On

Traditional weightlifting might make you sweat, but it won't make your heart race or your lungs expand as much as a run or bike ride. That's why aerobic exercises are an essential part of any prehike training. Fast-paced and rhythmic activities like running, climbing stairs, and cycling force your cardiovascular system (your heart, lungs, and blood vessels) to pump blood and oxygen to all the nooks and crannies of your body to keep your muscles working. Besides running—which you can do on a sidewalk, a treadmill, a track, or a trail—the following aerobic activities are guaranteed to get your heart pounding as well as toughen up the leg muscles that hikers depend on:

◊ Cycling

◊ Tennis

◊ Dance fitness/Zumba

◊ Basketball

◊ Soccer

◊ Lap swimming

 Safety Check   Before engaging in aerobic exercise, start with an easy 5-minute warm-up routine like a brisk walk or a slow jog.

To improve your cardiovascular fitness, you need to follow the same system of progressively harder workouts employed by strength training. After all, the heart is a muscle, too. Boosting your cardiovascular fitness, however, doesn't automatically happen when you run 1 mile, or even 5 miles. That's because how fast or how far you run isn't as important as how fast your heart is beating while you're doing it.

Follow Your Heart

Your pulse—the number of times your heart beats per minute—is like the RPM gauge for your cardiovascular system. The faster your heart beats, the harder it's working, and the more health benefits you'll gain. The fitness bonus really kicks in when your heart rate reaches a level known as the intensive training zone.

If you can keep your heart rate in this zone for at least 20–30 minutes, three times a week, your cardiovascular fitness will start to soar.

Here's how to find your training zone:

1. Subtract your age from 220. The result is your maximum heart rate, or MHR.

2. Multiply your MHR by 70 percent—this is the floor of your intensive training zone.

3. Multiply your MHR by 85 percent—this is the ceiling of your intensive training zone.

4. If you want to exercise at a slower pace, multiply your MHR by 50 percent and 70 percent to calculate the floor and ceiling of your moderate training zone.

 Trail Tips   To find your pulse, place the tips of three fingers on the palm side of your wrist, below the base of the thumb. You can also feel a pulse on the lower neck, on either side of your windpipe. Count the beats for 10 seconds, and multiply by 6 to get your heart rate per minute.

Using this formula, a 45-year-old man would have a maximum heart rate of 175 beats per minute. As a result, his intensive training zone will range between 122.5 and 149 beats per minute. To achieve the maximum cardiovascular benefits from aerobic exercise, he would need to stay in this zone. Keep in mind that it often takes several minutes of intensive aerobic activity to reach your training zone. In addition, people who are overweight and don't exercise regularly might have trouble reaching their training zone at first.

Purchasing a heart rate monitor—a wearable device that uses a wrist or chest strap to measure and record your heart rate during a workout—can give you more accurate results than manually checking your pulse. More advanced monitors can also record the distance, elevation changes, and speed of your aerobic workouts. High-end standalone heart rate monitors are made by Suunto, Garmin, and Polar, and they normally cost between $200 and $500. Cheaper versions can connect to heart-monitoring apps on fitness trackers, smartphones, and smartwatches.

Training for Ups and Downs

Hiking always gets harder when a trail goes from flat to sloped. Whether you're going up or down, uneven trails put more stress on your muscles and joints, especially your knees. Even steps and switchbacks, which are designed to reduce the impact of elevation change, can cause hikers' knees to rebel when climbing over the umpteenth rock. Training for ups and downs requires a combination of high-impact leg exercises along with pulse-raising endurance workouts to replicate the terrain you'll encounter on the trail.

Aim for Impact

First, use a stair-climber or practice box jumps to build strong quads and calves—the two main leg muscles that propel you up a trail and absorb the shock of going down. Repetitive, high-impact exercises can even prevent knee pain by strengthening the tendons around the kneecap. Start with low steps and increase the height as you improve.

Exercising at Every Age

Because the body of a 30-year-old hiker is different than that of a 60-year-old, it makes sense that their training goals should be different, too. Here's how you should train at every stage of your hiking career.

Age 18–35

Congratulations, your metabolism is wicked fast, your injuries heal quickly, and you can power up steep inclines without gasping for air. To maintain these advantages as you get older (yes, it will happen), you need to concentrate on building bone and muscle mass and staying flexible.

First, maximize your bone density and muscle strength, both of which peak around age 30 and then start to decline, by adding rapid, high-impact exercises like box jumps (see earlier in the chapter) and sprints to your workouts. These drills, along with aerobic workouts like running and swimming, will boost your muscle mass. Don't forget to stretch at the end of every workout, run, and hike. Maintaining the flexibility of your muscles will protect you from joint problems later on.

Age 36–55

You might have lost some of your power, agility, and hair from your mid-20s, but don't fret. Men and women reach their peak endurance in their late 30s. That's why the best marathoners and cyclists are much older than the best sprinters.

At middle age, you should focus on postponing age-related problems with aerobic training and healthy eating. Now is the time to start running, cycling, or swimming. Keep in mind that as you get older, you'll reach your training zone heart rate faster. To stop joint pain, which is a common problem at this stage, stretch after every workout, wear a brace, and battle inflammation with rest, icing, and ibuprofen. Drink plenty of fortified milk or add a calcium and vitamin D supplement to keep your bones strong.

Age 55 and Over

Getting your AARP membership card isn't a ticket to slow down. You might not be the strongest or fastest person on the trail, but you're probably the most experienced. Stay active by walking, swimming, and jogging, but don't ignore strength training. After age 50, bone density and muscle strength decline more rapidly. Protect your legs with three weekly 20-minute sessions of intensive, high-impact exercises. You should make sure your diet includes plenty of antioxidant-rich berries, which can reduce attacks of arthritis. At this age, heart attacks are also a major threat. Don't ignore chest pains or shortness of breath.

Realistic Training

If the first day of a big hike is also the first time you've worn your boots, pack, and equipment on an actual trail, you're in trouble. That happened to me on an 8-day backpacking trip in Scotland. Not only was I exhausted by the end of the first 14-mile day, but my inflexible leather boots had shredded my feet.

That painful experience taught me a lesson: take your training outdoors. The stair-climber at your local gym will thicken your leg muscles, but the plastic pedals on that machine aren't the same as rough and rocky terrain. Likewise, the forgiving rubbery bounce of a treadmill won't prepare your joints for the unyielding surface of a trail. In addition to gym workouts and weekend runs, you need to put in some miles on a real trail using your actual gear. These realistic practice sessions—called *shakedowns*—will not only improve your fitness, but they'll help you identify potential problems with your body and your equipment. (A shakedown is a practice hike undertaken prior to the main trip to check your fitness level, test gear, and make sure everything will go smoothly.) You should plan a shakedown at least a week before your actual trip to give you time to fix any problems that develop. Follow these suggestions to add some realism to your training routine:

◊ Run on a trail instead of a road or track.

◊ Use local day-hikes to practice for longer backpacks.

◊ Wear your regular hiking boots and socks during a workout.

◊ Add weight to a backpack using bags of rice, books, rope coils, or canned food.

◊ Use a shakedown to test alternative gear setups—like different socks or bug repellents.

SUMMARY

Like any sport, hiking is a physical activity you can't begin at full speed. Prepare your body for the trail with an exercise program that targets your legs, back, and overall flexibility. But don't run out and join a gym: integrate exercise into your work schedule and everyday activities, or check out easy-to-follow YouTube workout videos you can do in your kitchen. And remember, hikers don't need a certain "look" or have an expiration date. Some of the strongest people you'll meet on the trail will be old, heavy, and very fast.

CHAPTER 6

NAVIGATION ON THE TRAIL

When you're hiking in the woods, you won't find a gas station to stop at and ask for directions. Most hikers consider the absence of civilization a blessing. The downside is that anyone who hikes will occasionally get lost. It happens to everyone, even experienced trekkers.

Getting lost is easy. Getting unlost is the hard part. Finding the correct trail and pinpointing your actual location requires smart navigational skills, a calm approach, and the right tools. Anybody who hikes should learn how to read a map, use a compass, and understand how a GPS (Global Positioning System) device works. Besides first aid (see Chapter 17), these are the most important skills a hiker can know.

Types of Maps

Carrying just any map isn't enough. After all, there are many types of maps out there. Some maps provide a big overview, while other charts show tiny details. If you use the wrong map to get somewhere—like consulting a globe to drive in downtown Chicago—you'll end up lost. Topographical maps—the detailed charts that show trail markings, campsites, and terrain contours—are the best maps for hikers. But every map has its purpose, and you'll probably use several different types while planning and executing a hiking trip.

Road Maps
Use road maps or atlases in your car but not on the trail. They can guide you to a highway exit, trailhead parking lot, or scenic view, but they aren't detailed enough to help you find a backcountry campsite. Even if some road maps show hiking

trails as squiggly dotted lines, they aren't meant to be used for navigation.

If you can't find a physical road map for your destination, use the map app on your smartphone or a website like maps.google.com to generate and print turn-by-turn directions. Most apps and websites can direct you to specific trailheads, campgrounds, and park entrances.

Park Maps

Full-color maps are available for free at most park entrances and ranger stations and can be downloaded as high-resolution PDFs from each park website. These maps often provide a broad overview of the entire park and its amenities, including entrances, trailheads, campsites, and ranger stations. While most park maps are great for planning your visit, including selecting established campgrounds and hiking routes, they won't help you navigate trails or find backcountry tent sites. To maintain their simplified design, park maps often ignore trails and key terrain features like rivers, mountains, and ridges.

For hikes on short, well-maintained, and signed trails, these maps are usable—but they are not ideal. For example, these maps often lack distance measurements between trail intersections, which are a key feature for accurate navigation. Even on easy trails, you'll likely spend several minutes trying to decide which tiny dotted line on the map corresponds to the confusing trail junction you just encountered on the ground. Any situation when you have to guess which direction to hike is an invitation to become lost.

Topographical Maps

A topographical map is what you want in your pocket or backpack when you set out on a hike. Topographical maps, also known as *topos*, provide a comprehensive view of a trail and its surroundings. When you compare a basic trail map to a topo map, you'll realize that the difference between the two is like the difference between AM radio and HDTV. Not only are topo maps drawn with an enhanced level of detail, but they also use contour lines to project our 3D world onto a flat piece of paper.

These contour lines trace the elevation changes created by mountains, valleys, rivers, and ridgelines to help you visualize the surrounding terrain. Topographical maps become even more powerful tools when used in conjunction with a compass or GPS-enabled phone or handheld device.

 Trail Tips Reviewing a trail's elevation profile can help you judge how difficult a hike will be. Profile charts are found in most trail guidebooks and website trip reports and can be created with most online mapmaking software.

The U.S. Geological Service (USGS) prints topos for every square inch of the United States—a total of more than 55,000 separate maps, which are popularly referred to as *quads*. USGS quads serve as the baseline for almost all topographical maps, and they remain the most popular and accurate maps carried by hikers.

A Note on Scales

Want to know how much detail your map contains? You need to know its *scale*. This number, usually shown as a ratio like 1:24,000 or 1:75,000, determines map detail by indicating how a distance measured on the map compares to a corresponding distance on the actual ground. Topographical maps with scales between 1:24,000 and 1:50,000 are best for trail navigation.

For instance, on a 1:24,000–scale topographical map, a measurement of one inch on the map equals 24,000 inches—or 2,000 feet—on the actual ground. This means that if a trailhead and a waterfall are 1 inch apart on a map, they are 2,000 feet apart in real life.

Maps are designed with different scales for different purposes. A road atlas for the state of California might have a scale of 1:800,000, where 1 inch on the map equals 800,000 inches—or the equivalent of 12 miles—on the ground. If this map shows that the highway between two cities is 3 inches long, the driving distance is 36 miles.

Which of these two maps—the topo or the road atlas—would be better for hiking? The 1:24,000–scale topo map, of course.

Its scale is 30 times larger (and 30 times more detailed) than the road atlas of California. That's why road maps never show hiking trails or junctions—these features are too small to show up.

To compare map ratios and scales, keep this rule in mind: The smaller the second number, the more accurate the map will be. Therefore, a 1:24,000 map has a larger scale and provides more terrain detail than a 1:50,000 map. However, the drawback to larger-scale maps is that they cover less territory, and you might need to carry multiple maps to cover a single trail or park.

Which map scale is right for your hike? You might not need the most detailed option available if you're planning a simple day-hike or you're hiking a well-marked trail. Find your ideal scale by checking the following table.

Map Scale	1 Inch Equals ...	Best for
1:24,000	2,000 feet	Detailed route-finding
1:62,500	5,280 feet	Day-hikes on familiar terrain
1:100,000	8,448 feet	Planning, but not hiking
1:500,000	8 miles	Driving to the trailhead

 Trail Tips Most topographical maps display the familiar latitude and longitude grid system of degrees and minutes. However, some newer maps and most GPS devices will show coordinates for the Universal Transverse Mercator (UTM) system, a metric grid that divides the world into 60 zones that are each six degrees of longitude wide. Use one system or the other; don't use them together because converting between the two is a hassle.

Finding Topographical Maps

Finding the right topo maps isn't always easy, especially if you're looking for a USGS quad. With more than 50,000 individual quad maps to choose from, finding the charts to cover your hike could be daunting for a first-time navigator. The secret to success not only involves knowing what you're looking for but also where to search.

In a Store

If your focus is a major national park or local hiking area, check your local book shop or outdoor gear store first. Their map and guidebook collections will often cover popular destinations and local hikes, but a store in New Jersey won't sell topos for Wisconsin. Local hiking clubs also create guides and topo maps for popular destinations—from the Appalachian Mountain Club's White Mountain Guide (now in its 30th edition) to the Alpine Club of Williamsport's (PA) Loyalsock Trail Guide.

Another option to consider is the National Geographic *Trails Illustrated* series. Printed on waterproof paper, the 250 maps in this series cover major hiking destinations from California's Sierra Nevada range to Maine's rugged coast. While these maps aren't drawn at a small enough scale for complicated route-finding, they can guide you on day-hikes and other popular treks. Look for *Trails Illustrated* maps in outdoor gear stores or order them from the National Geographic's online map store at natgeomaps.com.

Order Custom Maps Online

If you want to consolidate several USGS quads into a single map, you can order a custom topo with specific boundaries from MyTopo.com. This website not only sells individual topos for each state (New Mexico is covered by 1,975 topo maps), but it also allows you to design a custom map for the area you want to hike. It's easy: search for the name of a park or trail, zoom out until you cover the boundaries you need, pick "Topo Maps" to lock in the 1:24,000 scale USGS grid, select the size of map you want, choose UV and tear-resistant waterproof paper, and order a custom topo map that will arrive to your mailbox in a week for under $25.

Ask the Government

If you're searching for a map of a more out-of-the-way trail, you should check with the nation's official mapmaker: the

USGS. From the USGS Map Store website, store.usgs.gov, you can use a web-based system to select specific topos. You can either download free images or PDFs of the maps or order paper copies for a nominal charge. To help you locate a specific map, all USGS quads are named after local geographical features, labeled with the year they were drawn, and assigned reference numbers. If you need assistance tracking down the right maps, you can initiate a web chat, or call a USGS researcher at 1-888-ASK-USGS between 8 A.M. and 9 P.M. EST. Unlike MyTopo. com, you can't combine topo maps on the USGS website, so you'll likely download a half dozen large-scale maps to cover your area of interest.

 Trail Tips Maps are important, but you should always talk to other hikers you encounter on the trail—especially if they are coming from the direction you are going. They can share up-to-date information and advice about the terrain that lies ahead.

Reading a Topographical Map

If you try to read a topo map like a traditional road map, you'll quickly become confused. Instead of roads and cities, you'll see forests, valleys, and mountains indicated by curving contour lines. After scratching your head, you might wonder why these maps are considered so helpful. A topo map, however, is more like a sketch of your immediate neighborhood than an atlas. Its detailed contour lines bring to life identifiable features like a steep ravine or a mountain. By learning to read those lines, you can use local features to pinpoint where you are and where you want to go.

Learn the Legend

To understand a map, you need to understand its legend—the small box of information often located in a corner. Not only does the legend tell you the map's scale, but it also gives you the contour interval (the elevation change between each contour line), a distance ruler, and the local declination—which we'll describe in the next section. The legend also explains each map's symbols, such as campsites, trailheads, and ranger stations.

Finding Yourself

The worst time to take out your map is when you're already lost. By that point, it's too late. Instead, review your map at home or at the trailhead before you start hiking. It's also a good idea to check the map at all trail junctions and summits, where it's easy to take a wrong route. If you notice a discrepancy between your trail perspective and the map—like you're climbing when you should be descending, or the setting sun is on your left when it should be on your right—don't ignore it. Open your map and review any recent turns or trail junctions. If you're carrying a topographical map, check your position by matching the map's contour lines to your surroundings using the example shown in the following section.

Reading Contour Lines

Topographical contour lines look a lot like fingerprints. Reading them, it turns out, also involves recognizing patterns. Each contour line on a topo represents a change in elevation, ranging from 10 to 100 feet depending on the map. Lines that are drawn close together mean that the terrain is very steep. Lines that are spread out indicate the terrain slopes gradually. A circle or oval could be a flat area like a meadow, or if it's surrounded by tight contour lines, it could be the broad summit of a peak.

For instance, the following illustration shows what the contour lines for a 1,800-foot mountain peak would look like on a topo map.

By recognizing what a mountain or another natural feature looks like on a topo map, you can figure out where you are on a trail.

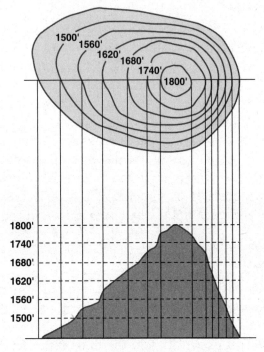

Each contour line represents 60 vertical feet on the mountain.

Getting Oriented

For everyone who spends time on a trail—but especially for the directionally challenged— finding your way in the woods requires a compass. Even with today's GPS-enabled smartphones, the compass remains a simple and reliable tool that every hiker should learn how to use.

 Safety Check Metal objects, power lines, and even buried iron ore can influence the magnetic needle on a compass. When using your compass, hold it flat and away from your body. Double-check with the time of day and the sun's position to make sure it's working right.

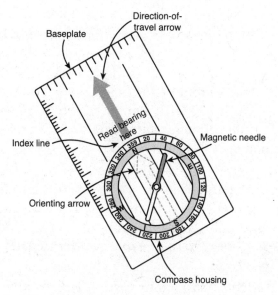

A hiker's orienteering compass has a rotating compass housing, an orienting arrow, and a flat plastic baseplate.

The Orienteering Compass

Land surveyors, ship captains, and pilots all depend on specialized compasses for their work. Hikers have their own special compass, too. It's called an *orienteering compass,* and it can be used on its own or along with a map. Unlike a cheap button or keychain compass, an orienteering compass will not only indicate north, but it can also help you navigate to a destination. A good orienteering compass will cost between $15 and $50, and it will contain all the elements needed to help you navigate:

◊ **Magnetic needle.** The needle of a compass is made from magnetized metal and floats on a pivot point. As you rotate a compass in your hand, the red end of the needle will constantly adjust itself to point north like an arrow. The opposite end of the needle will point south.

◊ **Compass housing.** The magnetic needle floats inside a rotating dial known as the *compass housing.* This dial is marked with the four cardinal directions (north, south, east, and west—sometimes labeled N, S, E, and W, respectively). The dial includes a series of degree markings from 0 to 359. Along with a map, the degree markings help you determine which direction you need to travel to reach a specific place.

◊ **Orienting arrow.** The second arrow inside the compass housing is the orienting arrow. This arrow moves when you spin the dial, and it is often marked with two lines with a space in between. As we'll see, taking a heading or bearing requires you to line up the orienting arrow with the magnetic needle.

◊ **Baseplate.** This rectangular foundation, usually made of clear plastic, often has a ruler along one edge to help you calculate map distances.

◊ **Direction-of-travel arrow.** This third and last arrow on a compass is fixed to point toward the top of the baseplate. When holding a compass in your hand or over a map, you should align the direction-of-travel arrow with your destination.

◊ **Index line.** This short line, located where the direction-of-travel arrow meets the compass housing, indicates a specific degree marking (for example, 45° 225°) depending on which direction you are facing. The index line helps you orient a map or take a bearing.

Compass Navigation

If you're new to compass navigation, prepare yourself for a shock. The red needle on your compass doesn't actually point to the geographic North Pole—called *true north*—at the top of the globe. Instead, that needle is attracted to the magnetic North Pole, which is currently located in the Canadian Arctic about 500 miles distant from Santa's workshop at true north.

For most of our everyday lives, the gap between true north and magnetic north doesn't matter. North is still up, and maps still indicate it with an arrow pointing to the top of the page. You also won't have a problem if you go on a hike and use a map to navigate a trail. It's only when you use a map and compass *together* that you need to correct for the gap between true north and magnetic north—a process called *adjusting for declination*.

Declination is the angular difference in degrees between true north (the geographic North Pole that aligns most maps) and magnetic north (where the magnetic needle on a compass points). Declination varies from place to place and must be corrected when using a map and compass together.

About Declination

This is going to sound technical, but it's actually not. If you can visualize a fade-away jump shot in basketball, or understand what "leading your target" means in sport shooting—you can understand declination. All three involve simple but important adjustments using angles to make sure your shot—or your compass—is on target.

Declination is a fancy name for the angular difference between true north and magnetic north—the gap in degrees between the two poles. It occurs because wherever you stand, your compass needle will point to the magnetic North Pole roaming somewhere inside the Arctic Circle, and not toward true north at the top of the globe. This means that the declination in Waitsfield, Vermont, is different than the declination in Sacramento, California.

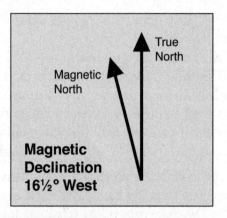

The V-shaped diagram indicating a map's declination correction is often located in its legend. In this example, the map has a declination of 16½ west.

Fortunately, you don't have to guess what the declination is for most maps because it's listed in the legend. Look for two V-shaped arrows like the previous diagram or a tilted compass dial in the corner of the map. The local declination will be marked in degrees east or west, depending on which region of the country the map depicts.

Trail Tips   Because the magnetic North Pole is slowly moving across the Canadian Arctic, local declination can change as well. To check whether an older map's declination correction is still accurate, look up the declination for a specific zip code or latitude and longitude position at the National Geophysical Data Center (NGDC)'s website: ngdc.noaa.gov/geomag/calculators/magcalc.shtml#declination.

In general, if your map depicts a location west of the Mississippi River, you'll have an east declination. Likewise, any map showing an area east of the Mississippi will indicate a west declination. For example, a map of New Hampshire's White Mountains indicates that the local declination is 16½° west. This means the compass needle in New Hampshire aligned with magnetic north is actually pointing 16½° west—or to the left—of the actual direction of true north—or the geographic North Pole.

Correcting for Declination

The easiest way to correct for declination is to purchase an orienteering compass that has an adjustable dial setting on the back of the housing. By shifting this setting at the beginning of every hike, you can fix your compass so that it will automatically show the correct bearing for true north. You do this by manually adding or subtracting the local declination indicated on the map with the adjustable declination dial.

If the declination on the map is labeled *west*, turn the adjustable declination to *add* the number of degrees to 0°. If the declination on the map is labeled *east*, *subtract* the number of degrees from 0°. You can remember when to subtract or add declination by using the following rhyme in which least means subtract, and best means add: *East is least; west is best.*

To make the adjustment for the White Mountains example I mentioned earlier, a hiker would *add* a correction of 16½° west to his compass so that the magnetic needle would indicate true north even as it pointed toward magnetic north. Once the compass was corrected, a hiker could use his map and compass together without problem.

If your compass doesn't have an adjustable declination setting, you'll need to add or subtract the local correction for every compass bearing that you take. For that reason alone, you should go out and buy a new compass that has an adjustable declination dial on the back.

Orienting Your Map

Have you ever stood in a city and turned a map round and round trying to get it lined up with the streets in front of you? Now imagine doing that in the backcountry where there are no streets or buildings to guide you. That's why getting your compass and map to work together—also called *orienting* your map—is an important navigation skill. Without it, you can't be sure that your map and your eyes are speaking the same language. You can only orient your map after you've figured out the local declination. So, if you skipped that section, go back and read it.

The best place to orient a map is when you have a good view of your surroundings. You should be able to see several identifiable terrain features like hills, rivers, or lakes. These features will confirm that you've lined it up correctly. To orient your map, follows these steps:

1. Either set your adjustable compass with the correct declination or manually turn the compass dial until the degree at the index line corresponds to the correction. Remember, "East is least (subtract); west is best (add)."

2. Place your map on a flat surface.

3. Lay the compass on the map so that the direction-of-travel arrow is pointed toward north, which is almost always at the top of the map.

4. Rotate the compass and the map together, often by rotating your body, until the red tip of the magnetic needle and the orienting arrow are lined up. This is sometimes called "Putting red Fred in the shed."

5. Congratulations. Your map is now aligned with true north and the world in front of you. Check the terrain to verify that you've done it correctly. If some landmarks look off, recheck your declination adjustment or make sure your map hasn't shifted.

Headings and Bearings

Unless you're a pilot or a boater, the words *heading* and *bearing* are probably familiar to you only from World War II submarine movies. Your heading is the direction you are currently moving. A bearing is the angle in degrees that an object or a location is in relation to you. These two terms—which describe the direction you need to travel to reach a specific destination— are as important for land navigation as they are for shooting torpedoes.

In fact, thinking about war movies is a good way to understand headings and bearings. The concepts are very similar to the clock-face method that fighter pilots use to describe the location of enemy aircraft. For instance, if you were facing due north (a heading of 0 degrees), an enemy plane approaching from your right side would be at your 3 o'clock and would be at a bearing of 90 degrees. Likewise, an enemy behind you would be at your 6 o'clock and at a bearing of 180 degrees. The two enemy planes would be heading (the direction they are traveling from their perspective) at 270 degrees and 0 degrees, respectively.

On land, taking headings and bearings is important for figuring out which direction you need to hike. For instance, a waterfall you want to hike to might be at a bearing of 145 degrees from your current location. Following that specific bearing will help you find that waterfall. Because learning how to find headings and bearings using a map is somewhat advanced, I'll cover it in detail in Chapter 20.

Upgrading to a GPS

Handheld GPS devices have come a long way since they first appeared in the mid-1990s. Not only do modern GPS units sport color touch screens and Bluetooth connectivity, they've become much easier to use, too. Whether you're a person who gets lost often or you like acquiring the latest high-tech gadgets, you'll probably appreciate the advantages of carrying a GPS on your next hike.

But before you spend $400 on a hiking GPS, you should know that you might be carrying a comparable product in your pocket right now. That's because iPhones and Android smartphones contain GPS chips able to do many of the same navigational tasks as a stand-alone GPS—and they can order pizza, too. Starting with the iPhone 6 in 2014, Apple even added a barometric pressure sensor to measure minor elevation changes. When connected with offline maps and routes downloaded from hiking apps like ViewRanger or Gaia GPS (see Chapter 1), your smartphone can function like a GPS far outside cell coverage. As useful as your phone is, however, it still lacks the durable, waterproof construction, powerful receivers, and replaceable batteries that make GPS devices ideal for trail use. For these reasons, I recommend acquiring a handheld GPS device if you hike a lot or you plan to tackle complex routes, mountaineering, or trips longer than a weekend.

A GPS pinpoints your location to within a few yards using satellite triangulation.

How GPS Works

Although it seems complicated, a GPS chip determines your location by playing an electronic version of tag with a network of more than two dozen orbiting satellites. When a GPS is switched on, it attempts to contact three or four satellites to triangulate your position and pinpoint your location to within a few dozen yards.

Choosing the Right GPS

Today, you can find GPS technology embedded in lawn mowers, drones, and dog collars. However, if you're looking for a GPS to carry on the trail, you should limit your search to devices specifically designed for outdoor use. These units run on replaceable AA-size batteries, are protected by tough impact-resistant covers, and contain sensitive satellite receivers that can peer through tree canopies. Here's a test: if a GPS unit looks flimsy, is built for a car dashboard, or can convert U.S. dollars to euros, it's not designed for hiking.

Most new GPS units today come with color screens, baseline topo maps, route tracking, and expandable memory slots. Other features—like a digital compass, barometric altimeter, and access to satellite images and weather alerts—are found only in high-end models. When deciding which GPS to buy, you should ask the same questions you would for any expensive gadget. What features do I need? How often will I use it? Where will I use it? And will it work with my phone or computer?

You should also consider your favorite outdoor activities. Most GPS makers sell models designed for specific recreational activities like biking, fitness, boating, or geocaching that can double as a hiking device.

Digital Maps

Almost all GPS units designed for hiking feature small 2- to 3-inch screens—many of them touch screens—that display a color map of your location. However, the 1:100,000–scale baseline maps preloaded onto devices aren't detailed enough for accurate route-finding. Before a trip, you'll need to purchase and import more detailed topographical maps via the device's microSD card slot or download the maps through a website or app.

Barometric Altimeter

All GPS devices can estimate your elevation by plotting your location on a map and referencing the nearest contour line. But devices with a built-in altimeter measure changes in barometric pressure to provide a more accurate elevation fix—a useful feature for mountaineering and predicting weather changes.

Electronic Compass

A typical GPS uses satellite fixes to determine your location. But a unit with an electronic compass can also tell you which direction you are facing to help identify landmarks and untangle trail junctions. However, you should still carry an orienteering compass as a backup because it doesn't require batteries to work.

Waypoints

A GPS waypoint is like a digital thumbtack stuck in a virtual map, and most devices let you save and name hundreds of waypoints to mark key locations like a water source or trail junction. If you ever need to return to a saved waypoint, the "Go To" function on a GPS can guide you back to the spot.

Routes

Downloading a route to your GPS lets you follow a digital dotted line of a trail on a screen instead of on a map. And if you diverge from the correct path, an alarm bell can sound and your GPS will direct you back to the trail. To add this capability to a GPS, download a trail route prior to your hike. Most devices can even predict your time of arrival to your destination based on your average speed. You can download GPS routes for hundreds of hiking trails at websites like backpacker.com, alltrails.com, hikingproject.com, and gaiagps.com.

Tracks

If you worry about getting lost, the "track" function on a GPS will be your guardian angel. Activate the track function at the beginning of your hike, and your GPS will lay a trail of electronic breadcrumbs wherever you hike. If you get lost or need to backtrack, simply turn around and retrace the digital trail. Most GPS devices use the data from your track to calculate your average speed, time spent stopped, elevation gain or loss, and even rate of climb—all of which are useful for planning future hikes.

SUMMARY

Topographical maps, which show physical features and elevation changes using contour lines, are the gold standard for trail navigation. But a map's scale—the level of detail it shows—matters, too, with 1:24,000 topographical maps being the most useful for route-finding. Although an orienteering compass points north, it also does a lot more, especially when you pair it with a map. But first make sure to adjust for magnetic declination (the angular difference between magnetic north and true north). If this sounds complex, it is. But it's still easier than getting unlost.

PART 2

GEARING UP

Equipment can be both an entry and an obstacle to getting on the trail. A new pair of snowshoes might inspire a winter hike, but the high cost of a portable stove could discourage a backpacking trip. And how do you know if the gear you own is adequate for the hike you want to do? To bring order to the complex and expensive world of gear, the next five chapters will describe the basic kit of footwear, packs, and clothing you need to hike safely and successfully and which accessories are helpful but also optional.

GEAR ESSENTIALS FOR EVERY TRIP

Not all hiking rules are set in stone. Your personal preference still counts, such as which style of pack to carry or where to pitch your tent. However, there are several rules that shouldn't be ignored. For instance, never approach a bear—even if it *seems* friendly. Don't eat wild mushrooms, unless you have a PhD in botany. And one more rule you should always follow is to bring certain essential gear on every hiking trip—even a short day-hike. In this chapter, I discuss the vital hiking and safety gear that you don't want to leave home without.

What Are the Essentials?

Like the Seven Wonders of the Ancient World, the list of hiking essentials has stood the test of time with few changes or additions. It's persisted because of the inescapable limitation of hiking: you can only carry a certain amount of stuff. As a result, hiking gear must be prioritized, and only the most important and useful items will make the cut. In the case of the essentials, each of these items could save your life if you get in trouble on the trail.

What should be your essential gear? You can probably guess most of the items—but here's the complete list:

- ○ Map, compass, and GPS-enabled device
- ○ Headlamp and extra batteries
- ○ Knife or multitool
- ○ First aid kit
- ○ Butane lighter or waterproof matches and flammable tinder
- ○ Warm clothes, rain gear, and an emergency shelter

- Gear repair kit
- Signaling devices
- Extra food and water
- Sunscreen
- Insect repellent

Most of these items, like the extra food and clothing, you'd probably pack anyway. Others, like headlamps and butane lighters, you might forget at home or accidentally leave in the car. If you keep this list handy while you pack for a trip, you'll be less likely to leave important gear behind.

Who Should Carry the Essentials?

In reviewing the list of essentials, it's hard to justify a reason not to pack any one of them. Still, plenty of hikers find reasons to leave them behind. *It's only a day-hike. Why do I need to bring a headlamp?* Of course, when that day-hike turns into an involuntary overnight trip because of a missed trail junction and a twisted ankle, they'll wish they had some extra illumination to see the trail.

The purpose of the essentials is entirely precautionary. They seem like extra weight until you depend on them to keep you warm, guide your way, or protect you from the elements.

 Safety Check If you're hiking solo, be sure to carry all the essentials. Without a second person to go for help, you are entirely dependent on the gear you're carrying in case you become injured or immobilized. If you're hiking in a group, not every person needs to pack a first aid kit or a compass but having extras can help.

Let's review each of the essentials so you'll know what to bring and how to use it in case of an emergency.

Map, Compass, and GPS-Enabled Device

Let's say you find an amazing loop trail in a guidebook, and you review the route, check the map, and drive to the trailhead. Once there, you decide the guidebook is too heavy to carry, so you toss it on the backseat of the car and set off hiking. That's where the guidebook is 2 hours later when you realize the simple loop trail is more complicated than you thought, and now you're hopelessly lost.

I've encountered this scenario so many times that my wife, Jackie, and I now have an ironclad rule: we always bring multiple maps on every hike. No matter how heavy it might be, a detailed map is an invaluable insurance policy against getting lost. Of course, you don't need to carry the entire guidebook or an enormous fold-out map. Instead, make color photocopies or take photos on your phone of the relevant sections of the map, ensuring that important details like contour lines, trail markings, and place names are readable.

Along with a map, you should always bring an orienteering compass, described in Chapter 6. Even if you don't know your exact location on a map, the red magnetic arrow on a compass can tell you the general direction you need to travel to reach a known landmark like a road or another trail.

Adding a GPS or a smartphone with a GPS app to your navigation arsenal (see Chapter 6) is a great idea, but a map and compass are the original and real essentials. That's because electronic gadgets have a habit of breaking or running low on batteries just when you need them the most. For instance, the tumble that twists your ankle could also smash the screen on your phone. A low-tech map and compass can guide you to safety even after you accidentally dunk them in a stream.

A Light in the Dark

A bright light is more than just a good way to see at night. The ability to shine a light is also a major morale booster. That advantage becomes most important when the sun goes down while you're hiking and the campsite is still three miles away. For that reason, and many more, you should always pack a reliable light source and extra batteries, even on a day-hike when you expect to be finished before dark.

If you're still wondering whether you bring a *headlamp* or a flashlight on a hike, here's a newsflash: Headlamps are compact, adjustable lights that wrap around your forehead using an elastic band. Wherever you look, it shines a beam of light to illuminate your field of view. Headlamps are far superior for lighting your way on the trail than a handheld flashlight. Headlamps are not only lighter and more durable, but they're also much more convenient. With a headlamp secured to your forehead, your hands are free to search through a backpack, grasp hiking poles, or hold a map.

Headlamps range in size from ultralight to heavy duty. In general, the size of the headlamp is determined by its battery pack, which range from watch batteries to AAs, and the number of bulbs, which can be either LEDs (light-emitting diodes), incandescent, or halogen.

 Trail Tips Protect spare batteries from moisture and corrosion by putting them in a plastic bag or covering them in plastic wrap. Store them in your first aid kit so you always have them handy.

For most day-hikers and backpackers, a small AAA-battery powered LED headlamp will provide all the light they need. LED illumination is sufficient to read a map, cook a meal, or navigate a trail in the dark. LED lights are also popular because the bulbs are small, are virtually unbreakable, and require much less energy to operate than other options. Most LED headlamps can remain on for 15 to 20 hours before needing new batteries. The bulbs themselves last for thousands of hours before burning out. Most headlamps combine several LEDs to boost overall brightness or allow users to adjust the beam's intensity level between several settings.

Knives and Multitools

Enormous knives might suit fictional characters like Crocodile Dundee and Rambo, but those blades won't cut it for hikers. Instead, the ideal hiking knife should feature a small, sharp, 2- to 3-inch-long blade.

Safety Check A dull blade is a dangerous blade because it can easily slip and cut you. If your knife can't cleanly slice through a piece of paper, you need to sharpen it using a whetstone.

Even better than hiking knives—but more expensive—are multitools. These devices combine knives with useful gadgets like pliers, files, and scissors. Knife manufacturers like Gerber, SOG, Victorinox, and Leatherman make the majority of stainless-steel multitools today. These devices can come with dozens of different implements, but the following gadgets are the most useful on the trail:

◊ A sharp blade for cutting and slicing

◊ A serrated blade for sawing fabric and wood

◊ Pliers for holding hot containers

◊ A ruler for measuring map distances

◊ A can opener for cooking

◊ Scissors for cutting bandages

◊ Tweezers for removing ticks and thorns

◊ Screwdrivers for repairing gear

 Trail Tips You wouldn't drive a new car without testing the brakes, right? Likewise, you should never use a first aid kit without knowing its contents. Before your first hike, open your kit and review all the items.

First Aid Kit

Tucked inside every backpack—preferably in an easily accessible pocket—should be a *small* pouch containing basic first aid gear. Notice the emphasis on *small*. Large kits stuffed with dozens of bandages, splints, ointments, and scalpels are impractical, especially when most hiking injuries are blisters, scrapes, and minor burns. (See Chapter 17 for more on first aid treatments.)

Instead, you should bring a kit that's most appropriate for the kind of trip you're taking. Wallet-size kits are adequate for day and weekend hikes, while toilet-kit-size pouches are more appropriate for trips that last a weekend or longer. Here are the types of injuries your first aid kit should be able to treat depending on the length of your hike:

- ◊ **For a day-hike:** Blisters, cuts, scrapes, sprains, insect stings, muscle aches and swelling, and allergic reactions.
- ◊ **For a weekend hike:** All day-hiking injuries plus bleeding wounds, burns, infection prevention, diarrhea, and dehydration.
- ◊ **For a weeklong hike:** All weekend hiking injuries plus severe bleeding and bone fractures. Note: Bring a first aid book on hikes of this length.

Solo hikers should carry a first aid kit on all hikes, even short day trips. Groups should carry at least one first aid kit for every two to three hikers. You can create your own kit by stocking a toiletry bag or zipper-lock plastic bag with items you purchase at a drug store, or you can buy prestocked kits in various sizes from suppliers like Adventure Medical Kits or I GO. Also, make sure you're packing a first aid kit and not a survival kit, as the latter has items like water purification tablets and fishing gear that are impractical for hiking. For a complete list of what your first aid kit should contain, see Equipment Checklists.

Before each trip, check your first aid kit to make sure it contains an adequate supply of these critical items that can run out:

- ◊ Adhesive bandages—both butterfly and rectangular
- ◊ Painkillers (Advil, Aleve, or Motrin)
- ◊ Moleskin, SecondSkin, or other blister bandage to treat blisters
- ◊ Sterile gauze pads
- ◊ Adhesive tape
- ◊ Antibiotic ointment
- ◊ Burn salve or aloe vera skin lotion

Many prestocked first aid kits lack simple items that can be extremely useful for wilderness first aid. Check your kit, and add these items if they aren't already there:

◇ Packets of sugary drink powder for instant energy
◇ Benadryl (diphenhydramine) to stop allergic reactions
◇ Moist towelettes or baby wipes to clean wounds
◇ Safety pins to secure bandages or make slings

Fire Starters and Tinder

The ability to make fire hasn't diminished in importance since the Stone Age. But coaxing a blaze from a damp pile of twigs is difficult, even for a cave dweller. Because the ability to make a fire is critical to survival, all hikers should carry a reliable ignition source and easily burnable tinder.

A simple and inexpensive butane cigarette lighter is the fire starter of choice for many backpackers. Not only are they handy for igniting gas-powered cook stoves, but they can light regular fires, too. Don't be tempted to purchase a jet-flame lighter, an electric torch, or a fancy lighter marketed as survival necessity, and use the money you save to purchase more useful gear.

Another reliable option is a ferrocerium fire starter consisting of an iron oxide rod and a metal striker that, when scraped together rapidly, produce a white-hot shower of sparks capable of igniting a gas stove or a pile of tinder. One more old-school option is waterproof matches stored in a plastic case. These are regular wooden matches with the flammable ends dipped in wax, nail polish, or another impermeable coating. Before using the matches, you must scrape off the coating to expose the striking surface. Regular wooden and paper matchbooks aren't reliable fire starters because damp weather turns matchbooks into mush.

Besides an ignition source like a lighter, a fire also requires highly flammable tinder. Packing a small quantity of tinder ensures that you can light a fire in wet, windy conditions when you need it the most. (See Chapter 16 for fire-starting tips.) Store your tinder in a waterproof container, like a zipper-lock plastic bag or empty pill bottle, and stash it inside your first aid kit.

You can buy commercial tinder products like Ultimate Survival Technologies' WetFire Tinder cubes or Coghlan's Fire Sticks. Or you can create your own from simple household items like the following:

◊ Dryer lint
◊ Cotton balls soaked in petroleum jelly
◊ Steel wool
◊ Birthday candles
◊ Wax-coated strips of cardboard

Additional Clothing or Emergency Shelters

Carrying extra warm clothing or an emergency shelter is smart insurance against an unplanned night outdoors. It doesn't take much—a wrong turn, a busted knee, or a raging river—to make your trip last longer than you expected. Backpackers on a multiday trek have this contingency covered. All they need to do is pitch their tents, unroll their sleeping bags, and crawl inside. (You'll learn more about tents and sleeping bags in Chapter 12.) Day-hikers, however, should also bring additional clothing or a lightweight shelter in case they get stranded or lost.

When It's Warm

During summer day-hikes, when nighttime lows stay above 55°F, packing an extra insulating layer like a fleece jacket and a winter hat will help you retain body heat during an unplanned night outside, especially if you layer a windproof and waterproof shell on top. Why pack a winter hat for a hike in the middle of the summer? If your entire body is insulated but your head is still left bare, you are going to burn a lot more energy trying to keep your noggin warm.

In the fall or spring, when nighttime temperatures drop much lower, day-hikers should pack a space blanket, which is a poncho-like emergency wrap made from silvery metallized polyester like Mylar. These blankets weigh only a few ounces and reflect up to 90 percent of your body heat back to you. They can be found online and in most outdoor gear stores.

When It's Cold

If you are day-hiking during the winter or any time when nighttime lows approach freezing (32°F), you should pack a sleeping bag in addition to extra warm layers and a hat. Even without a tent, a sleeping bag that is insulated from the ground by pine branches and leaf litter can keep you warm during a very cold night. You can also use a sleeping bag to keep an injured hiker protected and warm while they wait for rescue or evacuation or to treat someone suffering from hypothermia. (See Chapter 17 for hypothermia first aid.)

 Trail Tips   To pack duct tape without bringing a heavy roll, wrap several feet of the tape around a plastic water bottle or trekking pole. Rip off pieces of the tape as you need it.

Gear Repair Kit

Fixing a broken pack strap on the trail is similar to changing a flat tire: you only need the repair to last until you get back home. As a result, a gear repair kit should contain a few basic but versatile items that can stabilize equipment problems. Repair kits are optional for day-hikers who aren't likely to experience a catastrophic gear failure. However, anyone attempting a weekend hike should bring the following items, storing them in a small nylon or zipper-lock plastic bag:

◊ Extra shoelaces
◊ Needle and nylon thread or fishing line
◊ Safety pins
◊ Plastic zip ties
◊ Tube of seam grip or rubber cement
◊ Nylon adhesive patches

◊ Small bungie or elastic cords

◊ Nylon repair tape

 Trail Tips You can improvise a signal mirror by using the hologram on a credit card, shiny gum wrappers, or the inside surface of an aluminum can.

Signaling Devices

Getting lost in the woods is a lot easier than getting found by a search-and-rescue team. To enhance your ability to be seen and heard, all hikers should carry a whistle at the very least, and preferably a signal mirror and cell phone.

Ounce for ounce, a whistle is one of the most valuable safety devices you can carry. It weighs so little that you might even forget that you have one. The sound of a whistle can carry for a mile—much farther than a human voice. If you ever get in trouble, three sharp blasts from a whistle is the international signal for distress.

A signal mirror is a small, rectangular piece of reflective glass that turns sunlight into a bright flash of light that can be seen up to 10 miles away. These mirrors are especially useful for attracting search planes and helicopters. Most signal mirrors include a small aiming dot in the center of the glass that helps hikers direct the flash to a specific point. You can also improvise a signal mirror like the day-hiker who became lost in Arizona's Coconino National Forest and caught the attention of rescuers by triggering the flash on her digital camera.

The first edition of this book called cell phones a "valuable emergency tool," and that description has only gotten more accurate as phones have become more durable with longer-lasting batteries and better navigation technology. Nowadays, a smartphone can not only function as a standalone GPS device (see Chapter 6), but it can make emergency calls, send text messages, determine navigation points, and signal rescuers. Calling 911 from the trail can save hours of hiking and waiting to arrange an evacuation. Now that more backcountry areas receive voice and text message coverage, it's easier to make contact on the trail. So, instead of leaving your phone in your car's glove compartment, always bring it, and use a zipper-lock plastic bag or waterproof case to protect it from rain or water leaks. And remember to turn off your phone's Wi-Fi and Bluetooth receivers to conserve battery life on the trail.

Rain Gear

The most important task for any foul weather apparel is to keep your body—especially your torso and head—warm and dry. When clothing becomes damp or wet, it loses much of its insulating value and begins to steal your body heat.

Wearing a waterproof rain shell will not only protect you from moisture, but it will also protect you from wind, which removes heat through convection when it blows across your exposed skin. Waterproof shells are most effective when worn over an insulating layer like a wool or fleece jacket or sweater. Rain pants—a waterproof layer that hikers sometimes put on over shorts or pants—are generally unnecessary unless you know you'll be hiking through persistent downpours.

Extra Food and Water

The amount of food and water you bring on a hike should reflect how many days you plan to spend on a trail—plus a little extra in case of an emergency. For a day-hike, packing extra food requires bringing several more energy bars. On backpacking trips, you should bring at least one extra meal. This survival food should be packed separately from your meals so that you won't eat it for a snack. The kind of food you bring depends on your personal taste, but it should have the following characteristics.

◊ High calorie content
◊ Long shelf life
◊ Edible without requiring hot water

◊ Low protein content (for example, not beef jerky) because high-protein foods increase thirst

◊ Won't melt or freeze (for example, no chocolate bars)

Choosing nonperishable emergency rations ensures that you won't need to replace it every time you go for a hike and that it will still be palatable when you need to crack it open. Here are several popular choices for emergency foods:

◊ Energy bars

◊ Tuna foil-packs

◊ Mac and cheese packets

◊ Freeze-dried mashed potatoes

◊ Dried fruit packets

You can survive for weeks without food, but only a few agonizing days without water. To avoid running dry, plan to carry 2 to 3 liters of water for any hike that will last longer than a few hours. If you'll be traveling in hot or dry conditions or the terrain will be strenuous, you should bring 4 to 5 liters.

Store your water in hard plastic 1-liter bottles or hydration reservoirs. Most hikers find that plastic soda bottles are too flimsy to stand up to the rough handling they'll get on the trail. Insulated flasks, although they carry less liquid, can keep beverages warm or cold against opposing outside temperatures. They are especially welcome on cold-weather trips.

Refilling your empty water bottles from streams, springs, and other natural sources is a common way to reduce the number of water bottles you need to carry on a hike. Backpackers and day-hikers often carry a treatment or filter system to make this water safe to drink. In Chapter 14, you'll learn more about different methods hikers can use to filter and purify water and also how much you should carry depending on the distance and conditions of your hike.

Safety Check Avoid wristbands, patches, and balms that claim to repel insects because they just don't work.

Sunscreen

Every hiker loves a sunny day on the trail, but too much sun can turn your face and arms red before you know it. To prevent a painful sunburn, hikers should apply a sunscreen rated at least SPF 30 on every trip—even during the winter when the sun's rays reflect off the white snow. Wide-brimmed hats, sunglasses, and long-sleeve shirts offer additional protection and should be worn during the sunniest part of the day. (Learn about clothing that doubles as sunblock in Chapter 10.) If you do get burned, read about treatment options in Chapter 17.

Insect Repellent

Few people appreciate products that repel mosquitoes, ticks, and biting flies more than hikers. However, with so many products out there, how do you know what works? The answer is just one word—or really, one chemical acronym: DEET. Numerous lab and field tests have proven that DEET is the most effective ingredient to keep biting insects at bay. In addition, the products that work best contain DEET concentrations of between 30 and 100 percent.

DEET, however, is corrosive to plastic and rubber, and it should be applied to your skin sparingly and according to the following guidelines:

◊ Avoid using concentrations stronger than 30 percent on children under the age of 12.

◊ DEET-based repellents will melt synthetic fabrics like spandex and rayon, so don't spray it on your clothes or gear. Nylon, cotton, and wool are unaffected.

◊ Keep DEET away from open wounds and scratches.

◊ Store DEET containers in double-layer zipper-lock plastic bags to prevent leakage.

Non-DEET alternatives include products with the active ingredients picaridin, citronella, or lemon eucalyptus oil. Another repellent popular among hikers is Avon Skin-So-Soft Bug Guard, which combines an SPF 15 sunscreen and the chemical IR3525 to create a nongreasy, pleasant-smelling lotion.

SUMMARY

Innovations in camping gear appear every year, but the basic essentials—the vital safety equipment you should bring on every day-hike and backpacking trip—have remained the same for decades. These essentials can prevent problems (a map and compass to keep you on the right trail) and stop a bad situation from getting worse (rain gear and warm clothing to reverse hypothermia). Don't skimp on this list because the trip where you decide to leave the headlamp in the car will be the one where you twist your ankle and have to travel after dark.

WELCOME TO GEAR WORLD

It's Thursday night before a weekend hike when you finally find the time to pack your gear. To your dismay, you discover your sleeping pad has a tear, your stove is on the fritz, and your shoelaces are frayed. Sound like a familiar last-minute scramble? You're not alone. Most hikers wait until the night before a trip to pack their equipment.

The better approach is to make organizing, maintaining, and restocking your outdoor gear a routine task. Whether you're preparing for the start of the spring hiking season or just getting outfitted for a single trip, the earlier you review your equipment, the better prepared you'll be. This doesn't mean packing weeks in advance. Instead, you should rummage through your gear to review everything you own a week before a trip or several times a year. You should also use this time to determine which items are wearing out and need to be replaced before your next hike. After all, Amazon doesn't have instant delivery—yet.

The next several chapters in this book will cover everything you need to know about gear—from matching your hiking boots with specific terrain to finding the perfect tent. But before diving into the specifics of which product is superior to another, you need to know how to navigate the world of outdoor gear. To get you started, this chapter provides an overview of how to make smart decisions about organizing and buying your gear. Before you spend a single dollar, you need to understand how to evaluate your needs, ask the right questions, read reviews, and find the best bargains. If you don't, you'll acquire a collection of expensive gear that you never use. To discover the tools and insight you need to master the world of outdoor gear, read on.

Using What You Already Own

Before you pull out a credit card to order the latest and greatest titanium, ultralight camping gizmo, stop and ask yourself these questions:

◊ Do I really need this item right now?

◊ Do I currently own something that works just as well?

◊ What other gear could I be spending this money on?

These questions aren't meant as a killjoy. I know the thrill of walking out of a gear store carrying my latest purchase. But because most of us have a limited budget for camping and hiking gear, we need to prioritize what we purchase by focusing only on the essentials.

Making a List

The first step toward prioritization is to take a realistic inventory of what you already own and what you're missing. Grab a packing checklist like the one in Equipment Checklists and start sorting through your belongings. Use it to develop these four lists:

1. **Inventory:** Working, usable gear you already own

2. **Necessities:** New gear you need right away—usually for a specific hike or trip

3. **Replacements:** Upgrades to replace broken, failing, or outdated gear

4. **Wish list:** The nifty items you want but can't justify or afford now

These lists will help you focus on the items you need in the short term.

 Trail Tips Borrow gear from friends or coworkers to test it before deciding if you absolutely need it. Some outdoor retail stores also rent gear like tents, snowshoes, and backpacks.

Check Your Closet

New hikers are often convinced they need to spend hundreds of dollars to buy the latest, must-have gear. While beginners do need some essential items like comfortable footwear, hiking clothes, and a durable backpack, they might already own a lot of vital gear—and just not realize it. Before you spend a fortune outfitting yourself for the trail, check your basement and your closet for the following items that can be repurposed for the trail:

◊ Nylon or polyester athletic shorts

◊ Sports and bike water bottles

◊ Long underwear

◊ Wool sweaters

◊ Running shoes

◊ First aid supplies

◊ Winter hats and gloves

◊ Foam sleeping pads

◊ Emergency gear for your home or car

What Not to Bring

You're better off leaving some gear and clothing at home. For instance, my family photos from the 1970s and 1980s show everyone sitting around a campsite wearing cotton blue jeans. Being seen in those clothes today would be more than a fashion faux pas. When cotton gets wet from sweat or rain, it can take hours to dry. Of course, cotton clothing is just fine for warm-weather car-camping. But for most day-hikes and backpacking trips, you're much better off wearing clothes made from synthetic fabrics like nylon or polyester or an insulating natural fabric like wool. Here's a list of the gear and clothing that might seem okay for a trip in the woods but really should be left at home:

◊ Cotton and denim shirts, pants, and sweatshirts

◊ Any slumber-party sleeping bag or tent that has a cartoon character or brand on it

- ◊ School backpacks
- ◊ Any coat or jacket with leather
- ◊ Sandals, open-toed shoes, basketball high-tops, or dress shoes
- ◊ Trench coats or long rain jackets

Replacing Old and Broken Gear

I still carry the same compass I used as a Boy Scout to earn my orienteering merit badge. It points north just as well as it ever did, and I'll continue to use it until it breaks. However, not all outdoor gear is as durable or reliable. One purpose of your periodic gear reviews should be to identify and replace defective gear before it goes kaput in the middle of a hike.

Watch for Slow Leaks

As I mentioned, when gear gradually wears out, it should be replaced before it becomes a problem. If you don't replace it early enough, Murphy's Law ensures that it will break at the absolute worst possible time. Sleeping bags are one such item to watch. All sleeping bags lose their insulating ability over time, with synthetic fillings degrading much more quickly than down bags. Gas stoves, headlamps, and water filters also have a habit of sputtering along and then suddenly refusing to work. In some cases, you might have to completely replace a piece of gear. Fortunately, sleeping bags and most water filters can be cleaned and repaired to add a few more productive years to their lifespan. (Learn how to clean sleeping bags in Chapter 12 and water filters in Chapter 14.)

Out with the Old, In with the New

There are some categories of gear where you shouldn't wait for something to break or fail. Designers are constantly working to improve their products and occasionally, they can make amazing breakthroughs that transform the way people hike and camp. As a result, an item you bought 4 or 5 years ago becomes vastly inferior to a better model.

Generally, you should replace a perfectly good piece of gear if something newer will significantly reduce the amount of weight you carry or improve your quality of life on the trail. Here's a list of the gear categories that have shown significant improvements in design and performance over the last several years. If you're still using last generation's gear, consider upgrading:

◊ Smartphones with GPS apps (see Chapters 1 and 6)
◊ Lightweight backpacking tents (see Chapter 12)
◊ Fuel-efficient canister cooking stoves (see Chapter 13)
◊ Fast-acting water filters (see Chapter 14)
◊ Solar-powered chargers (see Chapter 16)

The Smart Hiker's Guide to Buying Gear

When you purchase an item for the first time—from a vacuum cleaner to new car tires—you should research the best brands and compare quality versus cost. The same goes for camping and hiking gear. Today's manufacturers embed so many high-tech materials into their products that you need to do your homework when shopping. Outdoor consumers should compare brands, read the reviews and the fine print, test different styles, and search for the best price. Like any shopping decision, try to avoid last-minute and impulsive purchases. Because buying a new tent, sleeping bag, or backpack often requires an investment of hundreds of dollars, you don't want to waste your money.

The Call of Retail

The best place to get equipped for hiking and camping is an outdoor specialty store. Not only are staff members at these stores knowledgeable about hiking and camping gear, but most are also avid hikers and campers who can give you tips based on their own experience. Another bonus is that they have the equipment and the expertise to properly fit boots, backpacks, and other gear that requires custom measurements. Every medium and large city will support one or two independent, mom-and-pop outfitters, especially cities located near popular recreation areas.

In many regions of the country, you can also find outdoor chain stores like REI and EMS or outlet stores for online brands like Sierra Trading Post and Patagonia. Stores that mainly cater to military personnel, athletes, and hunters also carry large inventories of hiking and camping gear. These include small local establishments, as well as chains like Dick's Sporting Goods, Sportsman's Warehouse, Cabela's, and Bass Pro Shops.

One of Seattle's most popular tourist attractions isn't a museum or a ballpark; instead, it's the REI flagship store, which contains 100,000 square feet of retail space that includes a 450-foot-long bike trail and a 65-foot-tall indoor climbing wall.

Every outdoor retail store has a different layout and atmosphere, but you can get better service and find more deals if you navigate them according to the following tips:

◊ If you're buying boots or shoes, try them on first so you can test them while walking around the store. Most stores won't allow you to wear footwear outside.

◊ The best deals and discounted items are usually placed in the rear of the store.

◊ To get more attention from store staff, shop midweek during your lunch break or midafternoon before the evening rush begins.

◊ Ask for personal recommendations from staff members— they've probably used most of the gear on the racks.

◊ Don't be shy about trying out gear; crawl inside sleeping bags and tents to discover how much elbow room you have. For a two-person tent, ask someone else to join you.

◊ Compare headlamp brightness in a dark closet, storage room, or bathroom with the lights turned off.

◊ When trying on backpacks, load them with at least 20 pounds of sandbags, rope, or tents.

◊ If something doesn't feel right, don't buy it. Gear doesn't magically feel any better on the trail.

Many outdoor specialty shops like REI and Cabela's offer free clinics and classes from compass navigation to wilderness survival. Check store websites and bulletin boards for schedules.

 Safety Check Tempted to buy outdoor gear at a local big box store? Don't do it. Even though prices are sometimes cheaper at big-box stores, you shouldn't buy there. First, you won't get much help from the salespeople who may have limited or no hiking experience. Second, even if the products are made by a recognizable brand, the quality of the materials and workmanship will be inferior to the products they ship to real outdoor gear shops. So, stick with big-box stores for buying stove fuel and toilet paper—not sleeping bags and tents.

Filling Your Virtual Shopping Cart

While websites lack the bricks-and-mortar sturdiness and helpful staff of a regular store, they do offer significant advantages like greater selection, online reviews, and often cheaper prices. So, if a broad search based on other people's feedback is your approach, and you don't mind buying gear without holding it first, you can shop online. And while Amazon.com sells camping gear in addition to everything else, it's worthwhile to review the selection and reviews at outdoor-focused online retailers to discover the best-selling brands and models as indicated by dedicated hikers and campers.

Here's a list of the most popular online gear stores:

◊ Backcountry.com

◊ Cabelas.com

◊ Campmor.com

◊ EMS.com

◊ LLBean.com

◊ Mountaingear.com

◊ REI.com

◊ SierraTradingPost.com

 Trail Tips When you buy online from gear retailers with actual stores like REI and Sierra Trading Post, you can opt for free shipping to one of their physical locations. You can either ship it to the store closest to you or to a location near your hiking destination.

Smart Ways to Save

In case you haven't figured it out already, outdoor gear is expensive. How else could Patagonia charge $99 for a hiking shirt? In Patagonia's defense, the shirt is made from hemp, recycled polyester, and cellulose, but $99 could also buy you a new water filter or a nice sleeping pad. For the savvy shopper, there are always techniques to save money—even in the overpriced outdoor market.

How much you can save depends on when and where you buy and whether you comparison shop. No matter what, you should always check the clearance, outlet, and overstock products at outdoor equipment websites and stores before paying full price. Even though the clearance racks don't carry the newest items or the widest selections, they do offer the best prices; you could get lucky and find a waterproof jacket marked down by 65 percent.

 Trail Tips   Being able to delay a purchase is also an advantage. For instance, if you want to buy a new camp stove, wait for a new model to be introduced and then buy the previous year's model at a reduced price.

Here are several more tips to save money while stocking up on gear:

◊ Avoid rushing out to purchase brand-new gear as soon as it's available. Not only will you pay top price, but the initial production runs often contain defects and problems that aren't identified during product testing.

◊ Shop out of season—purchase snowshoes and hats in March and camping equipment in October.

◊ Watch for end-of-season sales when stores try to get rid of their unsold inventory to make room for the next season's gear.

◊ Because selections of discounted and outlet items are often limited, focus on getting the right size rather than your favorite color.

◊ Get discounts on a specific brand by signing up for marketing emails and special promotions on the manufacturer's website.

◊ Purchase floor models or "irregulars," gear with minor cosmetic defects.

Buying Used Gear

Buying gently used gear is a smart way to save dough as long as you have a sharp enough eye to distinguish the trash from the treasure. Thrifty shoppers like you can benefit from other hikers' slightly worn but still workable cast-offs.

Instead of searching for used gear in newspaper classifieds, go online to find the biggest marketplaces and best deals. The website Craigslist.org hosts online classifieds for more than 400 local communities from Spokane, Washington, to Space Coast, Florida, with most outdoor gear offered under the category "sporting." You can also shop your social network by posting your gear requests to your friends on Facebook or other social media platforms. Consignment shops and Goodwill stores are also good places to snag gently used clothing, including hard-to-find items like wool sweaters and waterproof jackets.

Get Help from Product Reviews

Crawling inside a sleeping bag at a retail store will tell you how it fits, but not how warm it will keep you during a cold and windy night. To gain that insight, you need to rely on gear reviews.

Reading and watching gear reviews is a critical element of shopping for outdoor equipment. With so many available brands and models, you'll need reliable information to narrow down your choices. Gear reviews can be written by professionals who work for outdoor magazines or websites or by everyday consumers like you who record both positive and negative observations about equipment they own. Because most reviews are posted online, here's a list of the most popular websites that publish them:

◊ Backpacker.com/gear

◊ BackpackGearTest.org

◊ Outsideonline.com/outdoor-gear

◊ Outdoorgearlab.com

The best reviews and videos are written or produced by people who actually put gear through its paces on multiple hikes and camping trips. These reviewers will indicate where they tested the gear, how long the testing lasted, and how it responded to specific conditions. The most in-depth reviews are often written or produced by *gearheads,* people who could spend hours debating isobutane stove performance or the durability of 420-denier nylon fabrics.

On the other hand, steer clear of "armchair reviews," where it's obvious that the author never actually tested the gear in the field and is merely repeating the information provided by the manufacturer. Look for evidence that the reviewer tested the gear in realistic trail conditions before you trust his or her opinion.

 Trail Tips   One of the easiest and most useful DIY gear projects is a plastic footprint that protects the underside of your tent from water and punctures. Make your own footprint by tracing the bottom of your tent on a sheet of 2-millimeter-thick painter's plastic or Tyvek housewrap, and cutting it out.

Watching Video Reviews

Many professional and amateur gear reviewers, as well as outdoor-oriented magazines and writers, produce videos for their own YouTube channels. These videos are a quick way to get first impressions about the latest gear or new ideas on how to make your existing setup work better. Other channels focus on teaching skills like survival (see Chapter 16) and first aid (see Chapter 17). Nowadays, smartphone cameras enable many of these videos to be recorded on the trail with high levels of video and audio quality. But because there are literally thousands of YouTube personalities making millions of videos, look for channels that match your experience level, interests, and hiking style, and start with the videos that have attracted the most views. Some of the best and most prolific gear reviewers on YouTube are TheOutdoorGearReview, Darwin onthetrail, and REI.

Making Your Own Gear

If you can't afford to buy new gear, go ahead and build it. While the DIY option doesn't make sense for shoes and backpacks, it can be a fun and affordable solution to acquire smaller but still expensive items. After all, the DIY ethic is responsible for many gear innovations, from the hydration bladder to the headlamp. Here is a list of the hiking and camping gear that people commonly build:

◊ Ground tarp or plastic footprint for a tent

◊ Aluminum or plastic windscreen for a stove

◊ Alcohol-fueled stoves

◊ Rain tarps and shelters

◊ Wax and sawdust fire starters

◊ Bottle insulators and cozies

◊ Camper showers

If you're not someone who likes to tinker, then continue to buy your gear from a store or website. However, if you do enjoy designing and building useful contraptions, then DIY gear could be an option.

To get project ideas and learn techniques, watch some of the dozens of YouTube video channels devoted to DIY backpacking gear, including Nature Calls Backpacking and Homemade Wanderlust. Or you can borrow ideas by following crafty gear makers on Pinterest. Keep in mind that the gearheads who produce these DIY videos are often experienced backpackers whose skill level enables them to cut corners on weight and safety.

How New Gear Could Make You a Better Hiker

One of the best reasons to purchase new gear is to lower your pack weight. With less of a burden on your back, you can cover more miles each day—and your muscles will feel less tired when you're done. The type of gear you own and buy can contribute to the two main methods for reducing pack weight: carrying lighter, smaller gear and bringing less stuff to begin with.

The Rise of the Ultralight

Up until the 1990s, weight wasn't a major factor in how gear was designed. But ever since *ultralight backpacking* grew from a niche concept to a trendsetting category, the weight of tents, sleeping bags, and backpacks has dropped first by ounces and then by pounds. Ultralight backpacking is a hiking philosophy that emphasizes carrying extremely light loads, with full backpacks weighing 20 pounds or less. To achieve these weight reductions, ultralight hikers carry gear made from the lightest materials and leave behind any equipment that isn't essential.

Lighter gear has now become a constant demand of hikers and a major selling point for manufacturers. As a result, new lightweight materials are used to make all kinds of gear—from titanium tent stakes to Silnylon stuff sacks.

For these reasons, smart shoppers should consider weight when evaluating gear. Most product lines now include lightweight options, including less obvious gear categories like first aid kits and cooking utensils. Lighter gear isn't always more expensive. Headlamps and stoves with fewer features can be both lighter and less expensive than more complicated models.

Pack Only What You Need

Another technique to reduce pack weight—bringing less stuff— is so simple it doesn't sound like real advice. Just because there's extra room in your pack doesn't mean that you should fill it with nonessential or redundant gear. Here are some tips to prevent overpacking:

◊ Avoid redundancies; make sure your headlamp works and your knife is sharp rather than bringing two.

◊ Pack multifunctional gear like a waterproof stuff sack to haul water and tent guy lines that double as clotheslines.

◊ Leave a pillow at home and use a stuff sack filled with your clothes for the next day.

- ◊ Purchase a pair of convertible pants, which zip off below the knees to become shorts.
- ◊ Pack one T-shirt for every 2 to 3 days you'll spend on the trail, with a max of three shirts. Everyone you meet will smell the same.
- ◊ Bandannas and microfiber pack towels can serve many uses—from pot-holder to sunshade to dish rag.

Treating Your Gear Right

Buying a $250 down sleeping bag isn't just a purchase, it's an investment. If you take good care of that sleeping bag, it can give you 15 to 20 years of warm and comfortable nights. The same rule applies to your tent, backpack, and jackets, as well as gear like stoves and water filters that need occasional maintenance and cleaning. Just because most hiking and camping gear is made from durable materials like ripstop nylon and high-grade aluminum doesn't mean you can treat it roughly.

Keeping It Clean

Cleaning gear at the end of a trip is the first step to making it last longer. You want to remove any visible dirt and mud as well as stains and spills. A thorough scrubbing doesn't just make your tent or backpack look and smell better, but it also prevents problems from developing during storage. Over time, caked-on dirt will damage waterproof coatings on fabrics, while food stains and body oils will attract insects, mold, and mildew. Here are some additional tips:

- ◊ Never store gear that is dirty. Wipe mud off tents and backpacks, scrub carbon stains from stoves, and wash and dry boots and shoes.
- ◊ Recently washed tents, backpacks, or sleeping bags should be hung up for several days until completely dry before being placed in storage.
- ◊ Use a whisk broom or a vacuum to remove all crumbs, sand, dirt, and dead bugs from the inside of tents and backpacks.

◊ Jacket and pack zippers are often the first parts to fail on outdoor gear; scrub them after every trip with a toothbrush and warm water.

◊ Strong soaps and detergents can degrade fabrics with waterproof coatings; clean these surfaces using only warm water and a sponge, or use a diluted dose of a very mild soap.

Keeping It Organized

The outdoors can be hard on gear, like when a thorn punctures a sleeping pad or a rock scrapes the top of a backpack. But the most dangerous time for gear is actually the long months it sits in storage. As a result, you need to do more than just dump your stuff in a damp basement or a toasty attic. Here's how to set up the ideal home storage space for your outdoor collection:

◊ Store your gear in a cool, dry place like an extra closet, a recreation room, or a finished basement.

◊ Keep your stuff in one spot—including jackets and boots—to save time while packing.

◊ Install adjustable shelves, wall hooks, clothes rods, and towel bars to create multiple storage arrangements.

◊ Store loose gear in transparent plastic containers so you can see what's inside without opening the lid, and add labels to help you classify new gear and locate existing items.

◊ Combine similar gear into the same container: batteries with headlamps, gas canisters with stoves, water bottles with filters, and freeze-dried food packets with cook kits.

◊ Store lightweight items, like sleeping pads and bags, on high shelves and heavier items, like tents and snowshoes, down low.

◊ Instead of storing sleeping bags compressed in a stuff sack, place them in large mesh bags or pillowcases to hang in a cool, dry place, or stash them in large plastic tubs.

◊ Store water bottles with the caps open or off to enable air to circulate inside.

SUMMARY

Because you literally depend on your gear to prevent life-and-death situations—like whether a stove ignites, or a tent withstands a midnight thunderstorm—you should invest in high-quality, reliable products that earn top reviews. Once you own the gear, however, you need to maintain it by cleaning it after every trip—from scrubbing away carbon residue on a stove burner, to knocking the dirt off tent stakes. If you follow those two rules, you'll be able to trust your gear as you seek new outdoor adventures over many years.

CHAPTER 9

FOOTWEAR FUNDAMENTALS

Napoleon gets credit for the saying, "An army marches on its stomach." But how true is that? After all, Napoleon probably rode a horse. Had he walked like most of his soldiers, he would have realized that an army marches in its boots and that Moscow is a long, frozen walk from Paris.

The truth is that your choice of footwear will influence the success of your hike more than any other type of gear. If your feet aren't happy, you won't be happy either. As a result, selecting which boot or shoe to lace up before a hike shouldn't be a haphazard or last-minute decision. Instead, your choice of footwear should be the first gear decision you make. To get your hike started on the right foot, this chapter will give you the rundown on the best footwear options, from casual campers to intrepid hikers.

The Shape of Shoes

Basketball teams and tennis players don't wear the same style of athletic shoes, right? So, it makes sense that no pair of shoes or boots will work for both a day-hike and a weeklong trek. Instead, selecting the ideal footwear for each hiking trip boils down to three main factors:

1. The difficulty of the terrain and distance of the hike
2. The pack weight you will carry
3. Your sensitivity to blisters and other foot problems

If you like to go on both short day-hikes and long backpacking trips, you should probably own a different pair of shoes or boots for each activity. That might seem expensive, but comfortable footwear is worth paying for. Plus, big, bulky leather hiking

boots are going the way of the dinosaur as hikers switch
to lower and lighter options that increase comfort without
sacrificing support. Here are the two major styles available to
hikers.

Light and Fast

Lightweight, low-cut trail shoes emphasize speed and comfort
over support and protection, making them fine for short day-
hikes on smooth trails. These thin-skinned shoes and boots will
help you move quickly and assuredly on easy-to-moderate trails,
but they won't guard your toes from sharp rocks or give you
extra confidence on hazardous terrain. A comfortable, flexible
fit is another priority, which is made possible by their shoelike
appearance and extensive use of synthetic fabrics. This also
reduces the time required to break them in compared to larger,
more rigid boots.

Sturdy and Slow

If day-hiking footwear is designed to be nimble, then
backpacking boots are more like lumbering battleships. Instead
of speed and flexibility, they emphasize support and protection.
By wrapping your entire foot and ankle in a single rigid form,
backpacking boots give you the leverage to efficiently move
up steep, rocky slopes and added protection from stumbles,
twists, and stubbed toes. But just like no modern navy deploys
battleships anymore, bulky hiking boots are less popular on
trails today.

Even More Choices

The world of hiking footwear, however, isn't cleanly divided
between the two spheres of day-hiking and backpacking, or
lightweight shoes and bulky boots. Check out the shoe section
at your local outdoor store and you'll see enough styles and
sizes to make your head swim. Not only will there be trail shoes
and backpacking boots, but also dozens of crossover styles
incorporating aspects of both designs. You'll probably even
see running shoes on display. Driving this trend is a demand
by day- and weekend-hikers for smaller, lighter boots and

trail shoes that still provide meaningful ankle support and protection. Here are the four major styles—from light to heavy—you'll see on the shelves.

Trail Runners

Growing in popularity every year, these low-cut kicks are made from synthetic fabrics with mesh panels to enhance breathability. Trail runners offer excellent cushioning—including gel inserts in the heel—but less protection from jagged, rocky terrain. Key advantages include a comfortable fit, a short break-in period, and a lightweight design. Some models are made with waterproof membranes to keep moisture out, while others are designed with quick-drying fabrics and maximum breathability. Trail runners and running shoes are becoming more common on the trail, especially for experienced hikers. Case in point: my friend recently finished a 10-day backpacking trek in California's Sierra Nevada mountains and every hiker on the trail, including him, was wearing trail runners.

Best for: Ultralight backpacking, trail running, day-hiking, and blister-prone hikers

Trail runner shoes prioritize comfort and agility and over support and durability.

Light Hiker Boots

With a beefier build than trail runners, these hybrid hikers look like a cross between a shoe and a boot. A taller ankle collar provides additional support and protects your feet from wet and muddy trails. Thick, rigid soles help with rock scrambling and edging, while durable materials provide support for packs weighing up to 30 pounds. Most boots in this category also feature a a rubber toe cap on the front to shield your toes from rocks and roots. Lightweight boots are best for hikers who get blisters from traditional backpacking boots or who are looking to shave a few ounces without sacrificing ankle support.

Best for: Most weekend backpacking and day-hiking on rugged terrain

Light hiker boots match durable, waterproof performance with athletic shoe–style comfort.

Midweight Boots

Designed to take a licking and keep on hiking, these backpacking boots are protected from rocks and debris by a durable, scratch-resistant hide (often made from leather or tough synthetic fabrics) and a thick wraparound rubber sole and rand (the protective layer that rests above the sole). Higher collars and bulkier padding give your feet and ankles the leverage to heft packs weighing 50 pounds or more. Many also contain an internal shank—a plastic or metal support that runs along the bottom of the boot to provide more internal rigidity—while retaining some flexibility for comfortable striding. Waterproof membranes and ultrafine stitching enhance wet-weather performance so that you can ford shallow streams without getting soaked.

Best for: Backpacking on rugged trails while hauling heavier loads, hiking above the tree line, or for extensive rock scrambling

Midweight boots provide rough-trail support with higher, stiffer collars but remain comfortable for regular striding.

Trail Tips The stiffer and more rigid the boot, the more time you need to devote to breaking them in by softening the sole and heel cup through repeated wearing.

Winter and Mountaineering Boots

Challenging terrain calls for technologically advanced footwear, and these boots deliver with rigid soles designed to accept crampons and extra insulation to keep your feet warm. Superior waterproofing and high-cut collars repel snow and ice. Some winter boots are sheathed in hard plastic that surrounds removable, insulating liners. However, these unforgiving boots—the same footwear worn by climbers on Mount Everest—require several weeks of practice hikes to fully break in. Most hikers never wear these boots.

Best for: Hiking in snow and ice and for mountaineering

Finding a Good Fit

Fit is everything. A boot or shoe must feel good from the moment you first put it on to the last mile of a hike. Because fit is so important, buying boots and shoes from an athletic shoe store, an online retailer like DSW.com, or a catalog is a risky move. The better choice is to visit an outdoor retail store where you can measure your feet, try on multiple styles, and get expert advice from the staff. Most retail stores, however, don't allow you to return any shoes or boots worn outside. This makes any footwear trial runs in a store extremely important. To get the best results, shop for footwear first, and test each pair for at least 15 minutes—practice walking up and down stairs, on ramps, and while carrying a backpack weighing at least 20 pounds.

Don't assume that your regular shoe size will be identical to your hiking boot size. Just because a size-10 boot made by Brand A fits you doesn't mean that a size-10 boot by Brand B will also work. Try on multiple pairs and identify the brands that fit you best. Because feet tend to swell by the end of the day, shop for footwear in the late afternoon or evening. If your feet are different sizes, opt for the larger size.

Slippery Heels

Heels are ground zero for blisters—most are caused by moisture mixed with poorly fitted boots and not enough break-in time. Once your heel starts to rub against the back of the boot, the constant friction will quickly ignite a hot spot, followed by a blister. Making sure that your heel fits snugly in its cup at the back of a boot should be first on your checklist when shopping for boots or shoes. People with narrow or bony feet often experience the most trouble, and they sometimes need to experiment with various sock thicknesses, aftermarket footpads, or gel inserts to achieve a comfortable, no-slip fit. In addition to enhanced cushioning and support, some insoles wick away moisture and help control odors and bacteria. If bulky or midweight boots don't fit well, check out light hikers or trail runners as more forgiving alternatives.

 Safety Check When trying on boots, pay attention to subtle warning signs like painful pressure points or minor friction spots—they'll just get worse on the trail.

Getting Out of a Toe Jam

The front of your foot is the second most common spot for blisters to form. A cramped or narrow toe box can quickly lead to hot spots and smashed toenails, especially on steep downhill trails. To confirm that a boot has adequate toe room, stand with your feet flat on the ground and with your toes completely relaxed. You should be able to wiggle all of your toes up and down, and you should be able to feel half an inch of space between the tips of your toes and the inside edge at the front of the boot. A durable, rubber toecap surrounding the toe box will absorb the impact from buried rocks, logs, and roots and shield your little piggies from a painful bashing. Here are some other tips for shopping for new footwear:

◊ Get your feet measured every time you try on boots using a Brannock device—the flat metal tray with adjustable sliders that determines the length and width of your feet.

◊ If your feet are different sizes, try on footwear for the larger size and use thicker socks or footbeds to make the smaller foot fit the larger size.

◊ Bring hiking socks of varying thickness levels when trying on boots to determine which boot and sock combinations work best.

◊ Keep in mind key trouble spots as you try on boots: heel slippage, scrunched toes, and friction points on the ankle and the side of your toes.

◊ Remember that if it doesn't fit in the store, it won't fit on the trail. Breaking in boots reduces stiffness but doesn't improve overall fit.

 Trail Tips Tighten your shoelaces before long stretches of downhill hiking to prevent your toes from repeatedly slamming into the front of your boots.

Earning a PhD in Bootology

The quality of materials and workmanship that go into a boot or shoe can be as important as how it fits. After all, a boot that leaks in a light drizzle isn't tolerable even if it's comfortable to wear. Cost is one method to gauge the quality of footwear: most well-made trail shoes and boots are priced between $90 and $200. Expert reviews found online and in magazines (see Chapter 8) can lead you to reliable brands and models. The following sections will help you decide which materials and features matter to you.

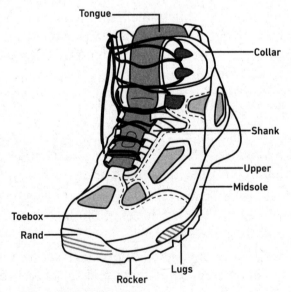

Today's hiking boots and trail shoes support and protect your feet from the lugs to the collar.

Judging a Boot by Its Cover

Durable brown leather was once the main material used in hiking footwear, but it's no longer the only one. The uppers (outer layers) of today's boots and trail shoes are constructed from many kinds of hides and fabrics—from ultra tough full-grain leather to soft, breathable synthetics. Here's a look at how each material stacks up:

◊ **Full-grain leather:** The thickest, most genuine type of non-processed leather that is also the most durable and water-resistant.

◊ **Split-grain leather:** The inner, more flexible layer of leather that has been split away from the durable top layer to make a thinner, but more pliable, hide.

◊ **Suede:** Split-grain leather that has been buffed to create a smooth, velvety surface.

◊ **Nubuck:** Full-grain leather with a top layer that has been brushed to create a softer fine-grain surface that is more durable than suede.

◊ **Synthetic fabrics:** Manmade fabrics that offer lighter weight, more breathability, and lower cost than leather hides but are generally less durable and abrasion-resistant than high-quality leathers.

◊ **Synthetic leather:** Plastic or fabric-based leather substitutes are cheaper and easier to clean but less durable than the real animal hides.

All About Sole

When examining a shoe or boot, grab it by the heel and the toe and flex the sole. The more it bends, the more comfortable it will be for walking but the less support it will provide on rough, rocky terrain. Light hikers and trail shoes are designed with soles that follow the flex of your foot, while heavier boots have rigid soles that resist bending. The level of stiffness is often determined by the midsole and shank—the flat piece of plastic or metal that runs along the bottom spine of the boot or shoe.

Weighing Your Options

A solid pair of boots doesn't need to be as heavy or dense as a brick to be effective on the trail. As average pack loads drop because of lighter, more compact gear, footwear manufacturers are responding by using lighter and stronger materials to build everything from agile runners to heavy clompers. It makes sense: lightweight footwear is more comfortable and easier to break in, and it requires less energy to take each step. So, when you're shopping for a new pair of shoes or boots, don't forget to factor in weight.

Keeping the Wet Out

Not all boots and trail shoes are waterproof. If protection from moisture is a feature you want, then you need to get savvy about the two techniques that keep the wet out: waterproof coatings and breathable membranes.

The easiest (and least expensive) waterproofing method is to coat the exterior fabric and seams with a thin, wax- or plastic-based sealant. Called a *DWR* (durable water-repellent) treatment, this waterproof coating is applied to the outside surface of boots, jackets, and tents to prevent rain and moisture from saturating the fabric. It works by causing water-molecules to bead up and slide away—just like water off a duck's back.

Footwear without a waterproof sealant, like tennis shoes, will quickly become soaked when hiking through rain puddles or damp snow. Any DWR-treated footwear, however, is considered "waterproof" and stays drier for much longer. Most DWR coatings wear away and degrade over time and must be reapplied about once a year. Also, no waterproofing is 100 percent effective. If you stand in a stream for several minutes, your feet are going to get wet.

Waterproof-breathable membranes work differently than DWR coatings. Instead of stopping water on the outside, the membrane is embedded inside the lining of a boot or trail shoe, where it creates a one-way path for moisture. Rain and snow from the outside can't soak through the barrier, while sweat and dampness on the inside can escape to evaporate into the air. The three major waterproof-breathable membranes on the market today are Gore-Tex, eVent, and Pertex Shield. Also, many proprietary brands are developed by footwear and apparel companies. While more expensive than DWR treatments, waterproof-breathable membranes often perform better and last longer.

End-of-the-Day Shoes

After many miles of hiking, your feet deserve some R&R by getting out of your boots and into some comfortable camp shoes. This second pair of shoes is designed to give your feet a rest and allow your boots to dry out. Camp shoes should be comfortable, breathable, lightweight, and sturdy enough to hike a few hundred yards to gather firewood, fetch water, or hang a bear bag. Sandals, but not flip-flops, can double as both camp shoes and lightweight footwear for crossing streams or rivers. During cold-weather or winter trips, many hikers prefer insulated booties, which will keep your feet warm and dry— even in several inches of snow. Note: If you hike in trail shoes or running shoes, you might not need camp shoes at all.

Slipping on Socks

In the battle against blisters, wearing the right pair of socks is crucial. Socks not only reduce dampness and chafing—the two major sources of blisters—but the right pair can provide the cushioning and support to make an uncomfortable boot feel better.

The best sock fabrics are quick-drying and comfortable synthetics like polyester and acrylic or natural fibers like wool and silk. Blends of synthetics and natural fibers are even better; they will wick moisture away from your skin in cold and hot temperatures, keeping your feet drier and less vulnerable to blisters.

Whether you wear one or two layers of socks depends on the sock fabric, the boots, and your personal preference. The logic behind the two-layer system—thin polyester liner socks under thicker wool socks—is to transfer friction away from your skin to the socks. With light hikers and trail shoes, however, it's often more comfortable to wear one pair. Plus, synthetic blends and finely woven wool socks are now comfortable enough to wear against bare skin.

The height of the socks you wear depends on your footwear and terrain. Calf-length socks are heavier but offer more warmth and protection against thorns, scrapes, and poison ivy. Shorter crew-length socks fit better with trail runners and light hikers and stay cooler for hot and arid terrain.

 Trail Tips   If you need to cross a deep river but aren't carrying a pair of camp shoes, remove your boots and pull on a pair of wool socks to give your feet more traction and protection. Dry them by placing them on the top of your pack.

Giving Dirt and Odor the Boot

Because your boots and shoes take a beating on the trail, they deserve some TLC at home. Cleaning, brushing, and waterproofing footwear will extend its life span. The worst thing you can do is stick a muddy, damp pair of boots in a plastic bag and throw them in the back of your closet until your next hike. Instead, air them out by loosening the laces and pulling back the tongue to create as wide an opening as possible. Remember to pull out any removable insoles, too. At home, stuff the inside of the boots or shoes with crumpled-up newspapers and place them in a cool, airy spot until dry. If any smells persist, spray the insoles with a disinfectant spray.

 Safety Check   Never dry out wet boots next to a fire or stove. The focused heat can crack leather, melt rubber, and singe fabrics—making your boots dry but unwearable. The same prohibition applies to hair dryers and ovens at home.

Cleaning Your Boots

Hiking boots collect dirt, scuffs, and dents like any object that gets pounded repeatedly against the ground. Because caked-on mud damages leather and synthetic fibers, regular cleaning will keep them from rotting away between your trips. Here's the proper post-hike procedure to follow for your footwear:

1. Brush away dried mud and dust with a plastic-bristle scrub brush. Use lukewarm water to remove tougher mud and stains.

2. Use a rubber mallet or a screwdriver to knock dirt from the rubber lugs and treads on the sole.

3. Remove persistent odors with a disinfectant spray.

4. For leather that appears dry, cracked, or lighter in color, check the manufacturer's guidelines for remoisturizing treatments.

5. Let boots dry completely after washing before storing them separate from any insoles or footbeds in a dry, cool place, such as a closet.

Revitalizing Waterproof Protection

Waterproof coatings don't last forever. Time, sunlight, dirt, and normal wear and tear cause them to break down. As a result, most manufacturers recommend reapplying a waterproof coating to footwear at least once a year—usually at the beginning of your busiest hiking season. Be sure to use the appropriate waterproof sealant for your footwear. A full-grain leather boot requires a different coating than synthetic trail shoes. Follow the product's instructions, remember to clean and dry all footwear before applying it, and wipe away excess drips with a cloth.

SUMMARY

Most hikers today lace up lightweight trail shoes or low-cut hiking boots instead of tall and heavy leather boots. However, your own footwear decisions should depend on personal preference and comfort. To avoid the moisture and friction that causes blisters, footwear must have a snug heel and adequate wiggle room in the toes. But you can improve the fit by inserting special insoles or by adjusting the thickness of your socks. Reapplying waterproof coatings to boots and shoes at least once a year, along with a consistent post-hike cleaning, will make your footwear last for hundreds of miles.

CHAPTER 10

OUTDOOR CLOTHING 101

Polyester clothing has come a long way since its heyday in the 1970s. After decades of neglect, the wrinkle-free fabric that defined the disco era has been reborn as the ultimate hiking apparel. The rebirth of polyester isn't just nostalgia; synthetic fabrics actually perform better in wet and cold weather than cotton. Now, instead of wearing worn blue jeans and a torn T-shirt, today's hikers can slip on waterproof pants and silky T-shirts with antibacterial membranes.

However, the synthetic renaissance has led to an explosion in hiking apparel found on store shelves. To help you get your duds in order, this chapter will cover everything you need to know about buying the right clothing, layering, and staying dry. After all, dressing for the trail isn't only about looking good (although it helps), but it's about feeling good, too.

What Not to Wear

There's just one rule for hiking clothing, and it's easy to remember: Cotton kills.

Of course, it's not a literal warning. Wearing cotton T-shirts doesn't attract lightning bolts or grizzly bears. However, it does put you at a disadvantage if you get wet, wind-blown, or cold. When cotton gets damp, it becomes a constantly soggy, heat-sapping reminder that you should have worn a synthetic fabric like *polypropylene*. Also called *polypro,* polypropylene is a synthetic polyester fabric used to make outdoor apparel, such as base layers, T-shirts, and shorts. Unlike cotton, polypro fabric wicks moisture away from the skin so it can evaporate and keep you drier.

Wearing any garment with a large percentage of cotton is a fashion mistake on the trail, but denim jeans are especially bad. Not only are they heavy and hot and take forever to dry, but they can also freeze solid in wet, cold weather. So, leave your blue jeans and these other items at home:

◊ Cotton or linen pants

◊ Cotton T-shirts and sweatshirts

◊ Cotton underwear

◊ Cotton socks

◊ Heavy belts

◊ Ski jackets

Be a Fabric Detective

"What is it made of?" should be the first question you ask when shopping for hiking clothes. Not only can the textile tell you how the clothing might perform, but it also gives clues on its quality. Here are the major fabrics and materials you're likely to encounter and how they stack up.

Synthetics

Polyester fabrics looked good in *Saturday Night Fever*, and they work even better on the trail as light base layers worn against your skin. Other synthetics besides polypro include nylon and spandex. However, all synthetics have one major drawback: they retain body odor more than cotton and wool.

Fleece

As a thicker and warmer kind of polyester, fleece is used to make vests and sweatshirts as well as liners for jackets, mittens, and hats. Like polypro, fleece is extremely comfortable to wear, is breathable, and dries out quickly. Not naturally waterproof, fleece is most effective as an insulating layer. Modern fleece garments are made with stronger microfibers that resist abrasion and last longer after repeated wearing and washing.

Wool

This natural and renewable fiber is a versatile insulator that works in hot and cold conditions—and even when wet. As a result, wool is a popular fabric for both insulating layers and lightweight shirts. Its secret is the natural crimp of the wool fiber that traps air in pockets and enables it to retain 30 percent of its own weight in moisture without appearing wet. Drawbacks to wool include its long dry time and scratchy fibers; however, merino wool is naturally soft, and new wool/synthetic blends combine the comfort and wicking advantages of polypro with the insulating and anti odor abilities of wool.

Silk

This soft and lightweight fabric is ideal for base layers worn next to the skin, especially in colder weather. Natural and renewable, silk can be treated with chemicals to enhance its wicking properties. Be aware that fragile silk threads are vulnerable to rips and abrasions, and garments must be hand-washed to prolong their life span and to avoid shrinking.

Down

Considered the warmest insulator per weight, down is made with soft, fine goose feathers. Down insulation is used in jackets, vests, and sleeping bags and is rated in warmth by its fill power—with 750-fill down being warmer than 650-fill down. While down compresses easily, making it easy to pack, it insulates poorly when wet, and it dries slowly.

Synthetic Insulation

This man-made substitute for down uses different arrangements of polyester fibers to accomplish the same purpose: trapping air close to the body to increase warmth. Unlike down, synthetic fibers retain their insulating ability even when wet, although they take up more space. Major brands of synthetic insulation found in jackets, vests and sleeping bags include Polarguard, Thinsulate, Primaloft, and Climashield.

Always Dress in Layers

As every hiker knows, or quickly learns, the secret to on-trail comfort is to wear multiple layers of clothing. From a scorching desert basin to a windy mountain ridge, layering not only helps to control your body temperature, but it also simplifies packing. Plus, bringing interchangeable layers gives you more flexibility than separate outfits.

The Layering Advantage

Chances are you already layer when you dress for work, school, or a cold day outside. Layering on the trail follows the same rule: You adjust your clothing to match your activity level, the weather, and the outside temperature. For instance, you should shed layers when you begin to sweat, but add more as soon as you stop for a rest break. Layering works by trapping pockets of air that are warmed by your body heat to act as an insulating barrier. And it works even better when you can quickly add or remove extra clothing to avoid becoming too hot or cold.

 Safety Check Always prepare for colder temperatures than you expect. Nighttime lows will often feel colder than you think, and you'll be chilled unless you bring enough insulating layers.

You've Got Options

The key to smart layering is versatility. The best hiking clothing works well alone and in combination with other layers; therefore, you should ensure that your clothing can fit over or under other layers. Two of the most versatile options for hikers are a long-sleeve polypro shirt with a half-zip down the chest and a pair of quick-drying nylon pants. By adjusting the sleeves and the zipper, the shirt can help you warm up or cool down. Nylon pants offer durability, water resistance, and comfort in all kinds of terrain and conditions. Convertible pants even enable the lower legs to be zipped off to create a pair of shorts. Combining tall socks or leggings with shorts can accomplish the same result.

Getting Dressed Layer by Layer

Layering isn't just about adding or subtracting random clothing. Wearing five polypro T-shirts doesn't do anything for you. To be effective, layering must incorporate these three categories of outdoor apparel—each of which plays a different role in regulating your body temperature:

1. Base layers include underwear (regular and long), sports bras, T-shirts, and hiking shorts and are made from synthetic fabrics that wick moisture away from your skin.

2. Insulating layers are primarily fleece or wool and keep you warmer by trapping the heat produced by your body.

3. Outerwear layers like jackets and rain shells block wind and rain from interfering with the performance of the base and insulating layers underneath and cover any exposed skin.

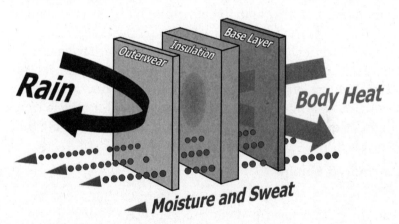

The right combination of layers will trap body heat, repel rain, and enable moisture and sweat to evaporate from your skin and clothing.

The next part will describe how these layers work together during a hike. For a detailed checklist on which clothing to pack for a hike, see Equipment Checklists.

The Foundation

Base layers are the first items you put on in the morning and the last clothing you take off in the evening. These shirts, shorts, and underwear are often sold in three thickness levels— lightweight, midweight, or heavyweight—that offer varying degrees of warmth and breathability. Most base layers are made with polyester-based fabrics like polypro and are occasionally mixed with spandex or nylon. Some manufacturers are also using micro weave wool or silk, which insulates and removes moisture while smelling better than synthetics.

 Trail Tips Long-sleeve shirts and full-length pants offer better protection from sunburn, poison ivy, bugs, and thorns than shorts and a T-shirt. And if you get too hot, you can always roll up the sleeves or cuffs.

The Thermal Barrier

Because humans lack fur or feathers, we need to re-create the same insulation by using vests, pullovers, sweaters, and jackets to trap warm air close to the body. Designed to be worn over base layers, these insulating layers are woven from water-resistant and breathable fabrics like fleece and wool or filled with fluffy synthetic insulation or goose down. Because you're likely to add or remove insulating layers multiple times throughout a day, you should store them in an accessible place in your pack.

The Armored Shield

The last layer to put on is your outerwear. This durable and weather-resistant layer is designed to protect you from the rough side of nature, including mud, thorns, wind, snow, and rain. While the most important outerwear option (and the one every hiker should own) is a waterproof rain jacket, there are plenty of other products available. Each of the following options can serve as the final barrier between you and the elements:

◊ Waterproof rain jackets and shells

◊ Waterproof pants

◊ Water-repellent soft shells (see the following note)

◊ Insulated snow pants

◊ Waterproof hats

◊ Vests

 Safety Check Despite their cheaper price, flimsy plastic ponchos won't keep you dry, are clumsy to wear while hiking, and are useless if the wind begins to blow. A waterproof rain shell and rain pants are always more effective.

The Proof in Waterproofing

Most outerwear can be divided into two categories: water-repellent and waterproof. A light drizzle or short bursts of rain are fine for water-repellent clothing like nylon pants or a fleece sweatshirt. But any persistent rain requires the comprehensive waterproofing found only in rain shells and pants.

Staying Dry

Like hiking boots (see Chapter 9), outerwear is made waterproof using two methods: an internal membrane or an external water-repellent coating. Under the first method, a waterproof-breathable membrane like Gore-Tex or eVent is sewn into the fabric. Microscopic pores in this layer enable sweat and moisture to evaporate from the inside, while blocking rain from penetrating on the outside. The second method involves applying a durable water-repellent (DWR) coating to the outside layer of fabric. This thin polyurethane barrier repels water, while also enabling internal moisture to escape. But because DWR treatments degrade over time, they need to be periodically reactivated or reapplied—usually at the beginning of each season. Many waterproof jackets employ both a waterproof membrane and a DWR coating for double protection against internal moisture and rain-saturated fabrics.

 Trail Tips To prevent water from seeping through the stitches in a jacket, higher-end shells are sometimes glued or welded instead of sewn, or the seams are sealed with waterproof tape on the inside.

There's Nothing Soft About Soft Shells

A soft shell is a water-repellent, insulating jacket that resembles a hybrid between fleece and a rain shell. They are best for dry spring and fall hikes when you need a little extra insulation at night but when a down or synthetic jacket would be overkill. However, if you get caught in a downpour, a soft shell will keep you warm but not dry. For that reason, you should always carry a waterproof rain jacket in addition to a soft shell.

It's Okay to Accessorize

Layering is the first step to dressing for the outdoors, but it's not the only one. You still need to cover your hands, feet, and especially your head—all of which tend to suffer first when the temperature drops. Here's what else you should wear from head to toe.

Head Gear

Pack a wool or fleece hat for any day-hike or backpacking trip in any season—even in July. That's because no other piece of clothing provides more essential warmth for its size. Plus, a hat is a simple way to regulate your body temperature on the trail. You've probably heard that people lose 90 percent of their body heat from their head. However, it's not as if your head is some super-radiator of heat. But if the rest of your body is covered with clothing, most of the heat your body sheds will be from your exposed noggin. Cold sleepers and winter campers should also consider a balaclava—a wrap that completely covers the head and neck—to ward off the overnight chill.

Gloves and Mittens

Lightweight gloves made from a blend of polypro and spandex are ideal for early spring and late-fall hikes, providing just enough warmth to ward off the nighttime chill. For any serious cold-weather hiking, however, bring mittens or gloves that surround fleece insulation with a water-resistant nylon shell. And remember, not only are mittens much warmer than gloves, but you can use them for simple hiking tasks like gripping trekking poles and opening a tent zipper.

Gaiters

Originally worn by medieval knights, modern hiking *gaiters* are thankfully made from fabric instead of steel. Gaiters are flexible footwear coverings designed to block rocks, sand, and moisture from getting inside boots.

Constructed from durable nylon, gaiters attach to your legs and boots with hook/loop tabs and a tough leather strap. They come in two general sizes. Low gaiters, which cover the ankle, are best for low-cut boots and trail shoes; high gaiters, which extend up to just below the knee, are made for midlength and tall footwear. Most gaiters are water resistant, and some higher-end models are made with waterproof-breathable membranes.

Rain Pants

In the hierarchy of waterproof accessories, gaiters are more versatile and effective than rain pants. But if you're ready for an upgrade, the key is buying a high-quality, waterproof-breathable pair of foul weather pants. Cheaper, nonbreathable pants will stop the rain but will also soak your legs in perspiration as you hike—especially in warm, humid rain showers. For this reason, don't purchase the cheapest, or even the second cheapest, pair of rain pants. Save up for a good pair made with a brand-name waterproof-breathable membrane. Rain pants are most useful in persistently wet and rainy climates, and they are less important in arid regions like the Mountain West or at high elevations.

Fabrics That Give You an Edge

Some hiking apparel does more than just cover you up. By experimenting with high-tech fabrics and chemical additives, manufacturers have given clothing special powers to enhance your hiking experience without you even realizing it.

Sun-Protective Clothing

Most hiking apparel doesn't provide as much UV protection as you think—especially any clothing that becomes wet or is thin or light-colored. Sun-protective clothing, however, is made with tightly woven fabric embedded with thin layers of chemicals that absorb UV radiation. Each article of sun-protective clothing is assigned an Ultraviolet Protection Factor, or UPF rating, which is similar to the SPF index. Clothing with a UPF rating of 30 means that the fabric will block $\frac{29}{30}$ (97 percent) of the UV radiation from reaching your skin.

Bugs Be Gone

Imagine a shirt that warns mosquitoes to stay away. Using a technology originally developed for the U.S. military, hiking clothing can be coated with permethrin, a man-made variant of a natural insecticide. Mosquitoes, ticks, and other insects that come in contact with these fabrics will either beat a hasty retreat or die. Long-sleeve shirts, pants, and hats are the most common types of bug-busting apparel, including the BugsAway products sold by ExOfficio, which the manufacturer claims will last up to 70 washes. You can also create your own bug-resistant clothing by applying permethrin sprays to shirts and pants you already own.

Leaving Odors Behind

Hikers have a well-deserved reputation for smelling "natural" after being on the trail for several days. The solution isn't more showers; instead, the solution is antimicrobial layers woven into base layers to block bacterial growth and reduce stink. Ionized silver, one of the most common antimicrobial agents, binds to bacteria to prevent them from reproducing. Look for these linings in polypro clothing like shirts, underwear, sports bras, tank tops, and shorts.

Caring for High-Tech Clothing

A waterproof shell can set you back $120. A good pair of rain pants can cost even more, and polypro shirts go for $20-$30 at outlet prices. Outdoor apparel isn't cheap. But instead of looking at new gear as a splurge, consider it an investment in comfort and safety. And to make sure your investment lasts, you need to periodically clean and maintain your gear.

Wash and Dry with Care

Despite their durable reputation, washing outdoor clothing like breathable jackets, soft shells, and fleeces is a delicate process. Liquid detergents, dry cleaning, and fabric softeners will degrade waterproof coatings and shorten a garment's life span. So, even if you're an expert at removing stains, you need to follow the manufacturer's directions on the garment label and remember these guidelines:

◊ Machine wash and dry most apparel, but use mild soap and lower temperatures.

◊ Delicate clothing should be hand washed in a utility sink or bathtub using lukewarm water and a mild powder detergent, then rinsed and air-dried. When in doubt, wash by hand.

◊ Wash down-filled jackets in a front-loading machine with cold water on a gentle setting, then tumble dry on low heat for several hours.

◊ Polypro clothing can be washed with other clothes, although air-drying will reduce the tendency for polyester and fleece to pill—the annoying creation of tiny fiber balls on the surface of the fabric.

◊ Never place any garment containing wool or silk in a dryer—unless you plan to shrink along with it.

Making Waterproof Barriers Last

When water begins to saturate a waterproof jacket (which occurs when the jacket's pores get clogged with dirt and sweat), it's time to reactivate its DWR coating by either machine washing or ironing.

1. To wash a jacket or shell, place it by itself in a washing machine set on cold water and a gentle cycle. Add a mild powder detergent like Dreft or Ultra Ivory Snow. Do not use liquid detergents or fabric softeners—both leave behind residues that impair DWR performance. Rinse twice to remove all the soap and dry in a standard dryer set on low or medium heat.

2. If washing fails to restore the DWR coating, run a warm iron over the fabric while on a low steam setting. The direct application of moderate heat will reactivate the DWR molecules inside the clothing.

3. Test a reactivated DWR coating by dripping water onto the garment. If the water beads up and rolls off the fabric, the coating is working. If the water soaks into the fabric, you need to try again or apply a new coating.

If neither washing nor ironing restores the waterproofing, you can apply a brand-new DWR coating. For jackets and shells with a waterproof-breathable membrane, it's best to use a spray-on coating on the outside of the fabric. For all other garments, a wash-in DWR treatment can be placed inside the washing machine to coat the fabric as it gets cleaned. You can find a wide variety of waterproof sprays and coatings made by companies like Nikwax, McNett, and Grangers at all outdoor retail shops and online stores.

 Safety Check   Before placing clothing in a washing machine or dryer, be sure to close all zippers and hook-and-eye fasteners to prevent their rough edges from abrading the fabric.

SUMMARY

Synthetic fabrics like polypro and nylon dominate the hiking apparel market, followed by traditional natural fabrics like wool (for insulation) and silk (for close-to-skin comfort). But the one fabric you should never wear on the trail is cotton because it steals the heat from your body when it becomes wet. Dressing in layers—ranging from base to insulating layer to outer shell—lets each garment level do its job, while also enabling you to add or subtract a layer to adjust to hot or cold conditions. To extend the life span of your outdoor clothing, wash it using mild soap and low temperatures, and always follow the manufacturer's cleaning instructions.

CHAPTER 11

HAULING YOUR GEAR

Wherever you find a hiker, you'll probably find a pack. The two go together like bears and honey. Fortunately, the cartoonish image of the towering, bulky backpack draped with sleeping bags, firewood, frying pans, and fishing poles is obsolete. New lightweight materials and efficient designs have transformed the look and performance of packs. Choices have gotten better, too. Now you can find separate packs for weekend jaunts, trail running, or ultralight trips. So, whether you're in the market for a new pack or want to improve the function of your existing hauler, this chapter will show you how to evaluate fit, form, and function to meet your needs.

Packing for a Single Day

You don't hop in your car to go to your next-door neighbor's house, right? Likewise, you shouldn't bring a gigantic backpack on a short day-hike. All that empty space translates into unnecessary weight. The better alternative is to carry a smaller pack designed for shorter excursions.

The All-Around Contender

The most versatile option for day-hikers is (surprise) called a *daypack,* and it resembles a miniature version of a full-size pack. While daypacks are similar in size to a school backpack, you shouldn't consider them equivalents. Unlike flimsy school packs, daypacks are made from durable *ripstop nylon* and feature padded shoulder straps and sturdy zippers to survive rough-and-tumble trail conditions. Ripstop nylon is a durable fabric used to make backpacks and other outdoor gear where the threads are sewn in a cross-hatched pattern to prevent holes and tears from expanding.

Most daypacks are large enough to handle all your day-hiking essentials, including snacks, water, and the 10 essentials (see Chapter 7). They can haul loads ranging from 5 to 15 pounds without any trouble, but most won't fit a sleeping bag or tent.

A Pack for Your Bum, but Not a Bum Pack

Called *waist packs, fanny packs,* and *lumbar packs,* these lightweight pouches attach to a padded, belt-like strap that circles the waist. Popular among day-hikers, trail runners, and other "light and fast" trekkers, waist packs can hold a rain jacket, energy bars, a map and compass, and a few other essentials. Larger versions come with side holsters to attach water bottles.

The Tanker Pack

Although hauling water in a plastic bladder is their primary role, hydration backpacks often have extra space to store a headlamp, snacks, or a rain shell. This makes them ideal for day-hikes where quick access to water is a necessity. Kids like hydration packs because they can carry their own water and drink through a hose, and parents like them because these packs help kids stay hydrated.

When You Need a Bigger Pack

Moving up from day-hiking to backpacking requires several adjustments, but the most obvious is a larger pack to handle your sleeping bag, tent, stove, and the extra food and water you'll be carrying. But because backpacks can range in size from super slim to gargantuan, you first need to narrow down how much carrying capacity you'll need for a typical hike.

The Right Size, Not Oversize

The worst approach to buying a pack is to pick the biggest one that you can carry. Instead, your ideal pack should be large enough to handle your typical trips but with a little extra room for a more ambitious hike. For instance, if your standard weekend trip lasts from Friday night to Sunday afternoon, you want a pack that could potentially haul your stuff until Monday or Tuesday. Because your pack should match your hiking personality, review these statements to discover which size works best for you.

 Trail Tips You can bring a backpack on a car-camping trip, but it isn't required. A couple of large duffel bags should be sufficient to transport your gear from the car to your campsite.

Consider a smaller pack if …

◊ Most of your camping gear is newer and lightweight.

◊ You eat freeze-dried food.

◊ You hike mostly with friends and share a tent.

◊ Most of your hikes are weekend trips.

◊ You're interested in ultralight backpacking.

Consider a larger pack if …

◊ Most of your camping gear is old and heavy.

◊ You prefer to cook food on a stove.

◊ You sometimes hike solo.

◊ You enjoy winter camping and weeklong trips.

◊ You tend to overpack.

◊ You appreciate creature comforts like a pillow.

Measuring Up and Down

Because a hauler's carrying capacity is often measured in both cubic inches and liters, this table shows which volume defines small, medium, and large capacities.

Pack Volumes Matched to Hiking Activity

Cubic Inches	Liters	Best For
Less than 2,199	Less than 35	Day-hiking and ultralight backpacking
2,200–4,499	45–75	Weekend trips in spring, summer, and fall
4,500–6,000	76–100	Extended

Fortunately, most hiking backpacks can accommodate slightly smaller or bigger loads than their rated volume. Making this possible are nylon compression straps, which can cinch down an empty pack or secure extra gear like stuff sacks, trekking poles, and sleeping pads on the pack's exterior.

Start with a Weekender Pack

The best beginner backpack is one that enables you to be self-sufficient for 2 to 3 days of *three-season hiking* and camping. Three-season hiking takes place in the spring, summer, and fall—but not the winter. In general, three-season tents and sleeping bags aren't strong or insulated enough for snowy or cold conditions.

Called a weekender pack, these medium-sized haulers range in volume from 45 to 75 liters and can stash your sleeping bag, a solo or two-person tent, and plenty of food and water. This is the most popular category of packs, so you'll have plenty of options to consider. The key is to narrow your search by focusing on the styles and features that match your needs.

The Right Stuff

With the exception of frame type, it can be hard at first glance to distinguish how one pack is different from another. Most display the same brightly colored nylon fabric festooned with straps, zippers, pouches, and clips. To find your ideal pack, however, you need to dig beneath the surface to discover which frame type and features will be the best match for your style of hiking.

Internal Frames

The vast majority of new packs sold today have internal frames featuring a vertical plastic sheet running along the back secured by aluminum rods called stays. Many hikers prefer these packs because the load is situated closer to their center of gravity, which improves overall stability on difficult terrain. The downside, however, is that internal frame packs are hot and sweaty to wear, although packs featuring suspended mesh panels and grooved channels enable better air circulation against your back.

External Frames
Instead of placing the suspension system inside the pack, external frame packs rely on a visible grid of aluminum tubing to support both the pack bags and straps. This design enables better ventilation and an upright walking stance—but it promotes a wide and wobbly suspension that is unsteady during climbs.

Top Loaders
These packs open at the top, usually through a waterproof drawstring collar. Top loaders are easy to stuff with gear and are lighter because of fewer zippers. Retrieving an item stashed at the bottom of the pack, however, often requires removing everything above it.

Panel Loaders
Zippers running down the sides or back of these packs provide easy access to items inside without removing all the contents above them. Panel loaders also make it easier to access and organize your gear but are heavier and more difficult to pack.

Load Lifters
These nylon straps regulate the tension between the shoulder straps and the top of the pack frame to adjust how the load rests on your body. Tighten them to pull the weight closer to your back for better control, and loosen them to allow the load to settle onto your hips for more comfortable striding.

Compression Straps
You can reduce or expand your pack's volume with these adjustable straps by either cinching down a bulky pack or attaching extra gear to the outside. They are especially helpful for securing sharp and extra long items like trekking poles, snowshoes, and tent poles.

Lid Pocket

Store smaller items you might need on the trail in this easy-access pocket located at the top of most packs. It's also a good place for breakable objects like sunglasses and cameras. Plus, lid pockets on some packs can detach to become waist packs for short day-hikes or scrambles to the summit of a peak.

Shovel Pocket

This expandable pocket is usually located on the outside of a pack and is best for storing sharp items like crampons or instant-access gear like a rain shell, hat, or snacks. A shovel pocket is also a good place to store wet clothing while it dries.

Water Bottle Holsters

To keep bottles close at hand, most packs feature side-mounted pouches that allow you to grab a drink without removing your pack. Because some bottle sleeves are too small for certain bottles, make sure your bottles fit before you purchase a pack.

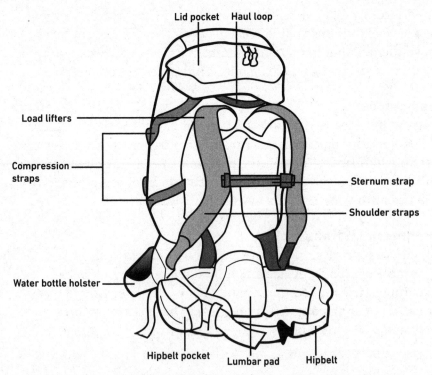

Each part of a backpack is designed to either hold gear or support the load.

Making Sure It Fits

Once you decide on the size and type of pack you want, the next step is to find one that fits. To do this correctly, you need to spend time in an outdoor retail shop trying on as many packs as you can.

A New Way to Measure Yourself

Just like your shoe size determines which footwear to buy, your *torso length*—and not your overall height—will determine which packs will fit the best. Torso length is a body measurement used to size and fit backpacks. It's the distance in inches between a person's C7 vertebrae at the base of the neck and the top of their hip bone.

Ask a store clerk to take your torso measurement, or do it yourself following these three steps. Note: to measure it correctly, you'll need another person and a soft tape measure.

1. While standing up, tuck your chin against your chest so that the knob on the bottom of your neck—actually your C7 vertebra—sticks out. Start measuring from this spot.

2. Place your hands on your hips and feel for a bony ridge on each side of your waist. This is the top of your hip bone— also called the iliac crest. Trace a level line from the top of the crest to the center of your spine. This is the bottom of the torso measurement.

3. Place the tape measure flat against your back and measure the distance between these two spots. Most adults have a torso measurement of between 16 and 22 inches.

Trying It On for Size

Most internal frame packs aren't one-size-fits-all; instead, they come in extra small, small, medium, and large sizes to accommodate different body types and torso lengths. The total volume of these packs could vary slightly between these sizes but not as much as between different pack types and models. In general, pack sizes adhere to the torso measurements shown in the following table.

Torso Length	Pack Size
Less than 15½ inches	Extra Small
16 to 17½ inches	Small
18 to 19½ inches	Medium
More than 20 inches	Large

The Testing Phase

Before you try on a pack, you need to make it heavier. Weigh it down with a load similar to what you'd carry on the trail—usually about 20 to 35 pounds—by stuffing it with dense, heavy objects like rope coils, tents, or sand bags. Most gear shops have these items in the backpack section for exactly this purpose.

The Smart Way to Put On a Pack

Getting a 30-pound pack from the ground to your back doesn't require brute force—just the right technique. First, loosen the shoulder straps and hip belt until they are very slack. Next, slightly bend one knee and lean forward to raise the pack by its haul loop so that it rests on your knee with the shoulder straps facing you. Then place one arm through a shoulder strap, lean forward, and twist your body to shift the pack around to land on your back. Once it's in place, put your other arm through the remaining shoulder strap. Finish by tightening the hip belt first, followed by the shoulder straps, the load lifters, and finally the chest strap.

 Safety Check Make sure there are no trees, people, or drop-offs near you while putting on a pack. A minor collision can send you—and your pack—sprawling.

Putting It Through Its Paces

A good-fitting pack should cling to your body without gaps or pressure points. Stand next to a mirror or have a friend or a salesclerk check out the following areas.

◊ **Shoulders** If you can see daylight underneath the shoulder straps, adjust the load lifters to form a 45-degree angle (a right triangle) between your shoulders and the pack so the straps show no visible gaps.

◊ **Back** The foam padding should rest snugly, but without discomfort, from your shoulder blades to your hips. If the curve of an internal frame pack doesn't match your spine, take it off and remove the aluminum stays—the flat bars that give a pack structure and support. Gently bend the stays to match the curve of your back and try the pack on again.

◊ **Stability** Walk around the store while varying your strides. Climb up and down steps and ramps. Lean sideways and forward to see how the pack might respond to challenging terrain.

◊ **Comfort** Make sure painful pressure points aren't sharp pieces of gear poking through the fabric before you try readjusting the pack. Watch out for numbness in your legs or arms, which could indicate a pinched nerve or constricted circulation.

Specialty Packs

For many years, most outdoor gear was designed for a single standard: the typical 5'10", 170-pound male hiker. Fortunately, those days are over. Now you can find backpacks and other gear proportioned for multiple body types and specific activities.

Women's Packs

More than just a marketing gimmick, backpacks designed for women offer numerous adjustments to better fit the female body, which is generally shorter than a man's and has a lower center of gravity. Women's packs come in shorter torso lengths, the shoulder straps are curved, the chest straps are raised, and the hip belt is canted to accommodate a woman's pelvis. Still, having two X chromosomes doesn't mean you're required to wear a woman's pack. A comfortable fit is still the goal—some women might prefer a man's pack, just as teenagers and some men might find that a woman's pack fits them better.

Youth Packs

Kids and backpacks present the same problems as kids and boots—they'll probably outgrow them before they wear them out. As a result, most youth packs accommodate shorter torso lengths and can adjust upward as a child grows. For most hikes, kids under 8 should only carry water, snacks, and some personal gear, while middle schoolers can shoulder daypacks and smaller backpacks without any problem. A fully grown teenager gearing up for a summer adventure trip or a college outdoor program can probably handle a regular adult pack. This can be a good time to make an investment in long-lasting gear.

Ultralight Packs

A typical unloaded weekender pack hits the scale at 5 to 6 pounds, but an ultralight pack weighs half as much and can still haul all your gear. The drawback: reduced durability and comfort and fewer features. To cut excess pounds, ultralight packs are made with super-thin waterproof nylon instead of higher *denier* nylon used in most other packs. Denier indicates the durability of pack fabrics by measuring the thickness of individual nylon threads. The higher the denier number, the thicker the fiber. Most backpacks are made with 150- to 300-denier nylon, but ultralight packs can feature 100-denier or less.

Also missing on ultralight packs are extra straps, pockets, and zippers. Shoulder straps and hip belts also are often smaller and thinner. In general, you should only purchase an ultralight pack if you have an ultralight tent, sleeping bag, and other gear to fill it because these packs aren't designed to carry heavy loads comfortably.

How to Load a Backpack

Loading a dishwasher is considered an art in some households, but filling a backpack is a science governed by a few crucial standards. An off-center pack is not only uncomfortable, but it can also be dangerous to carry. The general rule is that the heaviest items should be placed in the center of the pack and as close to your back as possible. Lighter gear can be stored higher up and on the sides. Here's how to fill a pack.

◊ Start by placing your sleeping bag in its own compartment, or at the base of the pack, to act as the foundation for everything else. Fill any empty space around the bag with other items you won't need until you reach camp.

◊ Position the heaviest items—tent poles, stoves, fuel, and food—in the center of the pack (not on the sides) and as close to your back as possible.

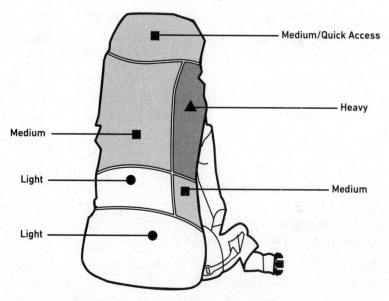

Placing heavier gear closer to the pack's frame—and your back—will make it feel lighter and improve your stability.

◊ For uneven, steep, or rocky trails, pack heavier items at the bottom of your pack to lower your center of gravity and increase stability.

◊ For smooth and level trails, place heavy items higher up— in the middle of the pack—to position the weight over your hips.

◊ Prevent heavy items from shifting by packing extra clothing around them.

Once the main compartment is mostly filled, you can add gear to the sides and top of a pack. This is where you should stash lightweight gear and anything you might need during the course of the day:

◊ Use the lid pocket to store breakable or frequently used items like snacks, sunscreen, maps, and bug repellent.

◊ Strap sleeping pads and other odd-size gear (like trekking poles) on the outside of the pack—but wait until the pack's interior is full before lashing gear to the outside.

◊ Place light and compressible items like rain shells and fleeces in a shovel pocket or at the top of the pack where they can be cinched down when you close the lid.

◊ Store containers with liquids—like flasks of white gas or water bottles—in an exterior side pocket in case of leaks.

 Trail Tips Packing your gear in multiple small stuff sacks instead of several large ones will speed up loading and allow you to squeeze gear into every corner of a pack.

Keeping Your Stuff Dry

Most packs aren't waterproof. They can withstand a light rain, but a persistent downpour will soak them. To protect your gear, you can buy a waterproof nylon cover that cinches over your pack. For the DIY crowd who doesn't want to spend an extra $30 on a cover, you can always line the inside of your pack with a large plastic garbage bag. And here's a tip: A white bag will make it easier to see the gear inside your pack.

Make It Last for Years

Most backpacks are built tough. On any given day on a trail, you might pass hikers with external frame packs that date back to the 1970s. Their durability, however, isn't unconditional. To survive for 10 or 20 years, your pack deserves the same TLC you

give your boots and clothes when you return home from a hike—
especially after a long, muddy, or rainy trip. Here's how to clean
your pack:

1. Brush or vacuum out any dirt, crumbs, or lint from all
   pockets; use a toothbrush to get at the nooks and crannies.

2. Clean zippers with a toothbrush and warm water, and trim
   any loose threads to prevent unraveling.

3. Remove stains and dirt from the inside and outside of a
   pack using lukewarm water and a sponge; avoid using soap
   or detergent.

4. Dry the pack fabric with a cloth or paper towels, being sure
   to reach into the corners.

5. Set the pack aside for several days to dry, and hang up in a
   cool, dry place.

SUMMARY

Fit and comfort are as important for backpacks as they are for footwear. For any pack
sized 35 liters or more, be sure to measure your torso length, and load the pack with
20–30 pounds for testing while you walk around an outdoor retail store. Always purchase
a pack with a little more space than you use for a typical hike so that you can extend your
trip length without requiring new gear. When loading a pack, place the denser, heavier
items at the bottom and close to your back, and put lightweight gear you might use during
the day at the top or in accessible pockets.

LIVING ON THE TRAIL

The next time someone suggests that camping is cold, uncomfortable, and grimy, invite them on a hike where you'll serve a dinner of chicken burritos, chips and fresh guacamole, with peach cobbler for dessert at a campsite with a view that no restaurant could equal. That should shut them up or at least encourage them to check their calendars for an available weekend. Hiking and camping are certainly rustic, but it doesn't need to be a suffer-fest, as the next four chapters will demonstrate. You'll learn how tents and sleeping bags protect you from nature's hazards, while your newly acquired camp skills don't just make trail life bearable, they raise the bar for style, comfort, and adventure.

CHAPTER 12

SHELTER FROM THE STORM

Imagine yourself in this scene: A full moon rises over a calm lake, momentarily dimming the stars—more than you've ever seen before—that plaster the night sky. After zipping shut the door of your tent, you lean back on your sleeping bag and study tomorrow's route with the glow from a headlamp. Outside, the hum of crickets is occasionally broken by the hoot of an owl perched nearby. Then you switch off the light and go to sleep, planning to wake just after sunrise to hike to your next campsite.

Sound enticing? A weekend spent hiking and camping can be the perfect antidote to your Monday to Friday grind, and it's actually much easier than you might think. To camp safely and comfortably, however, you need three things: a tent, a sleeping bag, and an insulated ground pad. This chapter will help you acquire those items and find the right balance of weight, space, insulation, and protection to create your ideal overnight shelter. The good news about your new portable home is that you don't need a mortgage and it never needs painting.

Why a Tent?

"The best roof for your bedroom is the sky." That's the advice Colin Fletcher gave in his 1968 backpacking bible, *The Complete Walker* (see Resources). Most hikers today, however, appreciate a waterproof tent between themselves and a midnight downpour. After all, insurance against rain, lightning, frost, and snow—as well as millions of biting bugs—is the primary purpose of a shelter. Your tent, however, is more than just a place to sleep at night. It can also be where you store your gear during the day, a playroom for kids, a cozy retreat, and your home away from home. You've got to love your tent to want to go camping. And you can only love your tent if it does its job to protect you.

This large dome-style family camping tent sleeps two parents and up to four kids with plenty

of leftover space for the dog.

Counting Heads, Feet, and Inches

Whether you're in the market for a portable backpacking tent or a cavernous car-camping tent, the first question to consider is space. More specifically, how many people will sleep in it? Whether you hike solo, backpack with a friend or your spouse, or have a family of six, it will determine how big a tent you need.

Every tent is classified as solo, two person, three person, and so on, to indicate the maximum number of people it can sleep. Of course, these standards aren't the same for all tents and all people. For instance, a two-person backpacking tent will be smaller than a car-camping tent for two. And any extra-large campers might find that a two-person tent is more like a solo shelter for them. The two key dimensions for judging the size of the tent are floor space (usually measured in square feet) and ceiling height (usually measured in inches). When shopping for tents, be sure to review these two numbers to compare different shelters.

Tents That Go the Distance

For backpackers, how much a tent weighs should be your number one concern. Just a few years ago, most two-person backpacking tents tipped the scale at 5 to 6 pounds. Innovations like tapered poles, lightweight fabrics, and narrower designs, however, have cut the average weight down to 3 to 4 pounds—with some ultralight models weighing 2½ pounds. This is great news for beginner backpackers because the ideal first shelter is a lightweight, three-season, two-person tent. Not only can you carry this shelter on most solo trips, but it can accommodate you and your best friend, too. A three-person backpacking tent is great for groups of friends to share or for a young family who wants to pile everyone into a single shelter. However, if backpacking with four or more people, it's better to bring several smaller tents instead of a single huge shelter because it's easier to divide the tent parts between several hikers.

 Trail Tips The most equitable way to carry a two-person backpacking tent is to have one person pack the inner canopy and footprint, while the other person takes the rainfly, poles, and stakes.

Room for the Whole Family

For car-camping tents, overall size (both floor space and height) trumps weight. After all, you're not going to be lugging this tent more than a few hundred feet. If you're shopping for a family tent, check product labels to determine the maximum number of adults and kids they can sleep. Besides a place to spend the night, large tents often become family activity centers—especially for trips with young kids. Make sure that family tents have durable floors with reinforced seams, a "bathtub" of thick fabric where the wall meets the floor, tall ceilings, and multiple doors to ease the constant comings and goings. Elaborate base camp tents sometimes feature partitioned sleeping areas and screened "porches" or "garages" for gear.

The Nuts and Bolts of Your Tent

A tent isn't just a single object but a system of interlocking parts that work together to make a reliable shelter. As a result, pitching a tent is much like putting together a 3D puzzle. Fortunately, most tents follow the same basic plan and involve the same parts—mainly a nylon/mesh inner canopy held up by poles and covered by a waterproof rainfly. Getting to know the parts of your tent—and what they do—will help you set it up faster when you're camping. Here's a quick summary of what's inside the stuff sack that holds your tent.

Inner Canopy

The tent's main sleeping chamber is usually made with a combination of breathable mesh and thin nylon. It can be a rectangle, square, or multisided shape, depending on the pole arrangements. Even the lightest tents feature a durable bathtub edge of nylon that rises several inches up the sides of the tent to prevent water from seeping inside, while a zippered door or doors provide access. Note: A canopy isn't waterproof unless it's covered by a rainfly or is a waterproof single-wall tent that doesn't need a fly.

Rainfly

A rainfly is a waterproof shield that covers the top and sides of a tent and repels rain and snow with polyurethane- or silicone-coated nylon. A properly pitched rainfly should reach down to within a few inches of the ground. Some tents enable fastpacking, which involves leaving the inner canopy at home and pitching the rainfly by itself with the poles and footprint to create a tarp-like shelter.

Poles

Poles are the lightweight aluminum or carbon-fiber supports for the inner canopy and rainfly. Most poles are segmented and connected by elastic shock cords that enable them to be folded and stored.

Guy Lines

These thin ropes tie down the tent or rainfly to provide extra stability. Guy lines are especially useful during windstorms or when camping on rocky terrain where stakes can't be used.

Stakes

These sharp aluminum, plastic, or titanium spikes pin down the corners and sides of a tent and rainfly. Staking tents keeps the rainfly taut, which helps shed rain and snow and prevents it from billowing in the wind. Tents that don't require stakes to stand upright are called *freestanding*. A freestanding tent can be pitched without stakes because the pole structure naturally supports the inner canopy and rainfly. Staking down a tent, however, is always a good idea to improve its stability.

Vestibule

A vestibule is a gear storage area covered by the rainfly but not located within the inner canopy. The number and size of vestibules vary between different tents, but the ideal space should be big enough to store the boots and packs for all the tent's occupants.

Footprint

This thin plastic or nylon sheet is placed directly underneath the tent to provide a barrier against moisture and abrasion. Tuck the footprint completely under the sides of the rainfly to prevent water from seeping underneath.

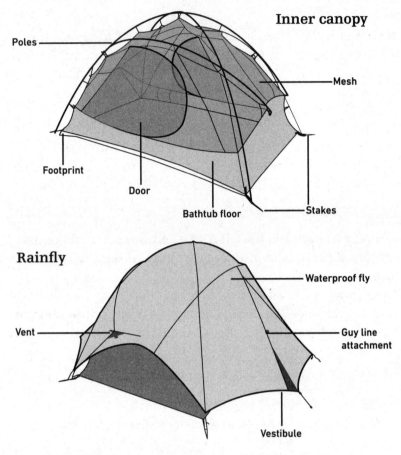

Inner canopy

Poles

Mesh

Footprint

Door

Bathtub floor

Stakes

Rainfly

Waterproof fly

Vent

Guy line attachment

Vestibule

All the parts of a tent work together to provide reliable support and waterproof protection.

Shopping for a Portable House

Once you determine how big a tent you want (that is, how many people it holds), the next choice is all about shape. Besides traditional tent styles like A-frames, domes, and hoops, there are also designs that resemble the drawings of Dr. Seuss. Not to worry—as strange as they look, today's unusually shaped backpacking and car-camping tents will still accomplish the main goal of keeping you warm and dry but with less weight and more interior space than tents made a decade ago.

The Shape of Your Shelter

Don't walk into a gear shop dead set on buying a specific shape of tent. Instead, evaluate all the styles to find the one that matches your requirements. The choice often boils down to weight versus interior space. For instance, if you're car-camping with kids, then you'll want a sturdy design with plenty of floor space and headroom—features most often found in a dome tent. A modified A-frame tent, on the other hand, is ideal for backpackers because it maximizes usable space without extra weight. Here are the advantages and disadvantages of each style of tent:

◊ **A-frame** These nonfreestanding tents are inexpensive and simple to set up, but interior space is limited by sloping walls and a cramped peaked ceiling.

◊ **Dome** This popular freestanding design maximizes square footage and height with curved walls and high ceilings, but these popular car-camping tents often weigh more than other models.

◊ **Half-dome** Combining the space efficiency of a dome tent with a narrower profile to reduce weight, these are ideal tents for backpacking.

◊ **Modified A-frame** Strategically placed poles extend the walls to improve interior space of these tents without adding more weight, but steeper sides are vulnerable to high winds.

◊ **Hoop** This low-slung tent offers superior wind and snow resistance, but all sides must be staked.

This lightweight backpacking tent is tight on space and has a single door but weighs less than three pounds with a rainfly.

Surface Matters

All tent canopies are made with a combination of two fabrics: transparent mesh, which is lightweight and breathable, and nylon, which is water resistant, heat trapping, and durable. Manufacturers mix and match these fabrics to create tents designed for different seasons and weather conditions. As a result, a tent designed for humid summer weather will have more mesh than a winter-camping tent, which might lack any mesh. You can also buy a convertible tent, a multiseason option that can be pitched with mesh sidewalls for warm-weather camping that can be covered by nylon walls that zipper up for more protection during winter conditions.

Safety Check   Never buy a cheap backpacking or family tent from a discount or big-box store. You'll realize your purchase was "all wet" the first time the weak waterproofing coating and flimsy stitching are subjected to a real rainstorm.

Stopping Moisture on the Inside

Pitching a tent isn't just about keeping the rain off your head. You also need to prevent the build-up of interior condensation generated by wet clothing and the moisture you exhale. If a tent doesn't vent well, overnight condensation can generate as much dampness as a leaky rainfly. Because mesh panels and ceiling vents can help condensation escape into the air, you need to make sure your tent has enough mesh and vents to breathe effectively and keep you dry.

 Trail Tips Before using a tent for the first time, apply a waterproof sealant to the seams on both sides of the rainfly. Even though these seams were taped and sealed in the factory, it's a good idea to rewaterproof them using a seam sealer (found at most outdoor stores) before your first outing.

Other Shelters

For the weight-conscious backpacker, the alternative to packing a tent is to opt for a much smaller, less protective shelter like a tarp, bivy sack, or hammock. These ultralight shelters are growing in popularity, especially among hikers on multiday treks and DIY gearheads who make their own products. A tarp is a waterproof sheet that you stake down and tie out with guy lines. It will give you overhead protection but won't shield you from sideways-blowing rain or biting bugs. A bivy sack is nothing more than a waterproof oversleeve for your sleeping bag for laying down on the ground. Breathable fabrics and bug screens make them a tolerable—although claustrophobic—sleeping option for weight-conscious hikers. Hammocks look like bivy sacks hanging in midair but require properly spaced trees to set up correctly. Beginning backpackers, however, should start with a traditional tent and only graduate to a tarp-like shelter after gaining adequate skills and experience.

Where to Stake Your Claim

Even when you're required to stay in a designated campsite, there's a lot you can do to maximize the advantages of where you pitch your tent. Here are some guidelines to follow:

◊ Choose dry, flat, durable ground like pine forests, rock slabs, or bare dirt. Select previously used or impacted spots if possible.

◊ Take advantage of shady places in the summer and sites that maximize southern exposure during colder seasons.

◊ Both water and cold air flow downhill, so make sure you're not in the lowest spot around.

Once you select a site, remove loose rocks or branches from the ground. You might not feel them underneath your sleeping pad and bag, but they could tear the bottom fabric. Next, unpack the tent. If it's raining, keep the inner canopy dry by placing the rainfly over it as you pitch it. Extend the poles gently because overstretching the shock cords or snapping the segments together violently can cause them to break.

 Trail Tips   When packing a tent, place the inner canopy in the bottom of the stuff sack, followed by the rainfly and the footprint so that you can remove them in the reverse order and keep the canopy dry if it's raining.

Organizing for the Overnight

Once you're done hiking for the day, your tent temporarily replaces your backpack as the place to store your gear. Here's how to turn a tent into a gear locker:

◊ Unroll or inflate your ground pad and unpack your sleeping bag outside your tent where you have more room—if weather permits.

◊ Keep food and scented toiletries outside your tent—either in a car trunk, in a campsite locker, or hung in a bear bag (see Chapter 18).

◇ Store overnight necessities like a headlamp, cell phone, glasses, water bottle, and tissues in the mesh side pockets inside most tents.

◇ Even if no rain is forecast overnight, place your boots and backpack inside the tent's vestibule; heavy dew can soak them as much as a storm. If the backpack won't fit, shield it with a rain cover.

◇ Store your waterproof rain shell and other outerwear in an accessible place inside the tent in case you wake up to rain or strong wind.

 Safety Check If you bring DEET-based bug repellent inside a tent, store it in its own zipper-lock plastic bag to prevent it from leaking and dissolving any mesh or plastic that it comes in contact with.

Building the Perfect Sleep System

A waterproof tent will protect you from rain and wind, but you need more to ensure a comfortable night. Your allies are a sleeping bag and a ground pad, which work together to create an insulated sleep system. Without one or the other, the quality and quantity of your overnight rest will suffer.

The Good Kind of Body Bag

Sleeping bags come in three general shapes: rectangular, semirectangular, and mummy. The first two are fine for car-camping, where weight and space aren't a concern. Backpackers, however, should opt for the form-fitting mummy bag. Not only is it made with less material and therefore lighter, but it also heats up faster. Sleeping bags, after all, don't generate heat; they use layers of down or synthetic insulation to trap warm air heated by your body.

Two Ways to Stay Warmer

Deciding between a down or synthetic bag is a classic and ongoing debate among hikers. The choice comes down to three factors: weight, wetness, and cost. Down compresses better than any other insulation (read: stuffs into a smaller space in your pack) and will last longer than a comparable synthetic bag—especially if it's washed regularly. But down loses its insulating ability when it gets wet. Synthetic bags will still keep you warm even when wet and are less expensive than down but are heavier and take up much more space. Most backpackers eventually acquire two sleeping bags to cover all options: a lightweight synthetic bag for wet conditions and summer camping and a warmer down bag for dry, cold-weather treks.

 Trail Tips To protect a down sleeping bag from moisture, place a plastic trash bag inside the stuff sack before packing the bag or use a waterproof stuff sack.

Ensuring Your Bag Is Warm (or Cool) Enough

How low can your sleeping bag go? When it comes to temperatures, you don't have to guess. Every bag is assigned a rating based on the lowest temperature for which it will still provide a comfortable night's sleep. Most bags are divided into three categories:

Temperature Rating	Bag Type
20°F and below	Winter
20°F to 40°F	Three-season (spring, summer, fall)
40°F and above	Summer

For a beginner hiker, a three-season mummy bag with at least a 30°F temperature rating is an ideal first sleeping bag. It can be either down or synthetic, depending on your preference. You'll find synthetic and down insulation in bags rated for all temperatures, although down is more common in cold-weather bags because it provides more warmth for less volume. One trend you'll notice is that cold-weather bags cost more than bags rated for higher temperatures because of the extra down or synthetic insulation required for winter-rated bags.

Sleeping bag temperature ratings are based on an average hiker, and they can be overly optimistic. If you're a cold sleeper—you feel cold at night when other people are warm—you should choose a bag with a conservatively lower temperature rating or use a thicker ground pad.

Why Cleaner Equals Warmer

As sleeping bags get dirty, they lose their insulating abilities. As a result, a grimy bag rated to 15°F might only be adequate for 20°F or 25°F. Airing out sleeping bags after each trip and properly cleaning and storing them will keep them cleaner and warmer, and it will extend their life spans to a decade or more. Here's how:

1. After each trip, unzip your bag and let it air out in your basement, garage, or living room for at least 2 full days.

2. Wash your bag at least once a year (usually at the end of the season) or if it gets especially dirty. Always follow the manufacturer's washing instructions.

3. Use only a front-loading washer (top-loading agitators can damage the insulation), warm water, and mild detergent.

4. Transfer the damp bag to the dryer carefully to prevent soggy insulation from tearing and dry on low for 3 to 5 hours.

5. Reapply a spray-on waterproof coating if your bag has a DWR shell.

6. Store your bag in a large cotton or mesh stuff sack and hang it in a closet. Never store it for long periods of time compressed into a stuff sack.

Between You and the Cold, Hard Ground

An often overlooked but critical element to your sleeping system is the ground pad. It's the foam or inflatable barrier that fits underneath your sleeping bag. Because the cold ground is extremely effective at stealing your body heat, ground pads (also called *sleeping pads* or *mats*) keep you from direct contact with the ground. In general, the thicker the pad, the more insulation it provides.

Sleeping pads fall into two main categories: closed-cell foam and inflatable. Closed-cell foam pads are lightweight, and cheap, and will never deflate, but they aren't as comfortable or warm as air-filled pads. Some foam pads have ridges or indentations that create air pockets and improve thermal performance. Inflatable pads are filled with one or more air chambers that when blown up increase their thickness and comfort. Higher-end air mattresses are often insulated, self-inflating, or made with lightweight materials.

After a hike, sleeping pads should be stored flat underneath a bed or hung in a closet. Inflatable pads should be stored with their valves open to encourage air circulation.

 Trail Tips Warm up your clothes for the next day by stuffing them at the bottom of your sleeping bag during the night.

SUMMARY

Choose a tent based on the number of people it can sleep, followed by considerations for weight, ventilation, height, and ease of setup. A two-person backpacking tent weighing 4 pounds or less is an ideal first tent, just as a three-season mummy bag rated to 30°F is the right sleeping bag for a beginning backpacker. A bag insulated with down is best for cold, dry trips, while you should opt for synthetic insulation if you hike and camp in a rainy climate. Tents and sleeping bags deteriorate if stored dirty, damp, or compressed, so remember to air out, clean, and store your sleeping system in a cool and roomy space.

CHAPTER 13

THE OUTDOOR KITCHEN

"Drop packs, it's chow time!"

For some hikers, those words mean a meal of multigrain bagels dipped in lukewarm baked beans. For others, it means a juicy grilled steak with baby carrots and red potatoes washed down with a glass of Merlot. Which is the better campfire meal? It depends what your goals are. If food is your passion, a steak dinner is worth the extra preparation and cook time it requires. If you seek your rewards on the trail and not in a frying pan, then bagels and beans will fill your stomach but not take up your entire afternoon.

No matter what you eat, backcountry cooking is a challenge. Instead of a kitchen sink and a fully stocked fridge, you make do with basic cooking gear like a small stove, a wood fire, and a few utensils. Most of the same limitations apply to both car-camping and backpacking, although access to a multi burner propane stove and ice-chilled cooler expands the range of car-camping cuisine. Still, as this chapter explains, you can create an outdoor menu filled with energy-rich foods and trail-friendly products. And the best part is that no matter what you cook and eat outdoors, food always tastes better the farther you are from civilization.

Big Effort Equals Big Hunger

The average backpacker needs to consume 3,500 to 4,000 calories per day on the trail—well above the daily 2,500 calories that's recommended for a normal, active adult. Day-hikers don't require as many calories as backpackers, but they should still pack high-energy foods for the trail. The easiest way for hikers to boost their energy levels—as crazy as it sounds—is to increase the percentage of high-fat foods in your trail diet. After all, eating more food isn't the best option when you need to carry everything you consume.

 Trail Tips Hard cheeses like aged Asiago, cheddar, and Colby last longer (and taste better) than softer cheeses when left unrefrigerated for several days.

Loading Up on Calories

Fat contains double the amount of calories per ounce than protein and carbohydrates, making these extra rich foods the ideal fare for hikers. Normally, you should try to limit your intake of fatty foods and snacks. But when you're carrying a backpack all day, you're going to convert those extra calories into more miles. The following list includes the most popular high-fat and high-calorie foods enjoyed by hikers:

◊ Chocolate

◊ Cheese

◊ Pepperoni, salami sticks, and beef jerky

◊ Nuts like walnuts, cashews, peanuts, and almonds

◊ Chocolate-covered raisins or peanuts

And Maintaining a Balanced Diet

While some hikers might enjoy eating chocolate bars for an entire weekend, it's not a wise or healthy plan. You should still seek a balanced diet that also includes grains, fruits, and vegetables. Packing rice, pasta, or bread covers the grain requirement, but fruits and veggies are often left out of trail meals because hikers think they'll spoil or get crushed. With the exception of bananas, fresh produce is not as hard to pack or preserve as you might think. Plus, vegetables are a good source of vitamins and minerals, and fruits contain complex sugars that boost energy levels. Apples, pears, oranges, cucumbers, carrots, avocados, onions, and bell peppers travel best inside a pack.

High-Energy Snack Attack

Bringing high-energy snacks isn't an option—it's a requirement for any hiking trip. Constant munching on a steady flow of snacks will prevent peaks and valleys in your energy level. Snacks should not only contain fat, but they also should contain protein and carbs, and they should be easy to eat on the go. One of the most popular trail snacks is *gorp*, a DIY mixture of nuts, seeds, dried fruit, and chocolate filling a zipper-lock plastic bag. Other snacks to munch on throughout the day include energy bars, granola bars, hard cookies, cheese sticks, dried fruit, and salami or pepperoni sticks.

Making a Menu

No matter if your meals are basic or gourmet, it's important not to wait until the last minute to plan them. Instead, several days before your trip, you should sit down and sketch out a menu for each meal and snack. For instance, a typical Friday night to Sunday afternoon backpacking trip involves six meals: two breakfasts, two lunches, and two dinners. Then break down each meal into the necessary ingredients, making sure to check your kitchen for items you already have.

Finding Trail-Friendly Recipes

Whether you're a fan of recipes or prefer culinary experimentation, you can find enough trail meals to keep your taste buds happy. First, it's not difficult to convert stovetop favorites like rice and beans, chicken burritos, and spaghetti with meat sauce into campfire recipes. Despite what you might think, you can bring meat, cheese, and fresh vegetables into the woods without it spoiling, which opens up a wide range of appetizing meals. This book suggests several meal options, but you can find more ideas in any recent issue of *Backpacker* magazine or archived in the "recipes" section at Backpacker. com. The Resources section also lists several books devoted to backcountry cooking and recipes.

Delicious Meals from Simple to Gourmet

The number one trail meal is probably a bagel sandwich made with cheese and peanut butter. It's uncomplicated, hearty, and easy to pack. If you prefer cheap and simple meals, here are some reliable backpacking foods that are easy to buy, pack, and eat—and promise a quick cleanup:

◊ Baked beans and rice

◊ Ramen noodles

◊ Macaroni and cheese

◊ Couscous

◊ Soup packets

◊ Oatmeal

Sometimes, it's fun to get out of a food rut by cooking at least one fancy meal on a weekend backpacking or car-camping trip. Unleashing your gourmet side often involves more ingredients, longer prep times, and multiple pots on the fire. The results, however, can be deliciously worth it, as these gourmet recipes suggest:

◊ Pan pizzas using just-add-water crust mix, a squeezable bottle of tomato sauce, and shredded Asiago cheese

◊ Quesadillas made with shredded cheddar and pepper jack cheese, canned olives, sliced bell peppers, salsa, and flour tortillas

◊ Veggie burgers on a toasted bun topped with grilled mushrooms and cheddar cheese

◊ Whole-wheat pancakes topped with fresh-picked berries

◊ Spicy curry made in a foil pouch with chicken, curry powder, rice, and a diced jalapeño pepper

Dealing with Perishables

Car-campers can throw beef patties, sausage links, and chicken breasts into a cooler full of ice and enjoy these tasty meats several days later. Although backpackers can't haul a cooler into the woods without a seriously sore back, they can employ a few tricks to make perishable foods last longer without refrigeration.

Plan to eat perishable foods—this includes fruits, vegetables, and meats—as early during a trip as possible to prevent spoilage. You can find white turkey, tuna, chicken, and salmon preserved in foil pouches, which don't require refrigeration. Uncooked beef and pork, however, should be placed in a zipper-lock plastic bag, completely frozen, and placed in an insulated bag deep inside your pack. These meats should thaw by dinnertime on your first day—which is when you should cook them. Protein-rich veggie burgers and tofu can be long-lasting alternatives to meat. Pack crushable foods, especially fruits and vegetables, inside a durable cooking pot, a spare water bottle, or lightweight plastic containers that can double as a bowl.

Trail Tips   To keep food and drinks chilled on the trail, place them in a mesh bag and submerge them for several hours in a cold-running river or stream near your campsite.

The Dehydrated Solution

The easiest meals to cook on the trail are pouches of dehydrated or freeze-dried foods that require only a half- liter of boiling water and ten minutes to cook. These meals are best for hikes where space, weight, and time are at a premium. Some of the better-tasting products include beef stroganoff with noodles, chili with beans, spaghetti with meat sauce, and vegetable lasagna. You can find dehydrated meals made by Mountain House, AlpineAire, and Backpacker's Pantry at your local outdoor retail shops and online at Campmor.com and REI.com.

From the Supermarket to Your Pack

Even if you choose freeze-dried meals, you'll still need to make a grocery run to buy snacks, breakfast foods, and other vitals. Write a detailed list before you go, then check the list for repeat items like cheese, rice, or pita bread that you can buy in bulk and use over multiple meals. Be sure to shop for food at least two days before your trip so that you have enough time to sort and pack it for the trail.

Backpacker-Friendly Ingredients

Shopping for trail meals requires more brain power than your typical grocery run. Not only do you need food that doesn't require refrigeration, but you also need to evaluate each product's size, weight, and sturdiness. Fortunately, most major supermarkets carry plenty of foods ideal for backpacking. Some of these items include:

◊ Chicken, tuna, and salmon in foil pouches

◊ Baked beans in foil pouches

◊ Pita pocket sandwiches

◊ Tofu packets and paneer cheese

◊ Boil-in-a-bag meals

◊ Instant rice

◊ Instant oatmeal

◊ Instant hash browns

◊ Noodle and sauce mixes

◊ Bouillon cubes and flavor packets

◊ Powdered milk packets

Raw ingredients often weigh more than freeze-dried pouches, but you can save a few ounces by choosing the right packages. For instance, choose foods that come in crushable plastic containers rather than glass jars and metal cans. And instead of bringing an entire jar of tomato sauce or olive oil, pour the amount you need into a smaller plastic bottle or container. Most outdoor retail stores sell plastic squeeze tubes and tiny vials designed to hold several ounces of an ingredient. And no matter how much you bring, your pack will weigh less than the baggage for the Lewis and Clark expedition, which started its trek in 1804 with 3,700 pounds of pork and 1,000 pounds of corn.

Filling Your Pack with Food

As you pack, you'll probably be surprised at how much space your food takes up and how heavy it is. Car-campers can just fill up another duffel bag or ice cooler, but backpackers need to get creative. The most important step is to divide the meals into separate stuff sacks or zipper-lock plastic bags to make them easier to slip inside a backpack. Here are several more space- and time-saving tips:

◊ Presort bulk foods like oatmeal and pasta into zipper-lock plastic bags according to the amount you need for each day and meal.

◊ Pour liquids like wine and tomato sauce into Lexan bottles that won't add a plastic flavor.

 Safety Check   To remember to clean your hands and face before handling food, store a small, squeezable container of hand sanitizer with your stove or cook kit.

◊ Take advantage of all empty spaces—like stuffing tea bags and instant coffee inside insulated mugs.

◊ Use condiment packets from fast-food restaurants and coffee creamer singles—despite the extra trash, they still weigh less than the smallest squeeze bottle.

◊ Store spices, powdered milk and drink mixes in empty pill bottles, and place semi liquid items like peanut butter, ketchup, jam, and honey in squeezable tubes.

The Outdoor Chef

Cold lunches—made without a stove—are the norm for campers and backpackers, but most breakfasts and dinners involve hot food. As soon as you get up in the morning or pitch your tent in the evening, cooking a big meal should be your next priority. To keep yourself energized as you cook, whip up some appetizers like cheese and pepperoni slices on wheat crackers or carrot or pepper spears, and brew some hot tea, or sip a sugary drink. A warm and partially full belly will help you enjoy cooking the rest of your hot meal.

Cook Kits and Utensils

To prepare most meals (besides dehydrated food pouches), you're going to need pots, pans, cooking utensils, and a plate or bowl. Car-campers can bring their secondhand kitchenware, but backpackers looking to conserve weight and space should bring only as much cookware as they need and cut corners when possible. Fortunately, newer cook kits are made with lightweight materials and nesting components for efficient packing. Some pots are also designed to hold lightweight stoves and fuel canisters. Here's a list of some extra items you might want to store with your cook kit:

◊ Extra butane lighter

◊ Pot gripper or small multitool with pliers

◊ Scrubber sponge

◊ Serving spoon

◊ Kitchen-only knife for slicing and cutting

 Trail Tips To make a small, packable cutting board, cut a thin piece of plastic into a circle that is the same diameter as your largest cooking pot and store it at the bottom of the pot.

Cleaning Up

Doing dishes on the trail can be as challenging as cooking meals. With no running water, sink, or garbage disposal, your goal should be to get dishes and utensils "as clean as possible" rather than spotless. Simple tricks like eating out of the cooking pot can reduce the number of dishes to clean, as can prioritizing one-pot meals and cooking rice and pasta in their own foil pouches.

Car-campers with access to ample water can utilize a three-bin soak, wash, and rinse system—using hot water heated on a stove to fill the plastic tubs for soaking and washing. Remember that a little bit of soap goes a long way, and too many suds will spoil your rinse water. Clean dishes can be left to air dry on a table or hung to dry in a nylon mesh sack.

For most backpackers, using precious stove fuel to heat water for a thorough dish cleaning doesn't make sense. As a result, backpackers and car-campers with limited fuel or water access should use plastic spoons to scrape away food residue from pots and plates before swirling a little bit of water around while scrubbing with a sponge. Dispose of the resulting "gray water" in a sump hole (at least 6 inches deep) or scatter it broadly at least 200 feet from campsites and water sources. Dip a bandanna or pack towel in hand sanitizer to wipe down knives and utensils. And remember, "clean" is a relative term for your dishes, as well as your body.

Cooking over Flames

A blazing fire can cook your dinner while also providing a warm glow. Ground fires are allowed in most developed campgrounds and in some—but not all—backcountry campsites. Be attentive to fire restrictions during drought periods, especially in late summer. Check Chapter 16 for simple tips on how to build a roaring fire with matches or a lighter.

Many backpacking cook kits are designed with nesting bowls and space to store a small stove and fuel canister.

Stovetop Cooking

Camp stoves range in size from picnic-table units with multiple burners for car-campers to tiny backpacking stoves no bigger than your fist. Stoves produce a hotter, more efficient flame than fires and leave almost no mark on the ground. To choose the right stove for your camping and hiking needs, you need to consider size, fuel type, and performance. Also, new tech has boosted stove efficiency and versatility in recent years, increasing the advantages of upgrading your old burner. Here are the main categories of camping and backpacking stoves.

Liquid-Fuel Stoves

Fuel: White gas in a refillable bottle, as well as kerosene and diesel fuel for multifuel stoves

Advantages: Durable construction; improved performance in windy and cold (under 40°F) weather; cheaper and more available fuel source

Disadvantages: Noisy; heavier than canister stoves; requires pumping and priming before lighting, as well as periodic cleaning and maintenance

Cost: $60–$150

Manufacturers: MSR, Optimus, Coleman

Best for: Four-season backpackers; international travelers

Liquid-fuel stoves like this burn pressurized gas stored in a separate fuel bottle.

Canister Stoves

Fuel: Butane, propane, and isobutane blends in a closed canister

Advantages: Backpacking models (including JetBoil-style systems) are smaller, lighter, and cheaper than liquid-fuel stoves; easy to operate; minimal maintenance; finer flame control

Disadvantages: Poor performance in windy and cold (under 40°F) weather; nonrefillable fuel canisters; fuel can be hard to obtain

Cost: $30–$150

Manufacturers: JetBoil, Primus, MSR, Brunton, Optimus, Coleman, Snow Peak

Best for: Car-campers (multiple burner units); ultralight hikers; summer backpackers

Canister stoves are the easiest to set up and operate and burn a blend of butane-propane gas.

This canister stove features a built-in heat exchanger and insulated bottle to boil water as quickly and efficiently as possible.

Alcohol- and Solid-Fuel Stoves

Fuel: Denatured alcohol or solid fuel tablets

Advantages: The smallest, lightest, cheapest stoves available

Disadvantages: Long boil times; poor performance in windy and cold (under 40°F) weather

Cost: $10–$60

Manufacturers: Trangia, Vargo, Esbit, TOAKS

Best for: Ultralight hikers; summer backpackers

Biofuel Stoves

Fuel: Twigs, leaves, forest litter

Advantages: Small, lightweight, and simple design; unlimited fuel supply; some models produce electricity

Disadvantages: Long cook times; wet and damp weather limits fuel supply; requires constant attention

Cost: $50–$130

Manufacturers: BioLite, TOAKS, Solo Stove

Best for: Ultralight hikers; arid climate backpackers; experimentalists

Stoves that burn twigs to heat meals eliminate the need to carry fuel but also require longer cook times.

Camp Stoves

Fuel: Butane canisters (16 oz.)

Advantages: Two burners shorten cook times; adjustable flame controls; sidewalls block wind

Disadvantages: Too heavy for backpacking; require a table or flat platform to operate

Cost: $60–$130

Manufacturers: Coleman, GSI Outdoors, Eureka, Primus

Best for: Car-campers; large groups; picnics and tailgating

Fueling Up

Most stoves will only work with a specific type of fuel, so before you purchase one, make sure you know what type it requires. Outdoor retail stores will sell fuel for most types—including compact 4-ounce and 8-ounce butane/propane canisters for backpacking stoves. However, supermarkets, big-box, and home improvement stores will generally only carry cans of white gas and the larger 16-ounce butane/propane canisters. When deciding how much stove fuel to carry, check the following table and always leave an emergency reserve.

Stove Fuel Consumption for Two People Cooking Two Meals per Day in Summer

Fuel Type	Fuel Amount	Burn Time	Days on Trail
White gas	20 fl. oz.	60–90 min.	2–3
Isobutane canisters	8 fl. oz.	60–90 min.	2–3
Alcohol	10 fl. oz.	60–90 min.	2

 Trail Tips To determine how much gas remains in a fuel canister, use a postage scale to compare the weight of the used canister to a full one—and write the result in permanent marker on the side of the used canister.

How to Prevent Singed Eyebrows

Despite their loud, jetting flames, backpacking and camp stoves are safer than they look. Still, to prevent any accidental fireballs, follow these safety precautions:

◊ Never light a stove inside your tent because of the risk of fire and the poisonous (and odorless) gases produced by combustion.

◊ Place stoves on durable, nonflammable surfaces like flat rocks or bare ground.

◊ Clean up any fuel spills before igniting the primer cup on a liquid-fuel stove.

- ◊ Double-check that fuel bottles are capped and sealed tightly before placing them into your pack.
- ◊ When priming a liquid-fuel stove, allow only a small amount of white gas to fill the priming cup to prevent flare-ups.
- ◊ Keep a water bottle handy when using stoves to extinguish any accidental ground fires.
- ◊ Wipe away carbon stains after every trip and let your stove air out before storing.

Flying with Stoves and Fuel

If you're flying to your hiking destination, your trusty backpacking stove and liquid-fuel bottle can't travel with you on a plane. Only new stoves in their original packaging will be allowed through airport security, and even empty and cleaned fuel bottles can be flagged as a potential hazard due to the presence of flammable vapors. Pressurized fuel canisters are never allowed on airplanes.

To avoid the risk of your stove and fuel being confiscated, you should ship them to a friend or outdoor gear store at your destination. Because you'll probably need to visit a store to stock up on food and fuel, anyway, call ahead and ask them to hold your stove until you arrive—most are happy to do so. Before mailing a stove or fuel bottle, clean them completely to remove any fuel residue and smell. The U.S. Postal Service, UPS, and FedEx can ship stoves and empty fuel bottles by air within 2 to 3 days without a problem, but you'll need at least 2 weeks to ship by ground. Shipping stoves and fuel bottles also requires filling out special hazard forms, so leave plenty of time to fill them out.

 Safety Check Additional hiking gear prohibited from airplanes includes torch-flame lighters, bear sprays, strike-anywhere matches, and spare lithium batteries not inside an electronic device. Regular butane lighters are allowed in carry-on luggage, as are hand sanitizer gels under the 3-fluid-ounce limit.

SUMMARY

When planning trail meals, don't limit yourself to bagels and oatmeal. Pick one meal on each trip to go gourmet, using tips like prefreezing meat and packing vegetables in a cook pot to make perishable food last longer. Snacks of fat-dense foods like nuts, chocolate, cheese, and pepperoni will keep your energy level high during the day by providing more usable calories per ounce than any other foods. Finally, when purchasing a cook stove, remember that isobutane canister stoves are lighter and easier to use, while white-gas stoves perform better in colder and windier weather.

CHAPTER 14

LIQUID REFRESHMENT

Drinking enough water to stay hydrated helps you hike quickly and safely by preventing muscle cramps, headaches, and stumbles. However, if you drink water directly from a lake or stream, you could ingest a nasty parasite or bacteria and become sick. So how do you resolve this conundrum? It's simple. You either carry all the water you'll need or you filter or purify water from natural sources to remove all the contaminants before you drink it.

Hauling all your water is only possible on short day-hikes. That's because water—weighing 8⅓ pounds per gallon—is heavy. For any trip that lasts longer than a day—and even some hot day-hikes—you'll need to refill water bottles along the trail. In this chapter, I'll cover the many methods to find and purify drinking water so you can stay hydrated while hiking.

Your Body Needs Water

Water for a hiker is like gasoline for a car. When your tank runs dry, you're not going anywhere. That's because liquids make up two thirds of your bodyweight. As you become dehydrated, your blood thickens, causing your heart to work harder and your circulation to slow down. Soon, your movements become sluggish and your brain goes foggy. A normal, healthy person can survive 2 to 3 days without water if they rest in the shade and don't move. If you're exposed to the sun and you are moving, your survival time would be much shorter. This is why hikers should never run low on water, let alone run out.

Trail Tips Bring an extra water bottle to drink in the car during the drive to the trailhead. This way, you'll start your hike hydrated and with your water bottles completely full.

How Much to Carry

Whether your hike is 4 miles or 10 miles, you should carry at least 3 liters of water in your backpack—the equivalent to one and a half large plastic soda bottles. Why 3 liters? Because it's the right balance between how much you need to drink and how much you can easily carry. Three liters of water weighs slightly more than 6 pounds, a load that even small daypacks can handle.

Occasionally, you'll want to carry more than 3 liters of water. This is true for multiday backpacking trips where water sources are scarce or when you're traveling in hot, humid, or dry terrain. You should bring more than 3 liters if any of the following conditions apply to you or your hike:

◊ Water sources on the trail or at campsites are far apart or unreliable.

◊ The trail is labeled strenuous or has a significant elevation gain.

◊ Weather conditions will be hot, humid, or dry.

◊ You tend to drink more than others to stay hydrated while exercising.

◊ You plan to overnight at a dry campsite—a spot with no water source.

◊ You're hiking with a child, a dog, or anyone who isn't carrying enough water for themselves.

How Much to Drink

Hikers lose about half a liter of fluids for every hour of hiking—and up to 2 liters per hour in extremely hot or sticky conditions. With all that water leaving your body as sweat, urine, and evaporation, you've got to constantly replace it to stay hydrated. How much to drink varies between people and conditions, but most advice follows two rules:

1. Drink at least half a liter of water per hour—and more if you're sweating profusely.
2. Start drinking before you become thirsty, and drink constantly throughout the day.

How much you need to drink beyond half a liter per hour depends on the local trail and weather conditions. As the temperature, humidity, and difficulty of the trail increases, the amount of water you carry (and the number of resupply stops you make) should increase as well.

How you drink is also important. Deep gulps are better than small sips because they rehydrate your core organs instead of just wetting your mouth and throat. You should also eat salty snacks like energy bars, nuts, or gorp when you drink to replace the electrolytes (or salts) you lose through sweat. Because plain water doesn't contain salt, you need to consume these snacks or mix electrolyte replacement tablets or powders into your water bottle. If you drink too much water without replacing lost salts, your body's electrolyte levels can become unbalanced, leading to a dangerous condition called *hyponatremia*.

The following table gives recommendations on how much water the average hiker (based on a healthy 170-pound male) should drink per hour in milliliters, depending on the temperature and the terrain. Note: 1,000 milliliters equals 1 liter.

Temperature

Terrain	Cool	Warm	Hot
Flat	350 ml	450 ml	650 ml
Hilly	450 ml	600 ml	750 ml
Steep	550 ml	650 ml	850 ml
Desert	700 ml	800 ml	1,000 ml

Source: U.S. Department of the Army FM-21-76(92); Backpacker.com, "The Hiker's Guide to Staying Hydrated and Treating Dehydration," September 2018.

Hauling Water on the Trail

Hikers today can choose among many containers to hold their water, but the selections fall into two general categories: bottles and bladders. Because these types each have their distinctive functions and advantages, many hikers choose to carry both at the same time.

Bottle It

Pastel-colored plastic water bottles might be as popular among soccer moms and schoolkids as they are among hikers, but that doesn't diminish their advantages. Lightweight, virtually indestructible, and easy to grasp, these 1-liter cylindrical bottles—often referred to as *Nalgenes* after a popular brand— are a backcountry mainstay. These bottles feature a wide mouth to reduce spills during filling and to accommodate pump and squeeze filters designed to attach directly to the threads on top. However, don't pack 2-liter soda containers or other crushable plastic bottles because they won't survive a trip. Some hikers also prefer bottles made from stainless steel, which is even more durable than plastic. As long as a water bottle is sturdy, leakproof, and easy to fill and drink from, you can choose any style or material that works for you.

 Safety Check   Beginning in the mid-2000s, the outdoor community became more aware of bisphenol A, commonly called *BPA*, which is a chemical linked to birth defects in animals and is used to manufacture plastic water bottles. Scratches and scuffs on some bottles could accelerate the leaching of BPA into the water, so consider replacing older plastic bottles with newer, non-BPA models.

Suck It Up

Once you try a hydration bladder—also called a *hydration reservoir*—it's hard not to be impressed by its simple but ingenious design. Here's how it works. Fill a long plastic pouch with water, place it inside your pack, and connect it to your mouth via a drinking tube with a closeable valve. When you suck on the valve at the end of the tube, the water is siphoned from the bladder into your mouth. Instead of reaching for a water bottle, unscrewing the cap, and taking a swig, you can suck water from your hydration bladder hands-free while you walk down the trail. Hydration bladders come in multiple sizes ranging from single-liter up to 3-liter bags, and they are all made from a durable but flexible plastic.

 Trail Tips To prevent improperly closed hydration bladders from accidentally leaking on your gear while driving to the trailhead, store bladders outside your pack in plastic bins or bags—and slip them into your pack just before you begin to hike.

Where to Find Water

It's one o'clock in the afternoon and the hottest part of the day. You're guzzling water to stay hydrated—as you should—when you realize that you're down to your last liter. You need to find a water source to refill your bottles. But finding water shouldn't depend on luck. As I explained in Chapter 4, you should either know if water access will be plentiful along a trail or preidentify sources that you can tap.

Refilling Along the Trail

Most trail descriptions will indicate reliable water sources and warn you if access could be a problem—as it might be in deserts, grasslands, and at higher elevations. If finding enough water will be a challenge, you should bring additional bottles or larger bladders to increase your carrying capacity and pay close attention to how much water you have remaining.

Normally, however, you don't need to mark or memorize every water source on your route. Most campsites are deliberately located near water, and trails often intersect with natural sources of waters like these examples:

◊ River, streams, and creeks

◊ Lakes, ponds, and pools

◊ Waterfalls

◊ Natural springs—a water source where an underground stream or river reaches the surface. Springs are marked on topographical maps by a small blue circle.

◊ Potholes and rock basins filled with rainwater

Refilling at Camp

The ideal campsite is located in the vicinity of a water source like a stream, lake, or spring. If you know your campsite doesn't have nearby water, you should fill up your bottles at another source before you get there. You also might discover that campsite water sources are often improved by park managers or other hikers to make them easier to access. This might involve placing rocks across a stream to create a catch basin or channeling a spring's output into a pipe. Be careful not to damage or disturb these structures so that other hikers can use them after you.

Making Water Safe to Drink

Two hundred years ago, the idea of filtering or purifying drinking water in the wilderness would have been laughable. Back then, however, surface water was not only cleaner than it is now, but people's stomachs were tougher, too. As a result, modern hikers need to operate like miniature sewage treatment plants—filtering or purifying their water to make it safe to drink using one of several methods.

Waterborne Contaminants

The reasons for sanitizing your water become apparent once you realize what it might contain. The most infamous pathogen is *Giardia lamblia,* a microscopic parasite that causes tens of thousands of cases of diarrhea each year. Giardia, however, is just one of the nasties you need to watch out for. Here's the complete lineup:

◊ *Giardia* (also known as *Giardia lamblia, beaver fever*)

    Type: Intestinal parasite

    Size: 6–10 microns*

    Remarks: Can survive 2–3 months in 50°F water

    Annual infections: 20,000–30,000

    Onset of symptoms: 2–12 days

    Symptoms: Diarrhea, abdominal cramps, headaches, nausea, vomiting, and low-grade fever

Treatment: Prescription antibiotic metronidazole (Flagyl)

◊ *Cryptosporidium* (also known as *Crypto, cryptosporidiosis*)
Type: Intestinal parasite
Size: 4–10 microns
Remarks: As few as 10–30 cysts can cause infection
Annual infections: 3,000–10,000
Onset of symptoms: 2–10 days
Symptoms: Stomach cramps, dehydration, nausea, vomiting, fever, weight loss
Treatment: Wait until symptoms recede, increase fluid intake

◊ **Bacteria** (also known as *E. coli, Salmonella, cholera, Campylobacter, Shigella*)
Type: Single-celled, rod-shaped organisms
Size: 0.5–2 microns
Remarks: Requires moisture to stay alive
Annual infections: Tens of thousands
Onset of symptoms: 2–5 days
Symptoms: Diarrhea, vomiting, cramps
Treatment: Antibiotics

◊ **Viruses** (also known as *Norovirus, Rotavirus, stomach flu, viral gastroenteritis*)
Type: Ultramicroscopic infectious pathogen
Size: 0.004–0.1 microns
Remarks: Pump filters cannot remove viruses from water—but waterborne viruses are rare in North America. Only chemical and ultraviolet treatments can kill viruses.
Annual infections: Millions
Onset of symptoms: 1–2 days

Symptoms: Diarrhea, vomiting, abdominal cramps, fever, hepatitis, meningitis

Treatment: Wait until symptoms recede, increase fluid intake

A micron is a millionth of a meter. For comparison, the period at the end of this sentence measures about 600 microns across.

 Safety Check Because bacteria and pathogens can linger in the untreated water droplets on a bottle's cap and threads, rinse those areas with filtered or purified water before taking a drink.

Chemical Purification

Once the mainstay of making water safe to drink, chemical treatments are less popular today as faster, easier filtration methods have become more widespread. Still, iodine drops or chlorine dioxide tablets—the two main chemicals used to treat water—are useful for international destinations and for purifying big batches of water. So I'll briefly describe how they work—and the key disadvantages that make them less popular today.

First, chemical treatments don't remove bugs from water. They just kill them. Ingesting a dead parasite might be unnerving, but it's also harmless. But while chemical tablets are lightweight and effective against bacteria and viruses (a feat filters can't match), they do have the following drawbacks:

◊ Chemical treatments like iodine and chlorine dioxide require waiting between 30 minutes and 4 hours to purify a liter of water, depending on the manufacturer's instructions. Cloudy or cold water takes more time to purify. You can reduce sediment levels by filtering water through a T-shirt or bandanna and heat up cold water by placing a bottle in the sun. However, if the water temperature is below 40°F, you'll need to double the dosage of tablets to treat it effectively.

◊ Iodine shouldn't be used repeatedly for more than several weeks and should never be used by pregnant women or people with thyroid problems.

◊ Iodine isn't effective against *Cryptosporidium*—a parasite with a tough outer shell—and most types of chlorine dioxide require several hours to knock out this bug. Both can effectively kill *Giardia*, however.

◊ Chemical treatments often have expiration dates and—in the case of iodine—degrade when exposed to sunlight and humidity. To ensure effectiveness, make sure your chemical treatments have not expired before you leave for a hike.

Chemical Treatment Details

Brand names: iodine tablets (Potable Aqua); iodine crystals (Polar Pure); chlorine dioxide (Aquamira, Potable Aqua, Katadyn Micropur)

Best for: Viruses, bacteria

Advantages: Inexpensive, lightweight, useful outside North America where water-borne viruses are more common

Disadvantages: Bad aftertaste (iodine), long wait time, effectiveness varies based on water temperature and clarity

Pump Filtration

The underlying concept for water filters is rather simple: if you build a door small enough, not everything can squeeze through. In water filters, those doors are tiny pores that trap harmful organisms like bacteria and parasites but let your drinking water pass. The force that pulls the water through these pores is provided by the filter's hand pump.

Most portable filters are designed with pores between 0.2 and 0.5 microns in diameter—small enough to block all parasites and most bacteria. Tiny viruses, however, will still pass through. Fortunately, most water sources in North America are virus free. You need to worry about viruses only if you travel in the Alaskan backcountry or to overseas developing countries. Most filters can be cleaned by reversing the flow of the pump or replacing the internal cartridge when its pores become too clogged.

Safety Check Combining both methods by first filtering water and then adding a chemical treatment like chlorine dioxide takes more time but ensures that even the smallest waterborne pathogens are eliminated.

Pump filters use hand levers and muscle-power to create clean drinking water.

Here are the steps for filtering water:

1. Place the prefilter—the small nozzle attached to the end of the intake hose—in the stream or lake where you want to draw water. Be careful not to stir up sediment.

2. Attach the filter's outlet hose to your empty water bottle or hydration bladder.

3. Pump slowly and deliberately so that you don't overload the pores or knock over your water bottle.

4. Switch to another bottle when the first one is full. It's more efficient to fill multiple containers in one session.

5. Because the prefilter and intake hose have been immersed in untreated water, treat them as contaminated and place them in a separate plastic bag when you store your filter.

Pump Filter Details

Brand names: Katadyn, MSR, First Need

Best for: Parasites, bacteria

Advantages: No wait time, no aftertaste

Disadvantages: Expensive, physically tiring, can freeze or break if handled roughly, ineffective against viruses

Squeeze Filters

Challenging pump filters for dominance in the hiking and backpacking market are simple screw-on filters that allow you to squeeze filtered water from a collection pouch into your drinking container. These smaller filters are gaining followers because they weigh less than hand pump models. Case in point: the most popular squeeze filter made by Sawyer weighs 8 ounces less than the most common pump filter made by Katadyn. Using a squeeze or gravity filter is even easier than pumping water out of a lake or stream, although filling the collection pouch is difficult in shallow or nonmoving water. To use a squeeze filter, follow these steps:

1. Fill the collection pouch (Sawyer can provide 16, 32, and 64-ounce bags) with water from a stream or lake. Some people carry a plastic cup to make the filling process easier.
2. Screw the filter onto the top of the collection pouch.
3. Squeeze the collection pouch to force the water through the filter and into your water bottle or hydration bladder.
4. Some squeeze filters include inline adapters to let you drink the water directly from the collection pouch, or connect it to a hydration bladder to create a gravity filter.

Squeeze filters save weight by using fewer moving parts.

Squeeze Filter Details

Brand names: Sawyer, LifeStraw

Best for: Parasites, bacteria

Advantages: No hand pump or moving parts

Disadvantages: Ineffective in shallow, stagnant water sources

Find the Cleanest Water

Whether you choose chemical treatments or a filter, you should try to reduce the amount of dirt and contamination lurking in your untreated water. Remove sediments by using a prefilter or straining the water through a bandanna. You can also attach a regular coffee filter around the intake nozzle of your water filter with a rubber band to screen out more dirt and debris. If the water is still dirty, let it stand for several minutes to allow the particles to settle to the bottom. Always collect water several yards upstream from any trail crossing to reduce contamination from hikers and animals.

Boiling

Heating water to 212°F will make it safe to drink, but this method often isn't economical for hikers because of the extra time and fuel required. However, if you need to boil water anyway to cook a meal, you can use untreated water and save some effort. According to the Centers for Disease Control and Prevention (CDC), water must be kept at a boil for 1 minute and then allowed to cool to kill viruses, parasites, and bacteria. Above 6,500 feet, water should be boiled for 3 minutes because of the lower boiling temperature.

Boiling Details

Best for: Parasites, bacteria, viruses

Advantages: Can be done anywhere

Disadvantages: Requires extra fuel and time to cool, does not remove sediment

Ultraviolet Light

When faced with microscopic adversaries like *E. coli, Cryptosporidum,* and hepatitis, it's hard to believe that a few seconds of ultraviolet (UV) light can save you—but it can. UV light will kill parasites, bacteria, and viruses in a liter of water in 1½ minutes. It's actually the same system that bottled water companies and major cities use to disinfect their water supplies. Most of the products designed for hikers are made by SteriPEN, which offers several models—all of which are the size of a small flashlight, run on AA or watch batteries, and work for several thousand uses. The newest model, the "Ultra," includes a rechargeable lithium battery linked to a USB charging port and an LED screen that tells you when your water is clean. There's no chance of irradiating yourself with this device—the light will only turn on when it's immersed in water.

However, like all high-tech devices, SteriPENs are expensive, rely on batteries, and are vulnerable to breaking. But for hikers concerned about pack weight, or those who want quick and comprehensive results, none of the other methods can compare to the power of UV light.

Ultraviolet Light Details

Brands: SteriPEN

Best for: Parasites, bacteria, viruses

Advantages: Lightweight, fast

Disadvantages: Less effective in cloudy water, fragile, expensive

Gravity Filters

The last method to acquire safe drinking water is similar to a pump filter but requires less energy and attention. Instead of hand pumping the water through a series of pores, you let gravity do all the work. After filling a large hydration bladder with untreated water, you hang it from a tree. The water seeps through a filter cartridge at a rate of 1 liter per minute to fill a bladder or bottle below it with drinkable water. Most gravity filters are designed with large capacities—up to 4 liters—and are ideal for hanging at a campsite to cook meals or serve large hiking groups. The main drawback is that they are difficult to fill from shallow water sources.

Gravity Filter Details

Brands: Platypus, Katadyn, Sawyer, MSR

Best for: Parasites, bacteria

Advantages: Autonomous, efficient for large groups

Disadvantages: Expensive, difficult to fill from shallow water sources

Cleaning and Storage

When you return home from a hike, try to resist the urge to toss your soggy filters, water bottles, and hydration bladders in a drawer. To make these water gadgets last longer, and to prevent mold and bacteria from colonizing them between your trips, you need to clean and dry them thoroughly before storage.

Bottles

Wash your bottles by hand with soap and warm water, paying close attention to the threads and the cap where dirt tends to collect. Do not place the bottles in a dishwasher; it reduces their life span. Let the bottles drain and completely dry overnight before storing them uncapped to allow airflow.

Bladders

The design of hydration bladders makes them hard to clean and vulnerable to mold growth on the inside. Instead of scrubbing, you need to disinfect and rinse all parts of the bladder and drinking tube using low concentrations of chlorine bleach. The following steps will clean out a hydration bladder after a trip or refresh one that's been kept idle for several months:

1. To disinfect, fill the bladder with warm water mixed with a teaspoon of chlorine bleach and let it soak overnight. Do not use soap or detergent, which can leave a sticky film on the plastic.

2. Drain the water the next day and rinse thoroughly with warm water until the bleach smell is gone.

3. Dry the bladder by hanging it upside down from a wire coat hanger. Insert the curved shoulder portion—not the hook—of another coat hanger inside the bladder to hold it open and increase airflow as it dries.

4. To clean the drinking tube, flush it several times with warm water. Next, find a wire longer than the tube and attach a paper towel to one end. Pull the wire through the tube to remove any sludge, replace the paper towel, and repeat until the tube is clean. To remove tough mold, fill the tube with water mixed with a few drops of bleach and let it soak overnight. Once it's clean, hang it to dry.

5. To remove odors, fill the bladder and tube with 2 cups of water mixed with ½ cup of baking soda and shake well. Let sit for 20 minutes, then drain and rinse with cold water until clean.

6. Clean bladder cap threads and tube bite valves with a toothbrush using warm water and bleach.

After the bladder, bite valve, and drinking tube are clean and dry, store them separately in your refrigerator—which slows mold growth—or in a cool, dry place.

Filters

Water filters are expensive tools, so the better you treat them, the longer they'll serve you. Start by choosing the cleanest and most sediment-free water sources you can find and use a prefilter to prevent sand and dirt from entering the filter. To prevent your filter from freezing on a cold trip—which can damage the tiny pores—stash it deep in your backpack during the day and store it in your tent or sleeping bag at night. When you return home at the end of a trip, clean your filter in the kitchen sink using these steps:

1. Wash the outside of the filter body, the prefilter, and the tubes with warm water and soap.
2. Fill a container with 1 liter of tap water and add 1 tablespoon of chlorine bleach.
3. Pump the disinfectant solution through the filter until the filter and tubes are empty.
4. Pump a liter of clean tap water through the filter and tubes to flush out any bleach.
5. Disassemble the filter and allow the separate pieces to dry completely.
6. Store all the filter pieces in a canvas or breathable bag in your refrigerator or in a cool, dry place.

Other Drink Options

To stay hydrated, hikers aren't limited to drinking plain water. The best alternatives to H_2O are sports drinks like Gatorade or Powerade, which replenish the salts and electrolytes that you lose by sweating—a benefit that water can't match. Don't rely on soda, energy drinks like Red Bull and Monster, or fruit juices because they contain too much extra sugar and caffeine that your body doesn't need. On the trail, you can convert regular water into an energy drink by mixing in packets of powder that add extra nutrients and electrolytes. Just be sure to mix flavored drinks in plastic or stainless steel bottles and not hydration bladders to avoid creating powdery, sugary deposits that are difficult to remove from inside the plastic reservoirs.

Another reason to avoid caffeine is that it actually increases dehydration by causing your body to get rid of excess water. For these reasons, choose decaffeinated teas and coffees, especially in the evening. Drinking a caffeinated beverage before bed will almost guarantee you'll need to pee in the middle of the night.

Still, there are many backpackers who can't greet the day without a steaming—and highly caffeinated—cup of joe. Even though you'll be dozens of miles (and hopefully farther) from the nearest Starbucks, you don't have to settle for boring old instant coffee. Gear makers like JetBoil, GSI Outdoors, and MSR sell products—from a portable French press to a mini espresso machine—that give hikers the ability to brew gourmet coffee on the trail. Just be sure to drink extra water with your morning coffee so that you don't start the day dehydrated.

SUMMARY

Because the average hiker should drink half a liter of water per hour (and more during hot and humid conditions), you should bring at least 3 liters of water on every hike and know where you can resupply. Most hikers carry both hydration bladders and water bottles, while handheld pump and squeeze filters—which easily attach to most water containers— are the most popular methods to make backcountry water sources drinkable. These filters can block the larger parasites and bacteria but not the smaller and rarer viruses.

CHAPTER 15

HYGIENE ON THE TRAIL

The absence of flush toilets and hot showers probably discourages more people from hiking and camping than anything else. Perhaps it's a concern of yours, too.

There are two answers to calm these fears. The first is "Don't worry." Staying relatively clean on the trail isn't that hard to do. The second answer is also "Don't worry." To truly enjoy yourself on a day-hike or backpacking trip, you need to relax your normal standards of cleanliness. Clean, it turns out, is a relative term. Instead of washing your hair, you'll wear a bandanna all day. And the "3-second rule" applies to food you drop on the ground, even if it lands in the dirt—and as you'll find out, dirt isn't that bad for you.

But lowering your standards doesn't mean living like a Neanderthal. You can maintain a decent level of hygiene while hiking and camping. Keeping clean, in fact, isn't only about maintaining appearances. Most trail-based illnesses and skin problems originate from poor hygiene. In this chapter, I'll tell you everything you need to know to keep your body, your clothes, and your camp as clean as possible.

Staying Clean in a Dirty World

Trying to stay fresh 100 percent of the time on a hike is impossible. When you're climbing a hill in 90°F heat, you're just not going to look your "red carpet" best. Because you can't avoid sweat and dirt, the solution is to wash it off at the end of the day, before eating a meal, or when going to sleep. Your goal should be keeping your personal hygiene at an acceptable level that allows you to enjoy your hike, stay comfortable, and reduce any opportunity to become sick.

Washing Your Hands

Drinking bad water isn't the only way bacteria and parasites can infect you (see Chapter 14). Sooner or later, the germs that stick to your fingers and hands will end up in your eyes or in your mouth. Cleaning your hands before you eat and after you go to the bathroom is the best method to reduce the spread of germs from the environment and between people.

 Trail Tips To reduce the spread of germs between people, pour trail mixes and other loose snack foods from the bag into a person's open hands rather than letting them reach inside the bag.

Because washing with soap and water isn't always convenient or available, carry a bottle of alcohol-based gel hand sanitizer. This clear gel contains a small concentration of ethyl alcohol that kills germs on contact. Just add a nickel-size drop to your skin, rub your hands together vigorously, and wait 20 to 30 seconds for the alcohol to evaporate.

Cleaning Yourself from Head to Toe

Gel sanitizer will disinfect hands—but you can't use it to clean your entire body. Not only is it impractical to carry that much gel around, but it would sting like heck. The bottom line is that you should wash your entire body at least once a day when you're on the trail. For most hikers, that involves either an improvised shower or spot-cleaning problem areas.

Showering in the Woods

Taking a trail shower can seem like a juggling act. You need two containers to carry water (the larger the better), biodegradable soap, a sponge or washcloth (often a bandanna), and a towel. If you plan to wash with soap, you should move at least 200 feet from any lakes or rivers to avoid adding suds to what might become your cooking and drinking water. Once you find a spot to shower, strip down as immodestly as the temperature and conditions allow and rub the soap onto your skin—paying special attention to your face, underarms, groin, lower legs, and feet. Dump one of the water bottles over your body while simultaneously scrubbing with the washcloth. Use the other bottle to rinse the leftover suds from your body and towel yourself dry.

If you want the deluxe shower option, you can pack a solar-heated water bladder to enjoy a longer, warmer shower. These products, made by companies like AdvancedElements, NEMO, and Seattle Sports, use the sun to heat several gallons of water in a black, insulated plastic bag. Once the water is warm, you hang the bag from a tree and use the attached nozzle to direct the flow over your body. While solar shower systems might be excessive for backpackers, they are a worthwhile luxury for car-campers.

Waiting until the end of the day to clean your entire body is often a good idea. Once you put your pack down and pitch your tent, the strenuous part of your day is over, and you won't be getting any dirtier. However, if you come across a deep stream or lake during the day, you shouldn't pass up the opportunity to rinse off. However, immersing yourself in water isn't as effective at removing dirt and grime as scrubbing with soap and a washcloth.

Sponge Bath 101

If it's too cold or impractical to take a trail shower, the next best thing is a sponge bath. This is also an effective way to clean yourself inside your tent before going to sleep. Start by stripping completely out of the clothes you wore during the day. Then coat the corner of a bandanna or cotton balls with alcohol-based gel hand sanitizer and dab it on your skin. Baby wipes or moist towelettes also work well but generate more trash. Focus on key trouble areas for inflammation, bacteria growth, and odors like the groin, armpits, between your toes, and inner thighs. Once the gel evaporates, put on new, clean clothing and hang up your soiled garments to dry. Eliminating the day's accumulation of sweat, dirt, and grime just before bed will also make it easier for you to sleep.

Don't Forget to Brush (and Floss)

Ultralight backpackers are famous for whittling down plastic toothbrushes to bare nubs to save half a gram of weight. The lesson here is that ultralighters—who quickly discard nonessential gear—still bring a toothbrush. They realize, as everyone should, the importance of brushing and flossing at least once a day on the trail.

If you use toothpaste, apply only a small amount and bury your spit in a small hole, or blow it from your mouth in a fine mist at least 200 feet from your tent and any water sources. Remember, most toothpaste has a strong, minty odor that attracts wildlife, so it should be stored with all of your food in a bear bag or canister where animals can't get it.

 Safety Check   Remember to wash your hands before cleaning your teeth to avoid introducing any germs into your mouth.

Nightly flossing is also important, even if you don't normally do it. Food particles from hiking snacks like peanuts and cheese are almost guaranteed to stick in your mouth. Plus, dental floss serves a dual purpose as a thread for repairing clothing and gear and shouldn't be left at home.

Inside a Hiker's Toiletry Kit

Car-campers can pack all the toiletries they would bring on a normal vacation, but backpackers should carry only the basics. You can leave behind the deodorant (attracts animals and who needs it, anyway?), shampoo (environmentally unfriendly), the razor (not practical), mirror (too fragile), and of course, the hair dryer (unless you brought a 5-mile-long extension cord). This leaves a few crucial items that can fit into a small zipper-lock plastic bag or toiletry pouch. Here's what it should contain:

◊ Toothbrush

◊ Toothpaste

◊ Dental floss

◊ Alcohol-based gel hand sanitizer

◊ Cotton bandanna or washcloth

◊ Moist towelettes or baby wipes

◊ Biodegradable soap

◊ Absorbent pack towel

◊ Toilet paper double-sealed in zipper-lock plastic bags

◊ Plastic trowel

◊ Extra quart- and gallon-size zipper-lock plastic bags for trash

 Trail Tips Three items essential for maintaining trail hygiene are hand sanitizer, moist towelettes, and quart-size zipper-lock plastic bags. Make sure you bring plenty of all three items on your hikes.

Hikers who wear contacts should opt for extended-wear models that can be worn overnight or be comfortable inserting and removing them without a sink or mirror. Packing a backup pair of glasses is always a good idea.

What Do You Mean, No Deodorant?

The absence of deodorant on the trail confuses most new hikers. Hiking up and down trails, after all, is when you need odor-fighting protection the most. However, deodorant does more than banish odors; its sweet smell also attracts bugs and other wildlife, including bears. After a few days without deodorant, you'll get accustomed to your new, "natural" odor, and it won't bother you as long as you continue to wash yourself regularly.

Bio Soap

When you wash at home, the suds vanish down the bathtub drain, but in the woods, the phosphates in those suds can harm the environment by promoting algae blooms in lakes and streams. To avoid contaminating water sources, hikers should never use soap in or near bodies of water—always wash at least 200 feet away. If you use soap, choose biodegradable soaps that revert back to their organic ingredients. Look for products made by Dr. Bronner's and Campsuds, two manufacturers that sell soap bars and liquids in backpacker-size 2-ounce and 4-ounce containers. You can choose natural scents (like citrus or eucalyptus) or unscented versions.

Drying Out

Instead of packing a heavy bath towel on your next hike, bring a lightweight towel made from a highly absorbent, quick-drying blend of polyester and nylon. Camping and outdoor stores sell these microfiber towels in many dimensions, but any size about 30 inches long by 16 inches wide will be sufficient to dry your entire body after a trail shower or a sponge bath.

Keeping Your Clothes Fresh

How can you tell when a hiker needs to change his pants?

When they keep walking down the trail after he takes them off.

Jokes aside, I've seen hiking clothes that were so dirty they could stand up by themselves. Washing your underwear and outerwear is just as important as scrubbing your skin. Maintaining proper trail hygiene not only requires packing enough clothing—a subject covered in Chapter 10—but also knowing how to keep your clothing as clean as possible until the end of your hike. On backpacking trips that last longer than 2 or 3 days, you don't change clothes as much as you rotate outfits by using the cleaning suggestions outlined in the next sections.

Changing Clothes

Most hikers choose to replace their sweaty shirts, pants, or shorts with cleaner, warmer clothes when they arrive at each night's campsite. You can also change into new socks and underwear at this time, although some people wait until taking a trail shower or heading to bed. If you don't remove your hiking clothes when you reach camp, you should change into clean and dry clothing before going to sleep. Wearing dirty clothing to bed not only sullies the inside of your sleeping bag, but it also creates a wonderful opportunity for rashes and other skin problems to develop.

Occasionally, you might need to switch into new clothes in the middle of the day. This occurs most often when your socks or underwear get wet or begin to chafe. One way to keep your feet happy is to remove your shoes and socks during rest breaks to air them out and check for blisters. To clean your feet, apply hand sanitizer to kill any lingering bacteria. If your feet sweat a lot, consider bringing foot powder to promote dryness. Many hikers also pack a comfortable pair of camp shoes to wear instead of boots once the day's hiking is over. (See Chapter 9 for more on camp shoes.)

Cleaning Clothes

If you rinse and dry your clothes on the trail, you can rewear the same shirts, pants, and shorts several times during a single trip. This process can be as simple as dunking your clothes in a stream or lake, wringing out the excess water, and hanging them on a tree branch or clothesline. To dry clothes while you are hiking, tie them securely to the top of your pack and let the sun and wind air them out.

 Trail Tips Create a miniature washing machine by stuffing underwear, socks, and other small garments into a water bottle, adding warm water, soap, and a few smooth rocks, and then shaking vigorously before rinsing and drying.

To freshen up clothes even more, wash them with a few drops of the same biodegradable soap you use on your body. Polyester and other thin synthetics will dry much more quickly than cotton or wool. This wash-and-dry system works best when there's plenty of sunshine or hot weather, but you can hang clothing inside a tent or under a tarp as well.

Keeping Kids Clean

Kids and dirt always seem to find each other, even if parents can't figure out how. It's just their nature. So don't fret about keeping them clean all the time. Instead, focus on the major concerns like cuts, burns, and splinters, and cleaning their hands and face with moist towelettes at meals, bathroom breaks, and prior to going to bed. Kids don't sweat like adults do, but they will get colder more quickly if they're wearing wet clothing because of their smaller body size. Check to make sure a child's socks and shirt are dry, and change them if they aren't.

Women's Trail Hygiene

Women are often more concerned than men about staying clean in the outdoors—and for good reason. Gals don't have it as easy as guys do when it comes to going to the bathroom or keeping their private parts clean. As a result, women need to take certain precautions, and men should understand why women can't just go pee behind a tree like they do.

First, women can use moist towelettes to clean themselves after going to the bathroom, wiping from front to back to keep bacteria away from the genitals. Women can also clean themselves this way when changing out of their soiled clothes and underwear. Using towelettes adds an extra line of defense against infection. Even if you wash your hands with sanitizer before and after going to the bathroom—which you should do—germs can still introduce bad stuff to a part of your body you want to keep as sterile as possible.

Most of the health concerns women have about hiking involve menstruation. The truth is that having your period on the trail isn't a major problem, and it can easily be dealt with by packing the right supplies and taking the time to stay clean. Be aware that the exertion of hiking can sometimes cause a period to start early or be delayed by several days—so be ready if you think it might occur. To handle a period on the trail, most women prefer tampons rather than pads because the latter can be uncomfortable when wet—especially in colder temperatures. Tampons also take up less space in your pack. Be sure to use tampons with applicators to reduce the opportunity for infections introduced by dirty hands. Double-bag all used tampons in zipper-lock plastic freezer bags and carry them until you can properly dispose of them in the trash. You can reduce any odors by adding a crushed aspirin or a wet tea bag to the bag. Do not attempt to burn or bury tampons, as they contain materials that won't completely decompose.

 Safety Check   Some people claim that bears are attracted to odors from menstruation, but the evidence from several studies is inconclusive. If women decide to hike while having a period, they should use tampons and store used ones in doubled zipper-lock plastic bags and treat as trash.

When Nature Calls

Relax. Doing your business in the woods isn't really such a big deal. Even though whole books have been written about it, following the simple advice listed below will not only help you remain clean and healthy but will also make trails and campsites more enjoyable places to visit.

Taking a Leak

On most day-hikes all you'll need to do is take a pee or two. In fact, *not* peeing on a hike could be a sign you're dehydrated. The process differs slightly between men and women, with women having a few more obstacles to overcome. No matter if you stand or squat, here are some basic rules to follow to keep yourself and the environment clean when going #1:

◊ Don't wait until the last moment; you'll need a few minutes to find the right spot.

◊ Use a latrine or pit toilet if one is available. If not, move at least 200 feet (70 adult steps) away from any trail, water source, or campsite; but watch out for poison ivy. (See Chapter 18 for an identification guide.)

◊ Clean your hands with gel sanitizer or a moist towelette before and after you go.

◊ Where vegetation is sparse and fragile—like in alpine zones and deserts—urinate directly on rocks. Not only can the nitrogen in urine harm plants, but animals seeking the salty residue will dig up the soil.

Using a Latrine

Trailheads and campsites that receive significant hiker traffic often have a latrine—a backcountry outhouse—located nearby. Latrines aren't optional. If there's one in your vicinity, you should use it instead of going into the woods. Latrines are designed to concentrate the waste generated by many people in a single, cleanable pit instead of scattering it throughout the area.

An increasing number of pit latrines are being replaced by composting toilets where the waste degrades more quickly and never or rarely needs to be removed. Instructions on these latrines instruct hikers to "flush" with a handful of bark chips after using them.

Digging a Cat Hole

Sooner or later, you're going to need to go #2 in the woods. Instead of holding it in (which your colon might do automatically at the beginning of a hiking trip), you need to dig a *cat hole* to bury your waste. A cat hole is a small hole 6 to 8 inches deep dug by hikers to bury their human waste underground. Why it's called a cat hole is a hiking mystery, but anyone who owns cats knows that they are extremely diligent about burying their waste—at least compared to dogs.

Here are the steps for digging a cat hole:

1. Find a place to do your business at least 200 feet from any water source, campsite, or trail. This distance prevents bacterial contamination and reduces the chance of someone accidentally "discovering" your deposit. Damp, dark, organic soil will speed decomposition, as will areas exposed to sunlight. Because you'll be squatting without the support of a toilet, look for a flat area where you can lean against a tree or hang on to a branch. Trekking poles can also be helpful in supporting your weight.

2. Dig a hole that is 6 to 8 inches deep and about 6 inches wide. You should carry a small plastic trowel exactly for this purpose.

3. Before you do your business, place your toilet paper, moist towelettes, and a zipper-lock plastic trash bag within easy reach. You should pack out all used toilet paper instead of burying it with the waste. Hard-core hikers will brag about using only leaves and ferns to clean their backside—but they won't tell you how uncomfortable they were for the next several hours. Cleaning yourself with a baby wipe or moist towelette will prevent most discomfort.

4. After you're done, fill in the hole with dirt and cover it with a rock or log. Place any soiled toilet paper or towelettes in the zipper-lock plastic trash bag to pack out, and then clean your hands thoroughly with gel sanitizer.

5. Occasionally, you'll need to go #2 where you can't dig a cat hole because of rocky or hard, frozen ground. Don't leave your "present" under a rock for someone else to find. Here you'll need to pack out your waste and your toilet paper in double-layer zipper-lock plastic bags or a purpose-built disposal bag made by Biffy Bag, Restop, or Cleanwaste (formerly WAG BAG).

Low-Impact Camping

Although Leave No Trace sounds like the title of a Netflix crime drama, it's actually a grassroots effort to promote low-impact camping and hiking. By following Leave No Trace (or LNT) principles, people can leave natural areas as good—or better than—they found them. LNT is best summed up by the saying "Take only pictures, leave only footprints." What does LNT mean for you? Think of them as a hiker's "rules for the road." The following seven guidelines should steer your actions on the trail and at camp:

1. Plan ahead and prepare. Know local camping regulations, be prepared to pack out waste, and travel in small groups.

2. Travel and camp on durable surfaces. Use existing trails and campsites, pitch tents in designated sites, and avoid creating erosion and destroying plants.

3. Dispose of waste properly. Bury human waste in cat holes, police your campsite for trash, and pack out toilet paper and other debris.

4. Leave what you find. Don't dig trenches around tents or build lasting structures, avoid disturbing flowers and plants, and respect historical and cultural artifacts by not touching them.

5. Minimize campfire impacts. Use established campfire rings, choose wood that's already dead and on the ground, and put out fires completely before leaving camp.

6. Respect wildlife. Keep your distance from animals, never feed wildlife, and store your food and trash securely.

7. Be considerate of other visitors. Yield to others on the trail, locate your campsite away from others, and avoid loud sounds and interruptions.

LNT guidelines work best when everyone follows them. It only takes one person to ruin a campsite by leaving behind a pile of trash. LNT is also a good way to teach children about protecting the environment. The best way to follow Leave No Trace is to adopt these ethics as part of your normal routine and always make decisions that will create the least amount of environmental impact.

SUMMARY

If showers aren't an option, practicing good hygiene—like using hand sanitizer before meals, changing clothes and underwear before bed, and brushing your teeth—will reduce your risk of spreading germs and getting sick. Make sure your toiletry kit includes moist towelettes, alcohol-based gel hand sanitizer, and a quick-drying pack towel. Following Leave No Trace principles will not only protect natural areas, but it will enhance the outdoor experience that you and your fellow hikers are seeking.

SURVIVING THE OUTDOORS

Everyone has fears. Whether yours are spiders, flying, snakes, or deep water, the only way to beat them is to face them. The same approach applies to hiking and camping, and these last five chapters describe the right responses to any "what if" scenarios you might encounter on the trail. This confidence-boosting advice can help you save yourself or other hikers you might come across. After all, confronting real challenges is one of the few ways we have left to remind ourselves that we're still alive.

CHAPTER 16

HOW TO SURVIVE

Every hiker gets in trouble. No matter how skilled or careful you are, sooner or later, you're going to make a mistake. When it happens, you're going to pause, look at your surroundings, stare at your phone or map again, and start to get worried. Then you're going to make one of two choices.

The first choice, and the one I wouldn't recommend pursuing, is to make hasty, poor decisions that will cause you to become frustrated, cold, wet, and more distant from a potential solution. The second choice is to make smart decisions that enable you to regain your bearings; stay warm, dry, and optimistic; and increase your chances of solving your problem.

Obviously, we all want to pursue the second option. But that's hard to do when you're stuck on a lonely trail surrounded by unfamiliar terrain as daylight fades. In this chapter, I'll teach you how to make the right choices to turn a potentially perilous experience into a great story you can tell your friends.

How to Get Lost

The division between knowing exactly where you are and being lost isn't a big, bold line that you cross on a trail. Instead, getting lost is a gradual process. Wayward hikers often don't understand how serious their predicament is until it's too late—even if the signs have been visible for a long time. That's because in most situations, the indications of trouble are only clear in retrospect.

This exact scenario recently happened to me. While descending an 8,300-foot peak in Utah, my wife and I missed a 90-degree turn in the trail (and a giant X of crossed logs designed to warn hikers about the direction change) and began scrambling down a steep gully. Even though I said "I don't remember hiking up this part" several times, and the terrain was much more challenging than anything we'd encountered on the ascent, we kept moving farther away from the actual trail and a safe position. Despite all the hints we passed along the way, we didn't recognize our predicament until the terrain became impassable and we almost started a rockslide. That brief but scary episode is a good reminder how tunnel vision can escalate one mistake into a dangerous situation.

The Common Causes

The process of becoming lost can start long before you arrive at the trailhead. A bad decision made at home—like failing to notify anyone of your route or forgetting a detailed map—can later snowball into big trouble. According to the search-and-rescue (SAR) statistics from national parks, "errors in judgment" was the primary reason (22.3 percent) people needed rescuing in national parks, followed by fatigue (16.8 percent) and insufficient gear (15.6 percent). Most of the mistakes people make are simple. In fact, the thousands of hikers who become lost on trails each year generally make the same half-dozen errors:

- ◊ Carrying improper maps or no maps at all and forgetting a compass
- ◊ Failing to download detailed maps to a smartphone's GPS app or a handheld GPS
- ◊ Starting a hike too late in the day
- ◊ Being ill-equipped for bad weather like rain, ice, or snow, or not being aware of obstacles like high water at river crossings
- ◊ Splitting up a group on the trail
- ◊ Leaving a known trail to take a shortcut
- ◊ Ignoring obvious signs to turn back

Day-Hikers Beware!

Day-hikers often believe that shorter routes are safer than longer ones, but are they right? It depends. As long as they stay on the correct path, their logic makes sense. However, if day-hikers become lost or injured, they can be at greater risk than backpackers because most don't carry shelter, extra food, and survival gear.

According to the same SAR study mentioned above, day-hikers accounted for 35 percent of all search missions at national parks, almost double the rescues for boating, which is the next highest category. You might assume that's because day-hikers are the largest percentage of park visitors, and that is true. But day-hiking is also inherently easier than backpacking, climbing, canyoneering, and dozens of other activities that people do at national parks. Because day-hiking is simpler doesn't mean that it is immune from danger.

Deciding When You're in Trouble

The best defense you have against getting lost is spotting the early signs of danger. This means being observant about the trail, talking about what you're seeing and thinking, and connecting the various dots of information. By the time you realize you're lost, you'll have already passed dozens of visual clues indicating something is wrong. Here is what to look for:

◊ A previously clear trail dwindles to a barely traveled path.

◊ You are retracing your steps and the trail and scenery don't look familiar.

◊ Blazes, signposts, and other markings disappear or change.

◊ The trail climbs when it should be descending, or vice versa.

◊ The sun is positioned in the wrong part of the sky for the direction you should be hiking.

◊ The middle of the trail is blocked by two sticks or logs crossed like an X—the symbol for "Not the way."

◊ You reach a river crossing or trail junction that shouldn't be there.

◊ Footprints and other indications of other hikers disappear.

In some instances, you'll soon reach a trail junction or spot a blaze or a terrain feature that you recognize, and everything will be fine. Other times, however, the chorus of clues and questions will continue growing. This is the point where you need to start making the right decisions:

1. **Voice your concerns.** If you're hiking by yourself, this means admitting that you might be in trouble. If you're hiking in a group, alert others to your concerns. You might be the only person paying attention and the first person to realize the problem. Or, your warning might echo what others have been thinking.

2. **Set a time limit.** Decide to continue on your current trail for a specific time limit—like 10 minutes—before you stop and reevaluate your situation. You might be hiking slower than expected because of difficult terrain, and the familiar landmarks you're expecting could lie just ahead. If you change direction or turn around too early, you can make yourself lost when you weren't beforehand.

3. **Stop and sit down.** Once you decide that you are lost, stopping is the most critical decision you can make. You'll often feel compelled to keep going or to turn around, but you need to stop and think first. Stopping and sitting down in a safe and sheltered spot helps you relax and mentally retrace your steps to the place where you might have made a wrong turn.

4. **Mark your location.** The place where you first realized you were lost is significant. Mark it by placing sticks across the trail or tying a bandanna to a nearby tree. That way, you can find it again in case you need to make a side trip to gather water or check your bearings.

5. **Conserve energy.** If you become lost, your hike will likely last longer than originally planned. As a result, you need to slow down and save your strength. When you sit down, place a sleeping pad or backpack under your body to insulate yourself from the ground. Put on an extra layer like a rain shell or hat as soon as you stop moving. If you're hungry, eat. If you're thirsty, drink. Keeping your body fueled will help you think more clearly.

Trail Tips Shifting to survival mode doesn't mean giving up on the map, compass, and GPS skills that you learned in Chapter 6. Instead, survival skills are like an insurance policy in case your navigation efforts don't work as planned.

First Priorities

As soon as you stop moving, the next step is to evaluate your basic needs like food, water, and shelter. Chasing after the first solution that presents itself can distract you from concerns like staying warm, dry, and hydrated. Keep signaling devices like a whistle or mirror handy in case you need them. If your cell phone doesn't have reception, turn it off to conserve its batteries.

Water

Staying hydrated will help you think more clearly. If you're low on water, make a plan to refill your bottles at the last water source you passed, or look around for nearby supplies like streams or lakes. If you're desperate for water in a dry environment, you can transform moisture from plants and soil into drinkable water using these survival techniques:

◊ Collect morning dew by wrapping a T-shirt or towel around your legs and wading through wet grasses; then, squeeze out the water.

◊ Wrap clear plastic bags around green leafy branches to collect plant condensation—though it can take many hours and several bags to collect enough water to drink.

◊ Even if a streambed is dry, dig for buried moisture on the outside banks of bends in the channel. Wring water out of damp soil or sand by wrapping it in a handkerchief or T-shirt and squeezing it.

Food

Munching on a snack as you consider your options will take the edge off your anxiety and give your body the sugars it needs to fuel your brain and muscles. You should also do an inventory of how much food you're carrying. Although water is a daily necessity, people can survive for days and even weeks with little or no food. In Chapter 18, I'll describe how you can find edible wild plants.

Shelter

Keep warm by avoiding wind and rain and insulating your body from the ground. If bad weather threatens, pitch your tent or seek cover under a natural shelter like a rocky overhang or dense pine tree. Stay as close to the trail as possible in case another hiker comes by.

If it's already late in the day, you'll need to start thinking about where to sleep. The idea of spending an unplanned night outdoors is often tough to accept, but you need to consider the option well before sunset if you want to find a warm, dry, comfortable place while you can still see and move easily. Techniques to build a shelter are described later in this chapter.

Morale

When a person becomes lost, maintaining a positive attitude often counts for more than muscle power and backcountry skills. Panic is a real threat that contributes to many hiking injuries and fatalities by clouding a lost person's judgment. Watch for signs of rising panic like rapid breathing, sweating, trembling, and throat constriction. Counteract these symptoms by sitting down, deliberately slowing your breathing, and focusing on concrete tasks like tightening your shoelaces or reviewing your equipment.

Leading the Lost

"Yup, we're probably lost." That announcement can send some people scrambling for solutions and others into paralyzed fright. Being lost is a high-stress situation that can inspire the same instinctive reactions as other crisis events—like the emergency evacuation of an airplane. Some people help the elderly and children exit first, while others barrel down the aisle to save themselves. You want to be the hiker who looks after others.

Despite advantages of more eyes, ears, and brain matter, hiking in a group can actually promote getting lost. For instance, a risk-taking individual can push a group to attempt a trail that's beyond the capabilities of everyone. If you are part of a hiking group with a wide span of abilities, you need to identify those ambitious hikers early on and channel their energy to more positive goals, like taking extra gear from a slower hiker. Other problems can arise from poor group communication and can lead to problems like a missed turn or ignoring signs of being lost.

Sorting Fact from Fiction

Unfortunately, most hikers are more familiar with folk tales about how to survive in the woods than actual facts. While some myths are based on real observations, most aren't true all the time, and some are just plain wrong. Here's the rundown on the most widespread fantasies about wilderness survival that you can now discard.

Myth: Moss grows on the north side of tree trunks.

Fact: Moss prefers damp, shadowy places—which could be the north, south, east, or west side of a tree depending on the terrain and the weather. Also, spiders do not always build their webs facing south.

Myth: Collect water by digging a solar still in the ground.

Fact: Solar stills require too much work to set up correctly and often don't work.

Myth: All streams and rivers will eventually cross a road.

Fact: Not necessarily. Water tends to flow in a consistent direction, but not always toward civilization. Streams and rivers often choose the steepest path down a slope, which might not be safe for hiking.

Myth: You can drink your own urine at least once.

Fact: Never drink your own urine or anyone else's. When you're dehydrated, your urine contains a higher percentage of waste products, which could cause you to vomit and become more dehydrated.

Myth: The insides of barrel cacti contain drinkable water.

Fact: Most cacti are bone dry most times of the year, and any fluid you do find after cutting through the tough, spiny exterior is likely too bitter tasting and toxic to drink and will cause vomiting and diarrhea.

How to Get Found

For every lost hiker who needs to be airlifted from a remote canyon, there are many others who manage to find their way out, return to their car, and enjoy a celebratory beer. Their stories don't get picked up by 24-hour cable news, and yet their experiences involve lessons that we can all learn from. Sometimes, these hikers are just lucky—a trait that everyone can use. However, most of them also made the right decisions to get out of a jam. Whether you are lost by 100 yards or 10 miles, your ability to rescue yourself mainly depends on these two skills:

◊ Your experience level as a hiker

◊ Whether you carry and know how to use a map, compass, or GPS device or smartphone app

These skills first come into play when you make your most difficult decision as a lost hiker, which is whether to continue moving or to stop and wait to be rescued.

Stay Put or Keep Going?

Most books and experts will advise lost hikers to stop and wait to be rescued. Stationary hikers are easier to find, and hunkering down conserves energy and prevents injuries. Plus, most search-and-rescue operations are resolved quickly. Between 2003 and 2006, national park search-and-rescue teams found 95 percent of all victims within 24 hours of initiating a search. But sitting tight doesn't make sense all the time. While it's true that lost hikers should always stop and consider their options—they might not choose to wait for a rescue.

Unfortunately, there's no magic formula to determine whether you should stop or keep hiking when you're lost. For instance, you might do both by moving to a more protected location to wait for rescue or spend the night. But one absolute rule that everyone agrees on is that you shouldn't hike in the dark or in poor visibility. Doing so skyrockets your risk of becoming injured or more lost. Here are factors you should weigh when deciding whether to stay or attempt to hike out.

Wait for rescue if ...

◊ Someone will quickly notice you are overdue.

◊ You're prepared to spend the night.

◊ Rainy or cold weather is imminent and you have a good shelter.

◊ You're tired or injured.

◊ Not much daylight remains.

◊ You're unsure of your location or which direction to hike.

◊ You're on a popular trail and have seen other hikers.

◊ You can't move without risking injury.

Hike out if ...

◊ No one knows where you are.

◊ You lack warm clothing or shelter.

◊ Rainy or cold weather is threatening and you lack shelter.

◊ You're prepared to hike.

◊ Several hours of good visibility remain.

◊ You have a map, compass, and/or GPS, and you recognize terrain features or landmarks.

◊ Few people hike in the area.

◊ You can handle the terrain or trails.

Attracting Attention

When you're lost, the last thing you want to be is silent or invisible. Unfortunately, the human voice doesn't carry very far outdoors. The piercing sound of an emergency whistle, however, can be heard more than a mile away. Three short blasts from a whistle are the universal signal for someone in trouble.

Visual signals are more likely to attract attention if they include bright colors, high contrast, and movement. If you decide to wait for rescue, select a spot that is visible from the ground as well as the air—like a clearing or bare ridgeline. Then try to attract attention using the following visual techniques.

◊ Signal distress by making a large X using rocks or branches at least 5 feet across that is visible from overhead.

◊ Put on your brightest, most colorful clothing—including rain jackets, hats, or bandannas. Color and movement attract attention.

◊ Use a signal mirror to periodically flash ridges, peaks, and other areas where people might be watching. To aim a signal mirror, hold the reflective surface next to your face with one hand. Then stretch out your other arm and point to your target. Adjust the reflective surface so that the light flashes across your extended hand, making it visible to your target. (Reflective objects like credit card holograms, foil wrappers, and metal containers are less effective but can still flash a light.)

◊ Make dark smoke—which is easier to see than white smoke—by covering a signal fire with evergreen branches, moss, or wet leaves. I'll discuss making a fire later in the chapter.

Calling for Help

As cell phone towers spread and signals grow stronger, more and more hikers will be able to get phone reception on remote trails and peaks. Some people might consider this digital expansion a depressing development. But when you're lost or injured, it could be your lifeline. If you own a smartphone, you should carry it on all hikes, and know how to use it to call for help.

Modern smartphones find your location through assisted GPS—a fast and accurate method that combines the satellite signals of GPS with radio signals bounced off three or more fixed cell towers. If your phone can communicate with cell towers (not always possible in many backcountry areas), it can not only make a call or send a text, but it can also triangulate your position from the cell towers' locations and give emergency responders a more accurate fix on your location.

To ensure that your phone works when you need it, keep it turned off when you're not using it. Phones lose battery power quickly while searching for reception and in low temperatures. To improve your chances of getting through to help, follow these tips when making an emergency call or text in the backcountry:

◊ Make calls from the highest ground available with an unobstructed view of the sky to improve your line-of-sight connections to cell towers.

◊ Hold the phone at arm's length away from your body and rotate around to find the strongest reception.

◊ Make follow-up phone calls from the same location because your cell phone will remember where the nearest towers are located.

◊ If your battery is low or reception is weak, send a text message to your emergency contact. Text messages require less power than a voice call.

◊ Provide the emergency dispatcher with as much information about your location—elevation, terrain, visible landmarks, position of the sun, and last known location.

 Safety Check Don't dial 911 for minor troubles that you can handle on your own, and don't exaggerate your predicament. Search-and-rescue teams are responding to an increasing number of calls from cell phone–equipped hikers who panic over insignificant problems.

Power from the Sun

Recharging your cell phone is a nightly ritual for most people. But on the trail, you'll be hard-pressed to find an electrical outlet. The solution is to carry a portable solar panel and storage battery to provide a daily boost to your phone's power level. But instead of recharging your phone at night, when cold temperatures reduce the efficiency of lithium batteries, top up your phone during sunny rest breaks or when you stop for lunch or first make camp. Using a storage battery ensures that your phone receives a consistent stream of electrons, as the output from solar panels can vary based on sun exposure. You can recharge the external battery while you hike by connecting it to a solar panel draped over your backpack or top it up at camp. Most products that combine solar panels with a battery often lack the surface area of panels to collect enough sun power; the ideal system should produce between 7 and 21 watts of power. Because the quality and durability of solar products can vary, opt for trail-tested devices made by Goal Zero, Anker, Nekteck, and RAVPower.

A solar panel and external battery can keep your GPS and smartphone at full power throughout a trip.

Call for Help via Satellite

Backpackers who hike solo, prefer backcountry terrain outside of cell coverage, or are just concerned about getting lost might consider carrying a personal locator beacon (PLB) or satellite messenger. These handheld devices are about the same size as a GPS and use satellites to alert search-and-rescue teams of your status and location in case of an emergency. Higher-end models include GPS mapping, allow two-way text messaging, and provide up-to-date weather reports. Companies that manufacture PLBs and messengers include Garmin, ACR Electronics, and SPOT, all of which charge a satellite service fee in addition to the cost of a unit, which ranges from $100 to $500.

How to Hike Out

Deciding you want to rescue yourself requires more than just enough energy. You need a plan to guide you, a route to follow, and the ability to evaluate new situations as they arise. First, however, you need to figure out your approximate location.

Finding Your Location

If you're carrying a mapping GPS, you've got orbiting satellites working on your team. The map screen of a GPS device will be centered over your location, and you can zoom in and out or scroll the map to locate nearby landmarks. To find your coordinates, create a waypoint on your current location. If you laid a track of waypoints as you hiked, the GPS's trackback function can lead you back to your starting point. Otherwise, place a waypoint where you want to go and follow the trails on the digital map to reach it.

A map and compass can also help you pinpoint your location, but first, you need to narrow down your general area. The two best methods are fixing the cardinal directions (north, south, east, and west), and reading the terrain. Start by figuring out which way is north using your compass. If you don't have a compass, that's a problem, but not an insurmountable one. You can estimate which direction is south by using an analog watch face and the sun. If you're wearing a digital watch or no watch at all, you can draw a clock face on the ground and follow the same method. This technique works best for North America below the latitude of Alaska:

1. Hold the watch face flat, with the hour hand aimed at the sun.
2. South will be at the point halfway between the hour hand and 12 o'clock on the watch face.
3. Adjust for Daylight Saving Time during the summer by using 1 o'clock instead of noon.

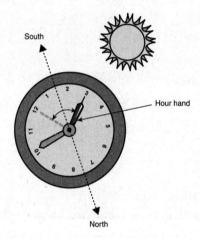

Aim the hour hand at the sun, and the direction south will be halfway between the hour hand and 12 o'clock.

You can find the cardinal directions at night in the Northern Hemisphere by locating the North Star, also called *Polaris*. Unlike other stars, the North Star remains stationary in the sky because it sits over the Earth's axis of rotation. Although the North Star is important for navigation, it isn't particularly bright. Luckily, one of the night sky's most recognizable constellations—the Big Dipper—points the way. Here's how to locate the North Star using the Big Dipper:

1. Scan the sky for the distinctive profile of the Big Dipper, which resembles a cup with a curved handle. Depending on the season, the Big Dipper could be sitting upright, on its side, or inverted.

2. Locate the two stars that form the front edge of the Big Dipper's cup—these are known as the pointer stars.

3. Extend an imaginary line from the pointer stars to locate the North Star. This line should be approximately five times the length of the gap between the two pointer stars.

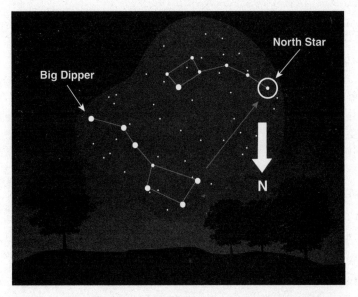

Follow the pointer stars on the end of the Big Dipper to locate the North Star.

Once you know your directions, you can use features like distinctive mountain peaks, lakes, and rivers to locate yourself on a map. You can also use the contour lines on a topo map to match visual features to points on the map.

How to Reach Your Goal

How far you need to hike to regain familiar ground can range from several hundred yards to many miles. For most lost hikers, however, the distance to a recognizable trail or location is fairly close—often less than 1 mile. Keep to regular trails whenever possible—even if it will make your route longer. You should only consider leaving a trail if the following are true:

◊ You can't reach your destination any other way.

◊ You can clearly see your destination.

◊ You are certain that you won't encounter impassable terrain on the way.

 Trail Tips You can estimate the remaining hours of daylight by counting the number of outstretched hands you can place between the bottom of the sun and the horizon. Each stack of four fingers represents an hour of daylight.

Spending the Night Outside

Bedding down on the ground without a tent or tarp for protection isn't ideal, but it beats the alternative: hiking until you collapse from exhaustion. Start seeking a place to spend the night an hour before sunset or when you encounter bad weather. Like choosing a tent site, there are advantages to certain locations:

◊ Look for places with natural protection from wind and rain—like a cluster of boulders, a stand of trees, or a depression in the ground caused by an uprooted tree.

◊ Overhead branches, bushes, or ledges provide an extra insulating layer above you to prevent heat loss.

◊ Avoid extremely high spots, which are more exposed to wind, and extremely low spots, where cold air settles at night.

◊ Stay above riverbanks in case the water rises during the night.

Building a Shelter

A tent should always be your go-to shelter for sleeping in the woods. But if you lack a tent, a wilderness shelter will keep you warmer, dryer, and more comfortable than sleeping in the open.

The goal of your shelter is to protect you from the outside elements and retain your body heat. For those reasons, you want your shelter to be small and cozy. Not only do large structures take more time and energy to build, but they also require more body heat to warm up. The ideal shelter should resemble a mummy sleeping bag and can be constructed from natural materials like leaves, branches, and vines, as well as these items from your clothing or pack:

◊ Plastic garbage bags to create a waterproof barrier for your body or a shelter

◊ Shoelaces to tie sticks together

◊ Trekking poles to support a canopy

◊ A belt to function as a rope

◊ A backpack to keep your torso off the ground

◊ Nylon or elastic straps to secure branches

The easiest backcountry shelter to construct is a basic lean-to that resembles a low-lying A-frame tent. Here's how to build one:

1. Create a ridgepole by leaning a 6- to 8-foot sturdy branch against a tree or rock at waist-level and placing the other end on the ground.

2. Build the shelter walls by leaning smaller branches against both sides of the pole. Secure some of these branches to make the shelter more stable.

3. Cover the framework with layers of dry, leafy branches, ferns, and other grasses at least 2 to 3 feet thick.

4. Lay several heavier branches or bark sections like shingles over the roof to keep the materials from blowing away.

5. Place a soft, insulating layer of pine boughs and dry leaves inside the shelter where you will lie down.

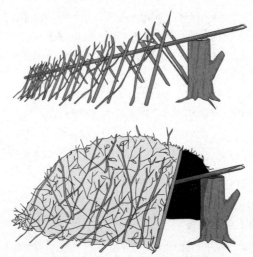

Building a small lean-to shelter makes it easier for your body heat to warm it up.

Making a Fire

Building a fire will keep you warm, create a visible signal for rescuers to see, and give you a morale boost. To maximize its benefits, you should build a fire as close to your shelter as possible, but also where it will be shielded from the wind. Scout around for a naturally protected place—like against a tree stump or inside a rock crevice.

 Trail Tips   If you place a fire between your shelter and a rock wall or embankment, the heat will reflect off the barrier and back toward your shelter.

To build a viable fire, you will need to collect three different types of wood:

◊ **Tinder.** Small twigs, dry needles and leaves, and bark. You can also use manmade fire starters like dryer lint and cotton balls soaked in petroleum jelly (see Chapter 7).

◊ **Kindling.** Dead sticks and branches the width of one finger. Dead wood is dry, will snap cleanly, and burns better than green wood that retains moisture. Break sticks into 6- to 12-inch pieces.

◊ **Fuel.** Dead branches and logs 1- to 3-inches thick. If the ground is damp, look for dead branches dangling from trees or buried under leaf litter. This is the type of wood the fire will consume the most. To make a fire last several hours, find logs 6 to 10 inches in diameter.

Log cabin method   Teepee method

Stacking small branches and sticks around the tinder provides the kindling a fire needs to sustain itself.

Once you've gathered enough wood, especially large branches to serve as main fuel, you're ready to make a flame. The key to a successful fire is lighting the smaller tinder and kindling first and letting them ignite the larger branches. Overloading a fire with too much thick wood at the beginning will cause it to fizzle out. Here's how to start small, and build up:

1. Make a small pile of tinder and stack the kindling around it, leaving small gaps for air to enter. Most hikers find that arranging the kindling like a log cabin or teepee creates a stable, open structure.

2. Ignite the bottom of the tinder with a lighter or match, and gently blow on the flames while blocking the wind.

3. As the flames begin to burn the kindling, add more on top, increasing the diameter and size of the wood as the fire grows.

4. Place wet wood in a pile near the fire to dry so that it will burn more easily when you need it.

Staying Warm and Dry

As the temperature drops at night, you can boost the insulating ability of your clothes by stuffing your pants, shirt, and hat with dry leaves, pine needles, and other forest litter. These lightweight organic materials will keep you warmer by trapping pockets of air against your body. Also, avoid sitting or lying directly on the cold ground by placing an insulating layer underneath you.

SUMMARY

No one is immune from making mistakes or getting lost—and sooner or later, it will happen to you. Smart planning and carrying the right gear (including the 10 essentials, see Chapter 7) can reduce the severity of your setback, as can stopping, sitting down, and suppressing feelings of panic. Always bring a cell phone in case you need to call or text for help. If you need to spend an unexpected night outdoors, start looking for a protected, snug, visible location well before sundown.

CHAPTER 17

FIRST AID

Mountain lion attacks generate first-rate drama for the evening news, but the actual danger from this threat is small. According to a 4-year study of backpacking trips led by the National Outdoor Leadership School (NOLS), sprained ankles and knees accounted for half of all outdoor accidents. So, instead of scanning the underbrush for cougars, you really should be watching your feet. (For advice on how to avoid mountain lions and other rare but fascinating wild animals, see Chapter 18.)

Day-hiking and backpacking are actually very safe activities. In fact, lacing up your boots and hitting the trail is less dangerous than a game of soccer or downhill skiing. Why? Because hiking is essentially walking—something that you do every day.

The challenge with hiking, however, is that your ability to treat injuries is limited to what you can carry—and more importantly, the first aid knowledge you hold in your head. You don't need to be an M.D., however, to know how to wrap a sprained ankle or stop a bleeding wound. What you do need is some common sense, a well-stocked first aid kit (see Chapter 7 and Equipment Checklists), and maybe some duct tape.

An Ounce of Prevention

Most first aid books will tell you how to treat injuries. Few, however, will explain how to prevent them in the first place. Because steering clear of a scrape is better than bandaging yourself afterward, here's how to stay out of trouble:

◊ Slow down while navigating difficult terrain, and use your hands or trekking poles for added balance.

◊ Test handholds and footholds before committing your full bodyweight.

◊ Tie the laces on your boots or shoes tightly and evenly.

◊ Keep your pack snug against your body, and tie down dangling gear like water bottles.

◊ Remove your pack for steep climbs and tight squeezes.

◊ Make sure you can climb down anything that you climb up.

◊ Stay adequately hydrated to prevent weakness and disorientation.

Blisters Be Gone

Blisters and hikers are like two old friends—rarely far apart. Almost everyone experiences these debilitating sores caused by skin-to-footwear friction. Even famous adventurers like Meriwether Lewis and William Clark complained about the numerous "bruses (sic) & blisters" they developed during their 2-year expedition to explore the American West.

Preventing Blisters

If you wait until the first mile of your hike to start thinking about your feet, it's already too late. Here's how to proactively stop blisters before they form:

◊ Break in footwear gradually, starting several weeks before your first major hike. Wear boots or shoes around the house and while doing yardwork, and take them on several practice hikes of at least 3 to 4 miles.

◊ If you feel a *hot spot*—painful, red skin irritations caused by excessive friction that can develop into a blister—cover it with a bandage and continue the break-in process to toughen up your skin.

◊ Experiment with several types and combinations of insoles and liner socks (see Chapter 9) to find the most comfortable fit.

◊ Keep your feet dry. Change out of wet socks and use foot powder if your feet sweat a lot.

◊ Apply lubricants like Bodyglide's Liquified Powder to your feet to reduce the friction that causes blisters.

◊ Blisters are dependent on temperature and terrain, so footwear that fits well on one hike might cause trouble on a different day or trail.

Treating Blisters

Because hot spots develop gradually, your first inclination will be to keep walking. But to prevent a full-blown blister (which will really slow you down), you need to stop and treat it:

1. When you feel friction, stop to inspect your feet for hot spots, especially on the heels and toes.
2. Clean the skin around the hot spot with a damp, clean cloth or an alcohol-based gel sanitizer and let dry.
3. Apply a self-adhesive cushioned bandage over the affected area and the surrounding skin. Common products available at drugstores include moleskin (a soft, feltlike fabric) or Second Skin. Secure the covering with several strips of tape or an adhesive bandage.
4. An alternative if the hot spot is too sensitive to cover with a bandage: cut a hole from the center of the bandage and place it over the hot spot—creating a raised "donut" of protection around the affected skin.

If you ignored a hot spot and you discover a squishy sac on your foot—you've earned yourself a blister. Your main goal now is to save skin and prevent infection.

In some cases, you'll need to deliberately pop an intact blister to drain the fluid inside. This technique—done with a sharp, clean needle or knife blade—prevents the blister from breaking on its own. To sterilize the needle or blade, place the tip in a flame for 30 seconds, or soak it in a solution of iodine or alcohol-based gel hand sanitizer.

Here's how to treat a fully formed blister on your foot:

1. If the blister is less than ½ inch in diameter and intact, clean the area and apply a large cushioned bandage over top of it. You might need to apply several overlapping layers. Secure with tape.

2. For blisters larger than ½ inch, or sacs that are about to pop, puncture the base with a sterilized knife or needle and drain the fluid. Keep the loose skin flap intact to protect the sensitive area underneath. Clean the wound with a damp cloth or an alcohol-based gel hand sanitizer. Careful, it's gonna sting!

3. To prevent infection, apply an antibiotic ointment and cover with a sterile gauze pad.

4. Cover the pad with adhesive moleskin and secure with tape or bandages.

5. Check the wound once a day to apply new, clean bandages.

Muscle Aches and Pains

When you finally drop your pack at the end of the day, your relief might be curtailed by the throbbing pain in your shoulders, calves, and back. To alleviate muscle pain both before and after it occurs, follow these tips:

◊ Stretch each morning by touching your toes, twisting at the waist, and doing several lunges.

◊ Take 400 mg of the pain reliever ibuprofen (known by hikers as "Vitamin I") at the first sign of muscle pain. If you know the day's hiking will be strenuous, pop some ibuprofen before you start.

Ankle Twists and Sprains

It takes half a second to sprain your ankle, but it can take several days for the injury to heal. You should be able to walk gingerly on a sprained ankle; if you can't, you've probably broken a bone and will need a splint—a first aid skill I'll describe a bit later.

To get back on your feet after a sprain, follow the RICE method:

1. **Rest.** Sit down to take all weight off the ankle.

2. **Ice.** Reduce swelling and pain by applying a cold water bladder or snow or ice wrapped in a T-shirt. Apply cold

for a maximum of 20 minutes, 3 to 4 times a day. Take ibuprofen to reduce pain and inflammation.

3. **Compression.** Wrap the joint immediately after icing to prevent swelling. Use elastic bandages, bandannas, a T-shirt, or a sock. Start at the ball of the foot and wrap backward toward the ankle.

4. **Elevation.** While icing, raise the ankle off the ground to reduce swelling.

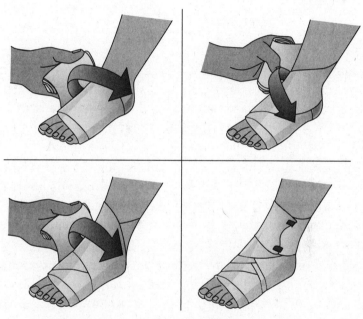

Wrapping a sprained ankle reduces swelling and enables the joint to support some weight.

You should follow the RICE method for 3 days. Icing and compression will speed the healing process, as will gently massaging the ankle and moving it around while walking. Keeping the ankle immobilized will actually impede recovery.

 Trail Tips If you can't stop to treat a sprained ankle, tighten the laces on your boots as much as you can, take a recommended dose of ibuprofen, and continue hiking. The pressure and medicine will reduce the swelling until you can properly ice and wrap it.

Wounds That Bleed

Any breaks in the skin are a concern in the outdoors because of the increased risk of infection. Cleaning a wound before applying a bandage will reduce the risk, but you should still check for signs of infection (redness, swelling, icky discharge) every day when you change a bandage. Here's how to treat a wound:

1. **Stop the bleeding.** Apply direct pressure to the wound with a clean cloth or bandanna. The purpose isn't to soak up the blood; instead, the purpose is to aid the natural clotting process. Elevate cuts on arms or legs above the heart.

2. **Clean the wound.** Remove dirt, bacteria, excess skin, and any foreign matter by washing it with a high-pressure stream of clean water generated by squeezing a hydration bladder or the narrow opening of a zipper-lock plastic bag.

3. **Close the wound.** For lacerations where the skin is separated, pull the wound closed by placing wound closure strips across the gap. Add more strips crosswise over the ends of the original strips to prevent them from curling. Adhesive bandages, duct tape, or super glue can be used as emergency alternatives.

4. **Apply a bandage.** Cover the cut with a nonadhesive sterile bandage, and then apply a gauze pad over the top. Hold the dressing in place using tape or a strip bandage. Applying tincture of benzoin, a red liquid commonly found in first aid kits that acts as a mild antiseptic, also helps secure bandages to skin.

Getting Burned

Serious burns are rare in the backcountry for the simple reason that stoves, flames, and fires are small and controlled. Because most burns are actually caused by the sun, shield your skin using the following methods:

◊ Wear a wide-brimmed hat and clothing that covers your neck and arms from 10 A.M. to 3 P.M., when the sun's ultraviolet (UV) rays are most powerful.

◊ Apply sweatproof sunscreen—at least SPF 30—throughout the day.

◊ Always use sunscreen on bright winter days, and at elevations above 5,000 feet, where UV rays are stronger.

◊ Use sunscreen in the winter and on water, where the reflected sunlight can still cause burns.

First-Degree Burns

Spilling a cup of steaming soup on your leg or brushing against a red-hot stove can cause red and sensitive first-degree burns. Luckily, treating these burns is simple:

1. Bathe the burned skin in cool water for several minutes. Do not apply snow or ice.

2. Don't use alcohol-based antiseptic or gel hand sanitizer, which will cause the parched skin to dry out even more.

3. Apply aloe vera or another nonalcohol skin lotion.

4. Take ibuprofen as needed to reduce swelling and pain.

Serious Burns

More serious second- and third-degree burns can be caused by steam, boiling water, and prolonged contact with flames or coals. The formation of white or pink raised blisters indicates second-degree burns, which require immediate treatment that is similar to treating blisters caused by friction:

1. Puncture and drain the base of large blisters (diameter of 1 inch or more) with a sterilized needle or blade.

2. Apply an antibiotic ointment to the burn.

3. Cover the blister with a nonsticking bandage and tape in place.

4. Take ibuprofen for pain and change the bandage at least once a day.

Third-degree burns are major medical emergencies that involve the complete charring of skin, nerves, and muscle. Caring for these burns is beyond the abilities of most hikers. Serious burns should be cleaned and covered, and victims should be treated for shock (see later in this chapter) as they are evacuated to seek medical attention. Remember to treat the first- and second-degree burns that often surround the more serious burned area.

Broken Bones

Fall hard and you'll get a bruise and a sprain. Fall harder or just land the wrong way, and your bones could fracture. Most breaks occur in the fingers, toes, arms, legs, and clavicle (also known as the collarbone). Broken bones are much less common on the trail than muscle sprains and tears, and treating them requires a splint to support the damaged limb and make the victim mobile again.

Distinguishing between a bad sprain and a fracture can be difficult. Here are several key characteristics of fractures:

◊ Sharp pain over a specific point

◊ Noticeable deformation of a limb or unusual protrusions beneath the skin

◊ Grinding sounds when the bone is moved

◊ The limb or joint is unable to support any weight

◊ Rapid swelling and black and blue discoloration

Once you identify a fracture, you'll need to splint it. You can improvise splints using many kinds of backpacking gear, including sleeping pads, trekking poles, tent stakes and poles, nylon compression straps, kitchen utensils, jackets, and elastic cords. Here's how to splint a forearm or wrist fracture:

1. Keep the elbow bent at 90 degrees and lay the wrist as flat as possible with the fingers curled around a sock.

2. Wrap the forearm in a U-shaped splint that stretches from the elbow to the wrist. Secure the splint to the forearm with tape or nylon straps.

3. Secure the forearm to the body by wrapping a sling—T-shirts and bandannas are just the right size—around the neck.

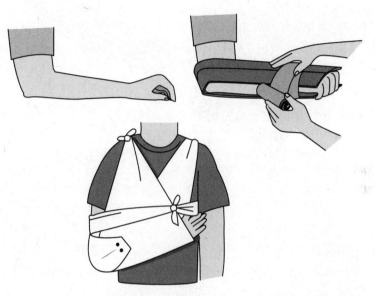

A padded arm splint and sling protects and immobilizes a broken bone.

Here's how to splint a lower-leg or ankle fracture:

1. Lay the victim on his back on a ground pad for insulation.
2. Loosen the boot or shoe, but keep it on to protect the foot. Remove the tongue so that you can check circulation and feeling in the foot.
3. Wrap the back and sides of the leg from the ankle to the knee in a U-shaped splint—a foam sleeping pad works best.
4. Secure the splint with adjustable nylon straps, rope, or duct tape.
5. Elevate the leg above the heart once the splint is secure.

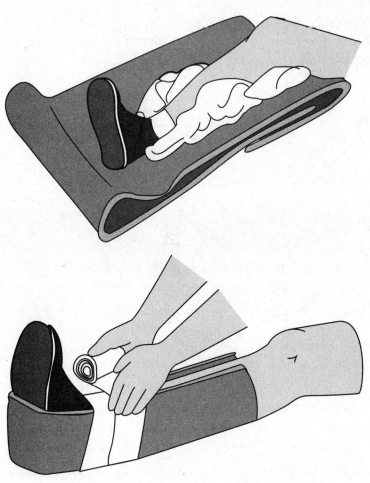

Use a folded sleeping pad to splint a broken ankle or lower leg bone.

Trauma and Shock

No, this isn't the shock you get from a frayed electrical wire. Shock is a medical condition that occurs when blood flow to a person's vital organs is disrupted. Shock doesn't usually occur by itself; it generally accompanies a serious injury like broken or crushed bones, severe bleeding, panic, or an allergic reaction.

Signs of shock include:

◊ Weakness, nausea, or vomiting

◊ Confusion or irritability

◊ Pale, clammy skin that is cool to the touch

◊ Rapid and/or weak pulse

◊ Shallow and irregular breathing

Because a person can die from shock even if their other injuries aren't life-threatening, you must treat it by following these steps:

1. Lay the victim on the ground, insulated by a sleeping pad and extra clothes.

2. Stop any bleeding by applying direct pressure to the wound with a clean cloth or bandage.

3. Immobilize broken arm or leg bones by applying a splint.

4. Once the bleeding stops, elevate the victim's feet to direct blood back to the core organs.

5. Give the victim small sips of water if they are awake and oriented.

Because shock is an internal malady, signs of it can be tricky to spot or remember during a first aid emergency. So it's a good idea to preemptively treat people for shock in cases of any serious injury.

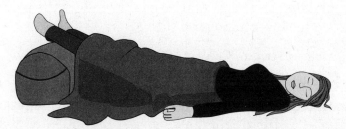

To treat shock, keep the victim warm and raise her feet to direct blood back to core organs.

Shock caused by allergic reactions to bee stings or certain foods is just as dangerous but requires different treatment. See the section on allergic reactions later in the chapter.

Hypothermia

There's an ominous saying among search-and-rescue teams: "Simple mistakes get you in trouble, but hypothermia will finish you off." Hypothermia occurs when a person's core temperature drops as the body runs out of fuel and can no longer keep itself warm. It often occurs after other accidents or mishaps have left a person cold, wet, or exhausted. Here's how to recognize the initial stages of hypothermia.

◊ Impaired muscle coordination and slurred speech

◊ Severe shivering and skin that is cold to the touch

◊ Irritability and confusion

 Safety Check You can spot the symptoms of hypothermia by watching for a person experiencing the "umbles": stumbling, mumbling, or fumbling.

At the first sign of hypothermia, follow these steps:

1. Stop hiking and place the person inside a shelter like a tent or sleeping bag.

2. Replace damp or wet clothes with dry, insulated layers.

3. Heat up sugary drinks and food like fruit juices and cookies so the person can generate their own internal heat.

4. Avoid using hot water bottles as they reduce the person's ability to shiver and warm themselves.

Heat Exhaustion and Heat Stroke

The opposite of hypothermia—excessive heat—can be just as dangerous as freezing. High temperatures and humidity combined with significant exertion (like carrying a backpack) and dehydration can overwhelm your body's ability to keep your core at 98.6°F—placing you at risk for heat exhaustion and heat stroke.

The keys to preventing heat-related illnesses are to recharge your body's cooling system with sufficient fluids and rest. Here are some other tips:

◊ Spend several days acclimating to hot climates or conditions before starting a hike.

◊ Hike in the morning and evening when temps are cooler, and take a break during noontime heat.

◊ Remove extra layers as soon as you begin to sweat.

◊ Keep your drinking water within reach while hiking. Cold water both quenches your thirst and cools your body—so insulate your bottles and bladders to keep them cool.

 Trail Tips The color of your urine is a reliable indicator of your hydration state. Clear urine indicates adequate hydration, while dark yellow urine means you aren't drinking enough.

Heat exhaustion is the first and less serious heat-related illness. It occurs as your body struggles to cool itself through normal methods like sweating and evaporation. Signs of heat exhaustion include:

◊ Profuse sweating

◊ Nausea, dizziness, and loss of appetite

◊ Occasional vomiting

To prevent heat exhaustion from advancing to the deadly condition of heat stroke, take these precautions as soon as you begin to feel overheated:

◊ Rest in the shade and remove extra clothing.

◊ Drink cool water.

◊ Cool your body by fanning yourself and splashing your head and neck with cool water.

Unlike heat exhaustion, the more dangerous heat stroke kills 80 percent of victims if left untreated. It develops when your body can no longer keep your internal organs cool. As they overheat and begin to fail, victims slip into a coma and die. Signs of heat stroke include:

◊ Confusion, agitation, and altered mental state

◊ Rapid heart rate (100+ beats per minute) and breathing

◊ Victim is no longer sweating, but sweat might still be present

Anyone experiencing heat stroke should stop hiking and seek immediate medical attention. Heat stroke victims should be cooled using similar methods as for heat exhaustion, but more aggressively and while being treated for shock.

Frostbite

It's 22°F with 6 inches of snow on the ground when you remove your gloves and notice that your fingertips are hard and white. You've got frostbite, a cold injury where the treatment requires thawing the frozen skin:

1. Rewarm frozen skin by placing it in lukewarm (100°F) water for 30 to 45 minutes. Add more warm water to keep the temperature high enough.

2. The thawing process is extremely painful, but do not rub or massage the skin. Give the victim ibuprofen or aspirin to manage the pain.

3. Recently frostbitten skin is vulnerable to refreezing, so protect it from further cold injuries.

Allergic Reaction

About 4 percent of adults who get stung by a bee experience a life-threatening allergic reaction known as *anaphylactic shock*—a rapid and dangerous response that causes immediate swelling of body tissues (including the throat), difficulty in breathing, and a sudden drop in blood pressure. This fast-acting and often scary—due to airway constriction—condition has the following symptoms:

◊ Rapid appearance of hives all over the body

- ◊ Difficulty breathing, wheezing, and pressure in the chest
- ◊ Swelling within the throat that inhibits breathing and swallowing
- ◊ Dizziness and fainting caused by a sudden drop in blood pressure

Anaphylactic shock can also be triggered by food allergies, and treatment should be administered immediately. Victims need a dose of epinephrine, a form of adrenaline that reduces swelling and reopens the airway. Epinephrine is injected via a spring-loaded cartridge known as an EpiPen, which is available with a doctor's prescription and should be carried by any hiker allergic to bee stings. Next steps include treating the person for shock and arranging immediate evacuation to trained medical care.

Even after administering a dose of epinephrine, give the victim a regular dose of an oral antihistamine like Benadryl (diphenhydramine) every four hours to reduce the allergic reaction. Administering Benadryl by itself, however, does not act fast enough to reverse the life-threatening symptoms of anaphylactic shock.

Intestinal Distress

There's an old campfire joke about a book called *100 Yards to the Outhouse*, written by Willie Makeit and illustrated by Betty Wonte. Bathroom humor aside, a bad case of the runs is a serious issue.

Most viral, bacterial, or foodborne illnesses last 1 or 2 days before subsiding. Backpackers suffering from diarrhea should stay in a camp with access to adequate sanitation facilities and increase their fluid intake to avoid becoming dehydrated. Water is okay, but water mixed with oral rehydration salts containing salt, potassium, and sugars is even better. Dilute sugary drinks like Kool-Aid or Gatorade to half strength because excessive sugar can worsen the diarrhea.

Waterborne parasites like *Giardia* or *Cryptosporidium* cause a nastier reaction. Both are microscopic bugs that live in water. Once ingested, they multiply in the gut, producing diarrhea, abdominal cramping, and severe gas for days or even weeks. Antidiarrheal medicines like Imodium A-D can reduce the severity of the fluid loss and cramping. However, because it takes 2 to 7 days for symptoms to appear after the initial infection, you might not experience an attack until after you return home. Standard treatment for *Giardia* is the antibiotic Flagyl (metronidazole), while Alinia (nitazoxanide) will clear up *Cryptosporidium.* Your best tactic, however, is to reread Chapter 14 on water hygiene to make sure these bugs ever get inside your gut.

Evacuating a Victim

Victims of serious injuries like broken bones and heat stroke need professional medical care. Getting a victim from where an accident occurred to a hospital, however, is often harder than it seems.

It's always better if the victim can walk out under their own power or with some assistance. To improve mobility, fashion splints to secure broken bones or sprained muscles and extend trekking poles to the victim's maximum height to create makeshift crutches. If the victim is unable to walk, hikers can create makeshift litters using trekking poles, ropes, backpacks, and other gear to carry the person out, although these devices are only safe on flat terrain. Most search-and-rescue teams use stretchers carried by up to a dozen people to evacuate seriously injured victims over rough trails.

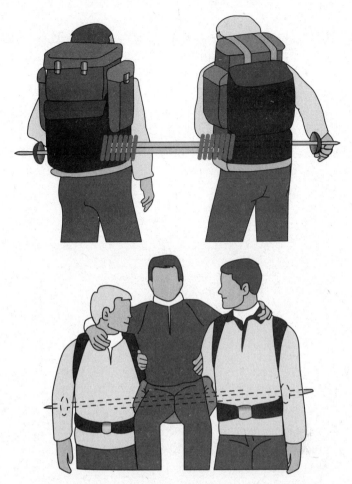

Threading trekking poles through the bottom straps on two packs and then lashing them together can create a sturdy seat for an injured hiker.

SUMMARY

Because sprained ankles and blisters are the most common medical problems that hikers encounter, your first aid kit should contain elastic bandages, plus plenty of inflammation-reducing ibuprofen tablets and adhesive bandages. More severe injuries are thankfully rare, but you should be prepared to apply pressure to stop bleeding, splint and immobilize broken limbs, and treat all serious injuries for life-threatening shock by laying the victim on the ground, keeping them warm, and elevating the victim's feet.

WHERE THE WILD THINGS ARE

I backpacked for five years before I saw my first black bear, yet I have friends who stumbled upon a crowd of bruins on their first hike. That's just the way it is on the trail: you'll encounter nature's wonders according to its own schedule.

The opportunity to observe wildlife in its own environment—rather than at a zoo or on a screen—is one of the prime attractions of hiking and camping. These authentic encounters are never dull, always revealing, and rarely forgettable. But not all members of the animal and plant kingdoms are cute and cuddly all the time. There are several species—like poison ivy and mountain lions—you never want to encounter. More common, but equally aggravating, are pests like squirrels and raccoons that raid your camp food. Whether it's a 600-pound grizzly bear or a deer tick smaller than a grain of rice, this chapter will help you identify the warning signs and take steps to protect yourself from harm.

Look, Don't Touch

Most people know that the warning "leaves of three, leave it be" refers to poison ivy's distinctive three-leaf profile. The same rule applies to poison oak, a poisonous plant common along the West Coast and in the Southeast. The one similarity between the two is that the leaves, roots, and vines are coated with urushiol, the oily toxin that causes skin blisters and rashes on 80 to 90 percent of people who come in contact with it. Since the only method to prevent an allergic reaction to urushiol is to avoid getting it on your skin, your first and only line of defense is to identify and avoid these poisonous plants.

Poison Ivy

Region: Eastern and midwestern United States and Canada (eastern poison ivy); Great Plains, Mountain West (western poison ivy).

Leaves: Clusters of three irregularly shaped leaves with notched edges; changes in color from pink/light green in the spring, to dark green and shiny in the summer, and to red, orange, or yellow in the fall.

Appearance: Eastern variety grows as a low shrub, a forest-floor carpet or a climbing vine, which sprouts dense clusters of reddish rootlets; the western kind only grows as ground vine; all parts of leaves, roots, and vine are toxic.

Habitat: Recently disturbed soil, edges of trails, lakes, wooded areas, and clearings.

 Safety Check Because clusters of three leaves are common to all species of poison ivy and oak, don't touch any three-leafed plant you see on the trail. Tuck your pant legs into your socks when passing through thickets of potentially poisonous plants.

Telltale sign: Clusters of three irregularly shaped notched leaves that appear glossy in summer and the longer stalk supports the central leaf.

Poison Oak

Region: Extremely common in California, as well as Nevada, Oregon, Washington, and into western Canada (Pacific poison oak); prevalent in the Southeast and mid-Atlantic states from Texas to New Jersey (Atlantic poison oak).

Leaves: Clusters of three leaves, 1 to 4 inches long, with smooth, slightly rounded edges (resembling white oak leaves) and offset on the stem; changes in color from reddish-green in spring, to dark green in summer, and to brilliant red or yellow in fall.

Appearance: Dense leafy shrub 3 to 6 feet tall, or climbing vine 30 to 100 feet tall often found on redwoods and Douglas fir trees (only Pacific poison oak).

Habitat: Disturbed areas, especially stream banks, grassy hillsides, and thickets in damp bottomlands, up to elevations of 5,000 feet.

Telltale sign: Clusters of three round-edged leaves that resemble oak leaves.

 Safety Check Never burn poison ivy, poison oak, or any plant that contains urushiol. Flames will vaporize the toxin into the air, where it can still cause serious allergic reactions when it comes in contact with skin.

Treating Skin Reactions

For most people, even brief contact with poison ivy or oak causes a burning, itching, and blistering rash within 2 to 48 hours. The severity of the reaction depends on a person's susceptibility to urushiol and the degree of the encounter—but even a tiny drop of the oily resin can inflame your skin. A person can also be infected by urushiol that's contaminated the fabric of dog leashes, shoes, or clothing.

Fortunately, you can fight back—but you've got to act fast before the urushiol is absorbed by your skin. First, rinse the affected skin with cold water. (Hot water enlarges your skin pores and intensifies the allergic reaction.) Then wash the area with soap and water or an alcohol-based gel hand sanitizer to dissolve any remaining urushiol. If you act within 10 minutes you can remove up to 50 percent of the toxin. After 30 minutes, only 10 percent can be washed off.

If you can't wash off the urushiol, the only realistic treatment is to wait for the skin reactions to clear up, which can take as long as 3 weeks. You can reduce the itching and inflammation by taking oral antihistamines like Benadryl and applying calamine lotion or cortisone-based creams. If the blisters start oozing liquid or break open, cover them with a bandage and keep them as clean as possible. Despite popular misconceptions, the skin rash caused by urushiol is not contagious.

Eat Shoots and Leaves

Not all plants produce rashes; some are actually good to eat. Of course, foraging for natural food isn't as easy as browsing a supermarket. Because some plants—like certain mushrooms and berries—are poisonous to ingest, you should only consume wild plants if you can absolutely, positively identify them as safe. Here is a list of common plants you can find along a trail that are okay to eat:

 Trail Tips   To learn more about making edible plants a part of your menu, check out the book *Identifying and Harvesting Edible and Medicinal Plants in Wild (and Not-So-Wild) Places* (HarperCollins, 1994) by "Wildman" Steve Brill, a New York–based naturalist and edible plant expert.

◊ Pine needles can be gathered all year round and boiled to produce a tea with a high dose of vitamin C, while the protein-rich pollen cones that appear on evergreen boughs in springtime can be eaten raw.

◊ Cattails grow in swamps and wetlands and produce the cigar-shaped tops, but the green leaves that shield the seeds in the late spring are the tastiest part—along with the underground root stems, which are most tender from late fall to early spring.

◊ Daisies produce green leaves that are edible raw, while the white flowers can be boiled to create a bitter-tasting but nutritious tea.

◊ Clover leaves are high in protein and can be eaten raw, or they can be boiled or steamed to make them easier to digest.

◊ Queen Anne's Lace is known for its umbrella-like, lacy white flower, but it's actually a wild carrot and hides a 9-inch-long white taproot underground with a carroty smell that is edible in spring and late fall.

The Bear Essentials

Encountering a bear on the trail is both exciting and terrifying. They are smart, observant, and curious, and can run 30 miles per hour. Like most wild animals, bears don't normally attack people. Any violent encounter is usually caused by a person provoking or scaring a bear or by the animal defending its cubs or a cache of food. Hikers are much more likely to be killed by wasps, domestic dogs, or a horse than by a bear. Still, you should know what to do if you hike around a blind corner and find yourself 100 feet from an equally startled bruin.

Excuse Me, What Kind of Bear Are You?

The first step of any encounter is to identify the bear—and I don't mean asking its name. Knowing whether you are facing a black bear or a grizzly bear will determine how you should react. Most encounters involve black bears, which live in more than 40 states from New Jersey to California. These bruins usually sport a narrow snout, pointed ears, and no shoulder hump, and weigh between 100 and 350 pounds. Black bears aren't necessarily black, however, as their bodies can range from black to dark brown to tan.

If you're hiking in Montana, Wyoming, Idaho, Washington, Alaska, or western Canada, you might be facing a grizzly, which is a type of brown bear. Grizzlies are generally much larger and taller than black bears, with a muscular shoulder hump, short rounded ears, and a dish-shaped face. Encounters with grizzly bears are much less common—and potentially more dangerous—than meetings with black bears.

How to React

If you're facing a black bear, your best defense is a strong offense. Stop moving, raise your arms over your head, and yell in a deep voice for the bear to leave you alone. Black bears will often bolt at the first sign of people. If the black bear doesn't retreat or starts to advance, make more noise, bang trekking poles together, and yell louder. Pelting the bear with sticks and rocks is another technique to drive it away. If a black bear charges (which is extremely rare), you should fight back as hard as you can. A black bear that attacks is looking to make you its next meal.

For grizzlies, your response should be completely different. You never want to provoke a grizzly bear because they are more likely to charge than black bears. However, their goal is to determine if you are a threat—not to eat you. For this reason, hikers should immediately back away from grizzly encounters while speaking calmly. Avoid looking the bear in the eye, which can seem like a sign of aggression.

 Safety Check   Before hiking in grizzly country, you should purchase bear spray as a precaution. A well-aimed blast of aerosolized hot peppers will stop most charging bears in their tracks—and it is much more effective than carrying a firearm. However, make sure the product is sold as a bear spray. Mace and other self-defense sprays aren't powerful enough to deter bears.

If a grizzly bear charges, you should either discharge your bear spray or fall on your stomach and play dead, placing your arms over the back of your neck. Lying down in front of a charging grizzly might seem like suicide, but it's a lot smarter than trying to fight an animal that has 6-inch razor-sharp claws.

Never turn around and run away during any bear encounter. Fleeing will trigger a bear's chase instinct and increase the likelihood that it will charge.

Bear Avoidance

The best bear encounters last under 10 seconds. You see the bear. The bear sees you. The bear vanishes into the trees before you can grab your camera. The best way to have those encounters is to alert a bear to your presence as early as possible. When hiking in bear country, take these precautions to prevent an unsafe encounter:

◊ Make noise as you hike either by talking loudly or by occasionally shouting, "Hey bear!" Bear bells are more annoying to humans than to bears.

◊ Be extra cautious in berry patches or dense foliage where visibility is limited or when you're hiking into the wind.

◊ Hang all of your food and trash in a bear bag (see the later section) or secure it in a metal locker or bear canister placed several hundred feet from your camp.

◊ The presence of a cub means that a concerned mother bear isn't far away. If you spot a cub, immediately retreat from the area.

Say Hello to the 150-Pound Kitty

While much rarer than bear encounters, meetings between hikers and mountain lions are on the rise. In North America, there have been 20 fatal and more than 90 nonfatal attacks in the last century, but the number of violent encounters has increased in the last two decades. Unlike bears, mountain lions might put you on their dinner menu, which means you need to be on high alert when hiking through their territory, especially when alone.

A mountain lion (also known as a cougar) is a large cat weighing between 90 and 180 pounds with a light-colored tan coat and a long tail. Currently, they are only found in the western United States, although there are confirmed sightings as far east as Missouri and Iowa. Still, only about 30,000 cougars are thought to exist in the United States.

Most mountain lions will flee when they spot a human, but some might be young and curious or driven by illness or injury to attack. Unlike bears, mountain lions are ambush predators and typically stalk their prey before leaping 20 to 30 feet for a knockout bite to the back of the neck. Now that I have your attention, here's how to handle a mountain lion that won't run away:

◊ Make yourself appear bigger by lifting your arms, holding a backpack above your head, or opening your coat. You should also shout, grab a branch or rock, and stomp your feet.

◊ If children are present, pick them up or place them behind an adult.

- ◊ Never run—not only does it encourage an attack, but it exposes your back and neck.
- ◊ Fight back aggressively if a mountain lion attacks. Use rocks, branches, trekking poles, and anything you can grab. In February 2019, a trail runner outside Fort Collins, Colorado, suffocated an 80-pound mountain lion that attacked him.
- ◊ Stay on guard even after the animal retreats—mountain lions are persistent predators and will continue to stalk you.

Venomous Snakes

Most of the snakes you see on the trail won't be venomous, including harmless grass, water, and garter snakes. To tell if you're facing a dangerous species like a rattlesnake, water moccasin, or copperhead, look for these characteristics of poisonous snakes:

- ◊ Scales that are shades of brown, gray, or black or have varying colors or stripes
- ◊ A triangular-shaped head
- ◊ A tail capped by a scaly rattle

Because they are cold-blooded, snakes often seek warm, sunny places to rest and regulate their body temperature. That's why hikers will often find snakes lying in the middle of a trail or sunning themselves on a rocky ledge.

If you spot a snake on the trail, back up and give it the space and time to retreat. If a snake won't move out of your way, go around it rather than trying to provoke it or move it with a stick. Remember: A snake can strike from a distance up to one third its body length.

Creepy Crawlies

The fact that there are more insects on Earth than any other kind of animal isn't good news for people who fear them. Since trying to steer clear of bugs is as impractical as trying to dodge raindrops, the best strategy is to minimize contact.

Mosquitoes

Known as bloodsuckers, Jersey bombers, and sand flies, the female mosquito is a heat-seeking insectoid missile with only three goals: mate, drink your blood, and lay her eggs. Peak mosquito season varies by region and climate, but the worst months are generally July and August when frequent rains cause mosquito populations to explode. An itchy bump is the most common result of a mosquito bite, but some species also spread West Nile virus—an infection that causes flulike symptoms and, rarely, a serious form of encephalitis. Protecting yourself from mosquitoes, chiggers, and other biting bugs on the trail requires a multilayered defense that includes these strategies:

 Trail Tips An insect repellent with 30 percent of the active ingredient DEET will remain effective for 5 to 6 hours—the higher percentage of DEET you apply, the longer the dosage works.

◊ Wear light-colored clothing, which is less attractive to mosquitoes and other biting bugs. Learn about hiking clothing embedded with insect repellents like permethrin in Chapter 10.

◊ Apply a bug repellent with at least 30 percent DEET at dusk and dawn, which is when mosquitoes are most active.

◊ Avoid wearing perfumes, fragrances, and scented shampoos and lotions that attract biting bugs.

◊ Mosquitoes prefer shade and have trouble flying when breezes exceed a few miles per hour, so seek out sunny, breezy areas.

◊ Burning mosquito coils or citronella candles can discourage biting bugs from lurking around a campsite, but don't use them inside a tent.

◊ Locate your campsite away from pools of stagnant water where mosquitoes may lay eggs.

Ticks

For a bug the size of a sesame seed, the deer tick creates some extra-large problems for hikers. That's because deer ticks transmit Lyme disease, a bacterial infection that causes joint swelling and fever. The major hot spots for the disease are New York, Connecticut, New Jersey, and Pennsylvania, as well as Wisconsin and Minnesota. But now that Lyme disease has spread to almost every state, avoiding ticks should be a mission for hikers everywhere.

Ticks lie in wait until a potential host—like a hiker or a dog—comes near enough for them to hitch a ride. To avoid giving them a lift, follow these precautions:

◊ Tuck your pant legs into your socks when hiking through tall grasses and dense underbrush.

◊ DEET also repels ticks, so apply it to your legs and arms—but keep it off any synthetic clothing containing spandex or rayon to avoid damaging it.

◊ Avoid sitting or lying down on damp or shady ground where ticks often lurk.

◊ Check your clothes and body for ticks at the end of each day—paying special attention to the backs of the knees, calves, armpits, and groin. Ticks will move to an optimal position on your body before taking a bite.

If you discover a tick on your body, you should remove it quickly. The risk for Lyme disease infection increases 24 to 72 hours after a tick bite. Here's the recommended technique using tweezers or needle-nosed pliers:

1. Grasp the tick by its head, as close to the skin as you can, to be sure to remove all of its mouthparts.

2. Pull slowly and firmly until the tick releases its bite and backs up—don't crush, squeeze, or jerk the tick from your skin.

3. Kill the tick, then clean the bite with an alcohol-based hand sanitizer and place a bandage over it. If a bull's-eye–shaped rash develops around the bite, see a doctor quickly to receive an antibiotic treatment for Lyme disease.

Protecting Your Camp Saves Wildlife

Teaching wild animals to associate food with humans is bad news for everyone. Animals conditioned to seek human food will continue to harass hikers and will teach their offspring to do the same. Bears who raid camps and lose their fear of humans often need to be destroyed. Break the habit by keeping a clean camp, placing your food and trash out of reach, and never feeding wildlife.

Common Camp Raiders

Tough nylon tent fabric might be waterproof, but it's no match for a rodent's sharp teeth. It only takes a few minutes for chipmunks, squirrels, or mice to chew through a tent wall or a backpack pocket to get at your trail mix. Larger mammals like raccoons, skunks, and bears are equally committed to finding your food—and more destructive.

Keeping a Clean Camp

To protect yourself and your campsite from these four-legged raiders, you should place food, trash, and items with strong odors beyond their reach. If you are car-camping, you can lock your trash in the trunk of your vehicle unless signs warn against it. You can also use metal lockers if the campsite provides them. Cabins and lean-to shelters will protect you from the elements but often attract marauding rodents. Suspend your food and trash from the ceiling, hang it outside, or place it in a locker. Here are some additional tips to keep your campsite odor-free and animal-free:

◊ Choose the cleanest section of campground to set up your tent.

◊ Because smells linger where you cook, locate your camp kitchen at least 200 feet (70 steps) downwind from your tent or sleeping area.

◊ Double-bag all of your trash and food scraps to reduce odors.

Hanging a Bear Bag

At most backcountry campsites, you'll need to hang a bear bag—a stuff sack filled with your food, trash, and smelly toiletries—at least 10 feet off the ground. You should hang a bag even when bears aren't present because this method will also protect your food from other mammals and rodents. Alternatives to bear bags when it comes to food storage include hard-sided plastic canisters (required in Yosemite National Park because the local black bears are experts at dismantling bear bags), or a tough, puncture-proof fabric sack such as Ursack's AllMitey. At night, these containers should be placed at least 100 feet from your campsite and away from ledges and bodies of water or rivers.

If hanging a bear bag is your chosen approach, the best time to do it is after you're finished with dinner but before the sun sets. Before you get started, you'll need to collect the following gear:

◊ 50 to 100 feet of ¼-inch nylon rope

◊ A large nylon stuff sack with a drawstring closure

◊ A metal carabiner to attach the stuff sack to the rope

◊ A small rock to help you toss the rope over tree branches

◊ A hiking sock to hold the rock—a glove also works

◊ All of your food, trash, and smelly toiletries

Next, you need to walk at least 200 feet from your campsite and find two tall trees at least 15 to 20 feet apart and with thick branches 20 to 25 feet off the ground. Once you find a good spot, follow these steps:

1. Place the rock in the sock and tie one end of the rope to the open end of the sock.

2. While holding on to the free end of the rope, throw the rock/sock over one of the branches. Watch out for ricochets.

3. Tie the free end of the rope securely around the first tree trunk, and then repeat the rock/sock throw over the branch on the other tree while keeping the middle of the rope on the ground.

4. Tie the carabiner to the middle of the rope and attach it to the stuff sack.

5. Untie the sock from the rope and pull on that end until the stuff sack is raised at least 10 to 12 feet off the ground. Because the weight of the sack will cause the rope to sag, you need to pick branches much higher than 10 feet.

6. Tie the end of the rope around the second tree trunk and check to make sure all knots are secure.

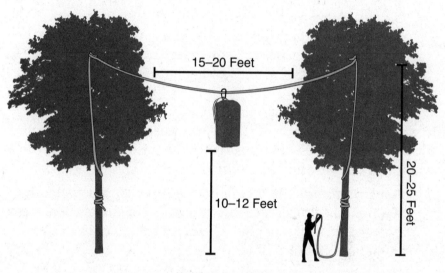

15–20 Feet

20–25 Feet

10–12 Feet

Hanging a bear bag.

Observing Wildlife

Wild animals are masters of concealment, stealthy movements, and quick getaways. If you want your animal encounters to involve more than luck, you need to adapt your hiking style to how nature works. Elk, bobcats, and red foxes don't punch a time clock, but they do follow certain patterns and routines that—if you know them—can increase your odds of a sighting.

Cowboy movies taught us to tread softly and stay upwind when sneaking up on someone. But when it comes to observing wildlife, your success will depend more on timing. Here are suggestions on the times of day you'll want to be on high alert:

◊ Dusk and dawn are the most active times of the day for most animals—except for raptors like hawks and vultures that prefer to soar on warm afternoon air.

◊ Overcast, drizzly weather encourages animals to move, while bright sunshine and storms send them under cover.

◊ Activity also varies by season, with elk and deer more visible during their fall mating season, bears gorging themselves on berries in September and October, and eagles flying high during spring migration.

Animals are almost always on high alert for predators or prey. To overcome their watchfulness, hikers need to take advantage of the terrain. These next tips provide advice on how to hide and where to look:

◊ Transition zones, like the edge of a forest or the beginning of a tree line (the elevation on a mountain slope where trees stop growing), create high-contrast backgrounds where animals are more visible.

◊ All animals are attracted to water, making the shores of ponds and lakes excellent places to lie in wait.

◊ Take a lesson from hunters and wear drab shades of green and tan instead of bright reds and yellows. Many animals, including birds, bighorn sheep, and black bears, can see colors.

◊ Animals with poor eyesight, including moose and deer, are better at detecting movement. Once you've picked a stakeout spot, remain as motionless as possible.

Stranger Dangers

It's generally a good idea to talk to people you meet along the trail, or it's good to at least nod and say hello. Hikers coming from the opposite direction can give you news about the trail ahead and tell you the distance to your objective. However, if you are hiking alone, or you feel uncomfortable stopping to talk to someone, trust your instincts and move on. Breaking contact and hiking away is the best solution. Other smart precautions include never camping within sight of roads, signing all trail registers, leaving your itinerary with a trusted friend, and never hitchhiking—especially if you are alone.

SUMMARY

You should be able to distinguish between a black bear (narrow snout, pointed ears) and a grizzly bear (dish-shaped face, muscular shoulder hump), but even more important is to spot and avoid the unevenly notched, triple leaves of poison ivy and poison oak. Keep mosquitoes, ticks, and biting insects at bay with spray-on repellents containing at least 30 percent of the active ingredient DEET—but avoid getting it on clothing containing spandex or rayon. If your goal is to see wildlife, stake out lakes, rivers, and the edges of forests and meadows at dusk or dawn. To keep bears and rodents from raiding your food, hang a bear bag at night or use a tough-sided bear canister or puncture-resistant sack.

CHAPTER 19

HIGH-COUNTRY HAZARDS

"Because it's there," is how British mountaineer George Mallory explained his desire to climb Mount Everest, the tallest mountain in the world. Any hiker who looks up at a high peak can understand why.

Seeking steeper, more advanced terrain is natural for an activity that's all about exploration. Standing atop a mountain summit provides a sense of accomplishment that few other feats can match. But how do you get up there? And more importantly, how do you get back down? Hiking a mountain trail isn't a walk in the park. Any route that gains elevation, even if it doesn't reach a summit, adds new risks. But if you can hike forest trails, you can make the transition to high-country ridges and scrambles. To help you tackle mountain trails, this chapter will identify and explain the unique challenges found at higher elevations. Every hiker should treat mountains with respect and know when the risks outweigh the rewards. After all, a year after Mallory uttered his famous quote, he disappeared while climbing on Everest.

So, let's be careful up there.

Finding Mountains

Before you climb a mountain, you need to find one. The tallest peaks are the most famous and tempting, but I suggest putting off the Himalayas for now. The closest most hikers should get to Mount Everest is to read *Into Thin Air*, Jon Krakauer's riveting account of the 1996 climbing disaster on that peak (Anchor Books, 1999). Instead, search for local summits with challenging trails within your skill level. Every state has a high point, and mountain ranges can be found in all regions of the country, not just out West. Most people forget the Ozarks in Arkansas, Michigan's Porcupine Range, and that West Virginia's nickname is the Mountain State.

 Trail Tips   The hands-down best resource for learning more about high-elevation hiking, scrambling, and climbing is *Mountaineering: The Freedom of the Hills*, now in its ninth edition (Mountaineers Books, 2017). For more information, go to mountaineersbooks.org.

If there aren't mountains nearby, check a regional trail book for hikes with the biggest elevation changes. Long ridgelines, a common feature in the Appalachian Mountains, can offer the same strenuous climbs and superb views offered by peaks but without a notable summit. And don't restrict yourself to looking up—some of the steepest and most challenging trails descend into river valleys, ravines, and canyons.

Two websites devoted exclusively to mountain hikes are summitpost.org and peakware.com. Both provide maps, routes, and up-to-date trip reports posted by everyday hikers. Although high-profile peaks like Mount Rainier get top billing on these websites, you can still find helpful information about lesser-known mountains in your area—including a trip report about climbing Campbell Hill, which at an elevation of 1,550 feet, is the highest point in my home state of Ohio.

Navigating Steep Trails

All trails go up and down, but when a trail gets steep or skirts the edge of a cliff, hikers face an increased risk of falling. This threat is called *exposure,* and its severity is determined by factors like the angle of the slope, the presence of drop-offs, and the difficulty of the terrain. Exposure is a hiking term that describes a hiker's vulnerability to falling at a particular spot. The more exposure a trail has, the more dangerous a fall would be. In general, a trail with significant exposure means you couldn't stop yourself if you tripped and tumbled down a slope.

All trails have some exposure, but it's more common on mountain and ridge trails because of the constant changes in elevation. How can you tell how challenging a trail might be? Most guidebooks assign trails an overall rating like difficult, moderate, or easy, but they might also rate specific sections of trails using a standardized approach like the Yosemite Decimal System. This rating system, shown in the following table, divides routes into five classes based on the difficulty of the terrain. The vast majority of hiking trails are categorized as Class 1 and Class 2. Steep and rocky approaches to high peaks, like the Keyhole Route on Colorado's Longs Peak or the Knife Edge Ridge on Maine's Katahdin, are considered Class 3 scrambles, while Class 4 trails are rare and generally unclimbable without safety ropes and harnesses.

Yosemite Decimal System for Trail Difficulty

Class	Difficulty
1	Flat terrain; no risk of falling
2	Regular hiking, with occasional use of the hands for extra balance; little risk of falling
3	Hiking that requires use of the hands with increased exposure; falls could cause severe but nonfatal injuries
4	Hiking and climbing on steep slopes with significant exposure; bad falls could be fatal
5	Technical climbing using ropes, harnesses, and helmets; falls would result in severe injury or death

Maintaining Balance

Whether or not you have a good sense of balance, everything changes when you put on a pack and hike a steep trail. Unlike flat trails, which you can often navigate on autopilot, rugged trails require constant adjustments to your body and balance. Follow these tips to stay upright and moving:

◊ Tighten pack straps against your shoulders, chest, and waist, so the load doesn't sway as you move.

◊ Lean slightly forward as you climb and slightly backward as you descend to keep your center of gravity over your feet.

◊ Walk slowly and loosely without jerky movements that could throw you off balance.

◊ Take small, measured steps instead of long strides, which strain your muscles and can upset your balance.

Fear Is a Good Thing

If you don't like heights, pat yourself on the back. Being acrophobic—afraid of heights—encourages hikers to be cautious. However, your fear doesn't need to hold you back. If you approach a section of trail that seems outside your comfort zone, stop, take a deep breath, and consider these options before you continue:

◊ Figure out how you will get back down before climbing any higher. If it looks too hard, don't continue.

◊ Make sure everyone in a group verbally agrees to continue hiking, and watch out for peer pressure.

◊ Recognize symptoms of summit fever—the drive to keep going that overrides more rational reasons to stop.

◊ Consider the time of day and forecasted weather—two factors unrelated to the terrain that still impact your safety.

◊ Imagine how things could go wrong and whether you are capable of dealing with them.

Getting in Pole Position

Adding a pair of trekking poles to your gear arsenal can temporarily make you a quadruped and absorb many pounds of pressure that would normally impact your joints during the course of a hike. Here are all the ways they can help:

 Trail Tips When hiking downhill, increase the length of your trekking poles several inches to give your arms additional reach. Likewise, shorten the poles when going uphill.

- ◊ Reduce the impact of each step on your legs and knees—especially while descending trails.
- ◊ Provide two additional points of contact to improve your balance on trails or while crossing rivers.
- ◊ Test rocks for stability and push away branches and thorns.
- ◊ Help establish a consistent pace.
- ◊ Boost your speed by engaging your arm muscles to push your body forward.
- ◊ Help construct splints, temporary shelters, or rescue litters (see Chapter 17), or fend off animals.

Most poles are made with two or three sliding sections of carbon fiber and aluminum that can be adjusted to different lengths and come with comfortable foam or cork grips, wrist straps, and durable carbide tips. To correctly adjust a pole to fit your height, stand on flat ground and hold the pole so that your elbow makes a 90-degree angle and then lock the sliding sections in place.

Basic Mountaineering Skills

On rugged trails, you're more likely to encounter sections that are steep enough to require the use of your hands for balance and extra protection. Called scrambling, this type of hiking is the most adventurous exploring you can do without technical equipment like ropes and harnesses. Although scrambling might seem dangerous at first, building confidence in your skills is the best way to tackle more challenging terrain.

How to Scramble

Anytime you need to use your hands while hiking, it's considered scrambling. Grabbing a rock or a tree branch isn't cheating—it's the natural way to overcome steep terrain. The ways to scramble are as varied as the obstacles you'll encounter on the trail. While descending a steep trail, grab roots and branches that you've identified as sturdy to help lower your body over drop-offs and slow your forward motion. You can even sit down to get over ledges or descend rocky slabs—a technique informally known as the butt slide.

The keys to safe scrambling are maintaining several points of contact at one time and keeping your center of balance directly over your feet. You can also maximize the amount of friction your feet create with the ground using these two techniques:

◊ Smearing allows you to walk up or down slanted rocks by pressing as much of your shoe's sole—not just the toes— onto the rock as possible to increase your traction. The steepness of terrain that you can ascend or descend using only the friction of your shoes will surprise you.

◊ Edging involves digging the inside or outside edge of your shoe or boot into the rock or dirt to give you a better grip. Edging is often helpful while traversing—cutting laterally across—steep slopes or trails.

Scree and Talus

Mountains have their own peculiar terrain, and two rocky challenges that you'll only discover where elevation changes abruptly are *scree* (small stony rock fragments) and *talus* (larger rocks and boulders that often have sharp edges). These are loose and unstable rock fragments that break off from slopes and cliffs and accumulate as large piles along trails, ridges, and cliffs. Hiking up and down slopes covered by scree and talus can be an exhausting and frustrating process unless you practice the following methods.

For scree:

◊ **Going up:** Prevent scree's "one step forward, two steps back" slippage by kicking secure steps into the loose rocks with the toe of your boot.

◊ **Going down:** Stay in control as you slide down scree-covered slopes by leaning back on your heels and taking long, plunging steps to push the rubble in front of you and slow your descent.

For talus:

◊ **Going up:** Avoid twisting your ankle on unstable rocks by tapping them with a trekking pole or hand (unstable rocks sound hollow) before placing your weight on them; step on the upslope edge to prevent rocks from rolling over onto your foot.

◊ **Going down:** Weave back and forth to slow your descent; lean back to keep your weight over your feet.

 Safety Check When scrambling up or down talus and scree slopes, avoid climbing directly above another person—any rocks you dislodge could strike those below. Climb line abreast, or diagonally, or stay very close together to prevent dislodged rocks from gaining speed before reaching another person.

Hiking on Snow and Ice

The air temperature drops 3.5°F for every 1,000 feet of elevation gain, which make mountains an excellent place to encounter snow and ice—even when you least expect it. During an early autumn hike at Mount Rainier National Park, my wife and I left the White River campground in a drizzle and arrived at our campsite—2,000 vertical feet later—in a ferocious blizzard. Hiking through snow requires not only wearing the insulated clothing mentioned in Chapter 10 but also strategies to save energy and stay safe. Whether you're prepared for snow or it catches you by surprise, here's how to keep your hike on track:

◊ If the temperature fluctuates around freezing, hike early in the morning on hard, frozen snow that can support your weight. By midafternoon, the sun will soften the snow so that your boots will punch through.

◊ On steep, snowy slopes, kick steps with the toe of your boot and edge as much as possible.

◊ Wearing snowshoes can enable you to walk on top of deep, unpacked snow (see Chapter 20).

◊ Add plastic baskets to the tip of your trekking poles to give them more traction on snow—or carry ski poles.

◊ Rotate the demanding role of breaking trail in deep snow among all members of a group.

River Crossings

Water can only flow downhill, which means that hikers on mountain slopes and ridges will often encounter rivers and streams—sometimes multiple times in a single day. Some trails have bridges, but most of the time, you'll need to cross on rocks and logs or wade. Because drowning is the second leading cause of death in the outdoors after falls, the first rule for river crossings is simple: never attempt a crossing where the water level is higher than your waist. Hike along the bank to find a safer place to cross or figure out an alternate route. Rivers and streams are often easier to cross at wider points, where the water is shallower and flows more slowly. Once you determine a spot to ford, follow this advice to keep yourself out of the drink:

◊ Always unbuckle the waist and sternum straps on your backpack and loosen the shoulder straps so you can drop your pack if you fall in. A pack on your back will force your head underwater.

◊ When wading, face upstream and shuffle sideways across the river, probing the bottom with a trekking pole or long stick.

◊ Wear sandals or shoes to protect your feet from sharp rocks and improve your traction—many hikers pack extra shoes to wear for water crossings.

◊ If you cross in your hiking boots or shoes, remove your socks to keep them dry.

◊ Protect electronic gear like cell phones and GPS devices by sealing them in plastic bags.

 Safety Check If you fall into a fast-flowing river, float on your back and point your legs downstream with your toes up. Use your legs to rebound off rocks, and don't try to swim or stand up until you reach calmer water.

Severe Weather

Thunderstorms are scary enough when they roll through town on a summer afternoon. Now imagine you're standing on a ridgeline watching menacing clouds advance your way. Sound scarier? It is. Hiking at high elevations, and especially on exposed slopes and ridges, increases your exposure to severe weather like thunderstorms, high winds, rain, and blizzards.

Trail Tips To calculate how far away a thunderstorm is from your location, divide the number of seconds between the lightning and thunder by 5 to determine the distance in miles. For example, a delay of 10 seconds means the storm is 2 miles away—which is extremely close. Start looking for cover when a thunderstorm is 6 miles (a gap of 30 seconds) away.

Knowing the weather forecast can tell you what to expect, but it won't tell you when you need to seek cover. Hikers at high elevations need to stay alert by scanning the horizon. Storms can develop and intensify much more quickly than you think.

Lightning Danger

Lightning is naturally attracted to tall, isolated objects. The fact that it's targeting a lone tree, a church steeple, or a person standing on a ridgeline doesn't matter much to lightning's 100 million volts of electricity. In 2018, 20 people were killed by lightning in the United States, including five struck while walking or fishing. More people die in July than in any other month, and Florida is the deadliest state. Besides avoiding Orlando in the summer, here are several tips on how to avoid becoming one of next year's statistics:

Safety Check Follow the 30/30 rule: Seek shelter when 30 seconds or less separate lightning and thunder, and remain under cover for 30 minutes after the last thunderclap.

◊ Stay off exposed ridges or above the tree line after 12 P.M., when most lightning strikes occur. This is especially true for mountain ranges in the West and during the summer months.

◊ Seek cover well before a thunderstorm is on top of you—bolts can travel 10 miles before striking the ground.

◊ Most people struck by lightning are standing under lone tall trees or in a body of water. Stay away from both during storms.

Avoiding Strikes

Once you determine a storm is heading your way, you should take cover. If you're in an exposed location, descend into valleys, gullies, and other areas lower than the surrounding terrain. Avoid tall, isolated objects (like trees, pinnacles, or cliffs) and any place with flowing water, which can conduct electricity. When you find a safe place to wait out the storm, follow these steps:

1. Remove your backpack and discard metal items like tent and trekking poles.

2. Place a sleeping pad or jacket under your feet and crouch down on top of it.

3. Stay at least 30 feet away from other people to prevent one bolt from incapacitating an entire group.

4. If you're in a tent, stay inside, crouch on your sleeping pad, and avoid touching any metal poles.

High Winds

It might be invisible, but a cold, harsh wind can steal your body heat faster than you think. The windchill created by a 25 mile-per-hour headwind can turn a 35°F day into a frigid 7°F freeze fest. If you're wearing clothes that are damp from a sweaty climb or a light drizzle, you'll lose heat even quicker. Hikers at high elevations should hide from chilling winds whenever possible. The unobstructed terrain means that gusts blow even stronger, turning mountain passes and ridge crests into ferocious wind tunnels. To protect yourself from high winds, follow these tips:

◊ Put on windproof layers before you reach the top of a ridge or mountain pass.

◊ Hike just below ridgelines on the shoulder of a slope to avoid gusts coming over the crest.

◊ Take rest breaks behind natural shelters like boulders and depressions that protect you from the wind.

◊ Protect extremities like your hands, feet, nose, and ears from exposure to frostbite.

◊ Recognize flying saucer–shaped lenticular clouds hovering over mountain peaks and ridges, which often indicate high winds.

Low Visibility

Fog, driving rain, and blizzards can not only block great views, but they can obscure landmarks and reference points and increase the risk of becoming lost. Low-level clouds and storms are common at higher elevations because air cools and condenses as it rises, creating a ground-hugging mist. If you're unprepared for low visibility or feel disoriented, turn around and return to the trailhead or stop and wait until visibility improves. In blizzard conditions, seek shelter on the leeward side (the side protected from the wind) of a boulder or stand of trees and wait out the storm. If you need to keep moving despite reduced visibility, follow these guidelines to stay on the right track.

◊ Mark your position on a map and note the compass bearing you need to follow to reach safety.

◊ Keep groups close together to avoid becoming separated and use whistles to find each other if it happens.

◊ Pay close attention to blazes and markings to stay on proper trails.

◊ Stop and check your position using a compass, map, or GPS more often than you would in normal visibility conditions.

 Trail Tips Mountain summits and ridge crests where trails meet and diverge are common places to lose a trail or get turned around. Before you reach the top, take a moment to memorize or mark your arrival route, and note its position relative to where you need to go next.

Overnight at High Elevation

Of all the places to spend the night without shelter, an exposed, high place is one of the worst. Not only will it likely be cold and windy, but the higher you go, the harder it is to find sheltering terrain. That's one reason why the majority of national park rescues occur in mountainous areas after hikers are waylaid by tougher-than-expected routes, injuries, or bad navigation. So, if the sun begins to set while you're still hiking up high, you need to make some tough choices. Should you:

1. Continue hiking?
2. Stop and find shelter where you are?
3. Seek out a more protected location at a lower elevation?

The right answer depends on many factors, including your hiking experience and navigation skills, and the distance to a safe place (using the same wilderness survival considerations mentioned in Chapter 16). But when you're hiking in exposed terrain, the stakes are much higher.

In most cases, you should seek shelter in the most protected place you can find before it gets too dark to safely move. Descending mountain trails after dark, even with headlamps in fine weather, isn't safe, especially on trails with significant exposure. Instead, you should hunker down. If you're carrying a tent or a solar blanket, set them up and crawl inside. Otherwise, make a shelter with what nature provides and follow this plan:

1. Seek out a shallow depression, a stack of boulders, or an overhanging rock. You can improve its protection by stacking rocks or branches on the windward side.
2. Place as much insulating material between you and the ground as possible to prevent heat loss.
3. Get inside a sleeping bag if you have one, or put on your warmest clothes and a hat.
4. Once you stop moving, drink and eat to help your body generate more heat.
5. Mark the trail or the route to safety so you know which direction to travel when morning arrives.

SUMMARY

Hiking peaks and ridgelines adds excitement to an outing, but it also increases the danger of falls and injuries caused by more exposure on steeper trails. Before climbing higher, make sure your pack is balanced, your footwear can grip angled slopes, and everyone in your group is okay to continue. Keep an eye on the sky and your map or GPS when hiking above the tree line, because up there you're more exposed to high winds and thunderstorms, and route-finding is more challenging without a well-blazed trail, especially in low-visibility conditions.

CHAPTER 20

EXPANDING YOUR SKILLS

If you find yourself asking "What's next?" as you plan another hiking trip, it might be time to raise the bar. By this point you've mastered key outdoor skills. You can light a one-match fire, navigate with a topographical map, and hang a bear bag on the first try—at least most of the time. In other words, you've gone day-hiking, camping, and backpacking enough times that you're looking for a fresh challenge. Fortunately, the great outdoors offers plenty.

This chapter explains how you can take your adventures to the next level. Some of these new adventures involve sports you already love—like biking or kayaking. Others build on basic skills—like wilderness first aid or avalanche safety—by seeking more advanced training. The list in this chapter is by no means exhaustive. You can combine hiking with almost any kind of outdoor activity you love—and maybe even invent some new ones. So, enjoy yourself—you'll never run out of fun!

Hiking at Night

Several years ago, I went on a backpacking trip to the bottom of the Grand Canyon. A late-afternoon start meant that our group was soon hiking in the dark. But when a full moon rose above the rim, we all realized that we could see better if we turned our headlamps off and hiked by moonlight alone. So, we hiked the last three miles to our campsite bathed in the blue-gray light of the moon reflecting off the canyon walls. It was one of the best parts of the trip.

Fun After Dark

Elsewhere in this book, I advise against hiking at night. Reduced visibility heightens the risk of a twisted ankle or a missed trail junction. However, if you plan ahead and bring the right gear, hiking in the dark can be an exciting way to experience a sunrise from a mountain peak or a beautiful starry sky.

 Trail Tips Your eyes require 20 to 30 minutes to completely adjust to low-light conditions. Any flash of bright, white light will instantly reset the process.

Illuminating the trail with headlamps is the most conventional way to hike at night. But because of the way your eyes respond to bright light, you won't be able to see much beyond where it shines on the ground. If your headlamp has adjustable brightness, setting it to a lower intensity can make it easier to see by allowing your eyes to partially adjust to the darkness.

Using Only Your Eyes

Hiking without the aid of a headlamp is more fun, but it requires the right conditions and a little daring. First, our eyes need some light and shadows to be able to distinguish terrain features. A full moon or ambient light reflecting off low-level clouds can increase the overall brightness to an acceptable level. If the conditions allow for it, here's how to hike without headlamps:

◊ Night hiking only works when everyone turns off their lights. Any bright, white light will dilate your pupils and ruin your night vision.

◊ Because red-tinted light doesn't damage your night vision, you can use a red LED bulb or tape red cellophane over a white LED to be able to read a map.

◊ To see an object better in low light, don't look directly at it. Instead, swing your head from side to side and use your peripheral vision, which is better for seeing in low light.

◊ You can improve your night vision through repeated practice.

Navigating Off-Trail

On most hikes, you'll follow an established trail from start to finish, but sometimes, it can be fun—or essential—to move cross-country. For instance, your map could indicate that a hot springs or a ghost town you want to check out is hidden several hundred yards from a trail. To reach those locations, you need to determine which direction to hike. With a GPS-enabled cell phone or device, it's easy—you create a waypoint for the destination on the base map and follow the navigation guides until you reach it. When using a map and compass, however, you need to take a bearing—a skill that builds on the navigation techniques I covered in Chapter 6.

Before you can take a bearing, however, you need to adjust your orienteering compass for the local declination and orient it to a topographical map—two steps outlined in Chapter 6. You should review both of those steps (and the parts of a compass) before reading how to take a bearing in the field using the following steps:

1. Place your map flat on the ground. Place your compass on the map so that the side edge of the baseplate is parallel to a straight line connecting your present location to your intended destination. A good way to check this is to make sure the compass's fixed direction-of-travel arrow is also pointed toward your destination.

2. Hold the baseplate stationary and rotate the compass dial until the orienting arrow is aligned with the map's north arrow and its north-south grid lines. Look for your bearing—a reading like 85 degrees—under the index line of the compass.

3. If your compass housing can't be adjusted for local declination, either subtract or add the declination (indicated in the map legend) from the initial bearing to determine your corrected bearing. Rotate the compass housing to reflect this corrected degree measurement.

4. To follow the bearing to your destination, stand up and hold the compass flat in your hand (without rotating the compass dial) and turn your body until the red magnetic needle is "boxed" inside the orienting arrow. Where the direction-of-travel arrow is pointing is the direction you want to hike.

5. Because you'll quickly drift off course if you try to follow a bearing cross-country, pick a landmark, like a rock or tree, several hundred feet ahead along the same line as the bearing. Walk to the landmark, and then pick another landmark along the same course. Continue walking from point to point until you reach your off-trail destination.

Hiking Long Trails

The Appalachian Trail (AT) and the John Muir Trail are two of the many long-distance footpaths that stretch hundreds—and sometimes thousands—miles across the continent. Some of these trails are new and still under construction, while others are well established and host hundreds of hikers a year. The most famous long-distance hiking route is the AT, a well-blazed 2,178-mile route that runs from Georgia to Maine and takes about 6 months to complete. The table on the next page summarizes America's most popular long trails.

At first glance, the mileage of these trails might appear daunting. Hiking 100 or 200 miles is an incredible undertaking, let alone trips of 1,000 or 2,000 miles—but not everyone attempts to hike a long trail in a single trip as thru-hikers do. You can also be a section hiker and break a longer trail down into multiple, shorter trips. Section hiking is also a good way to target the most scenic parts of a long trail.

Name/Website	State(s)	Length (miles)	Website
Appalachian Trail	GA-ME	2,178	appalachiantrail.org
Long Trail	VT	270	greenmountainclub.org
Benton MacKaye Trail	NC	300	bmta.org
Mountains-to-Sea Trail	NC	500	mountainstoseatrail.org
Florida Trail	FL	1,400	floridatrail.org
Buckeye Trail	OH	1,400	buckeyetrail.org
Ice Age Trail	WI	600	iceagetrail.org
Pacific Crest Trail	CA-WA	2,650	pcta.org
Continental Divide Trail	NM-MT	3,100	continentaldividetrail.org
John Muir Trail	CA	211	johnmuirtrail.org
Colorado Trail	CO	500	coloradotrail.org
Arizona Trail	AZ	800	aztrail.org

Given how intense thru-hiking can be, it's not surprising that an entire culture has grown up around the activity. For instance, thru-hikers don't use their real names on the trail but are assigned a humorous trail name like "Hotrod" or "Wrongway" by other hikers. Most become devotees of ultralight backpacking and learn to cook creative meals using Pop-Tarts, candy bars, and instant mashed potatoes. Hikers on long trails are all ages, but most are either in their 20s, having just graduated from school, or in their 50s and 60s, taking an active approach to retirement.

 Trail Tips Bill Bryson's book *A Walk in the Woods* (see Resources) is a laugh-out-loud account of his attempt to hike the Appalachian Trail that is also the quintessential example of how *not* to plan a long-distance trip. Read this book to laugh and learn.

Winter Hiking and Camping

Summer weekends between June and September are the peak season for hiking and camping. More experienced hikers, however, don't put away their sleeping bags and tents in October—or even in December. These hikers know how to enjoy winter's benefits—no bugs or humidity, fewer people on the trails, and more breathtaking views.

Stay Warm When It's Cold

Naturally, most people's biggest concern is how to stay warm when the temperature is 40°F, 30°F, or even 20°F. When you're moving on the trail, it's actually easy. As you hike, your body burns energy and produces heat in the process. If you are wearing the right layers of clothing, you should be able to keep your body temperature in a comfortable zone. It's only when you stop moving or when you're sitting around a campsite that winter's chill makes itself known. Here are several heat-preserving tips:

◊ Bring a four-season tent, which will have more fabric than mesh in the walls and strong poles to withstand high winds and snow accumulation.

◊ Pack a sleeping bag with a temperature rating at least 5°F below the predicted nighttime low—and lower if you get cold easily or expect a serious windchill.

◊ Sleeping on a cushy sleeping pad—at least one inch thick—will do more to keep you warm at night than anything else.

◊ Remove extra layers and increase air circulation against your skin the moment you notice yourself sweating—damp clothing will rob your body heat at a ferocious rate.

◊ Drink plenty of liquids, including soup and hot cocoa, because it's often difficult to notice dehydration in cold weather.

 Trail Tips Consistently cold temperatures on winter hikes make it possible for hikers to bring food like meat, soft cheese, and sauces that would normally spoil outside a refrigerator.

Shoes Built for Snow

Deep snow is great for building a fort or a snowman, but it's a serious obstacle for hiking. With every step, your boots break through the brittle surface snow in an exhausting process called *post-holing,* which can also soak your feet. The solution is a pair of snowshoes, which spread your weight over a larger surface area on snow so your feet don't punch through.

Snowshoes also come in various models and styles for different winter activities. Recreational models are designed to be light and fast and are used by day-hikers and racers. Expedition or backcountry models are designed for backpacking on steep, slick slopes. All major snowshoe manufacturers—including Tubbs, Atlas, MSR, and Redfeather—also sell women-specific snowshoes, which have a narrower frame to match a woman's stride.

Trips That Go Beyond the Trail

Hiking isn't only about the miles you hiked or the elevation you climbed. For some people, hiking and camping is a vehicle to explore other aspects of the outdoors. Hobbies like photography and birdwatching can be enhanced by spending time on a trail, as can stargazing and fly fishing. There are dozens of activities—including the ones described next—that are made even better by being outdoors.

Learn to Save Lives

No one starts a hike hoping they'll get to splint a leg or stanch a bleeding wound—unless that hike is part of a wilderness first aid course. Offered by organizations across the country, these courses teach first aid skills through hands-on scenarios, even using fake blood to make the training more realistic.

The first and most basic level of additional first aid training is a two-day course called Wilderness First Aid (WFA), which teaches students how to make splints, stop severe bleeding, and treat hypothermia. More advanced lifesaving skills are taught at weeklong Wilderness First Responder (WFR) and monthlong Wilderness Emergency Medical Technician (WEMT) courses. Here's a summary of the three types of classes offered:

◊ **Wilderness First Aid (WFA).** Type: Introduction to treating injuries in backcountry settings; duration: 2 days

◊ **Wilderness First Responder (WFR).** Type: Advanced care for diagnosing, stabilizing, and evacuating more serious injuries; designed for outdoor educators and guides; duration: 5–7 days

◊ **Wilderness EMT (WEMT).** Type: Professional-level urban and wilderness medicine certification; duration: 1 month

To find when and where wilderness first aid courses will be offered in your area, check out the websites for these major teaching organizations:

◊ Wilderness Medicine Institute: nols.edu/wmi

◊ SOLO: soloschools.com

◊ Wilderness Medicine Associates: wildmed.com

◊ REI: rei.com/events

Get Schooled on Avalanche Safety

Every winter, 20 to 40 people die in avalanches in North America. While backcountry skiers and snowmobilers are most at risk, hikers and climbers can also trigger these deadly slides. Learning how to assess avalanche risk is a science best taught by experts at schools like the Colorado Mountain School (coloradomountainschool.com), The Mountain Guides (jhmg. com), and The International Mountain Climbing School (ime-usa.com/imcs); you can also learn how to assess avalanche risk at popular ski areas or climbing mountains. Multiday courses teach students how to evaluate terrain risk, test snow conditions, and conduct rescue operations.

Get on Board with Geocaching

Geocaching is a fun and popular game that both adults and kids can enjoy. Like an outdoor treasure hunt, geocaching combines hiking and orienteering as players follow navigational clues to solve puzzles and locate small containers of trinkets hidden in parks and recreation areas. It's easy to get started with smartphone apps like Geocaching (freely available for iOS and Android) or Cachly (iOS, $5), or by downloading coordinates and clues from websites like geocaching.com or opencaching.us to a standalone GPS device. Thanks to the increasing accuracy and proliferation of GPS-enabled smartphones and devices, geocaching is growing like wildfire; there are more than 3 million active caches around the world today. Chances are there's a geocache less than 5 miles from where you're currently standing.

Each geocache is assigned a difficulty rating ranging from 1 (easy to find) to 5 (extremely well hidden). They can be concealed in tall grasses, inside hollow trees, and even underwater—but they aren't allowed to be buried. Each cache's GPS coordinates will get you within 20 to 50 feet of its location, and then you use the extra clues to find the actual box. Remember, it's important that anyone searching for a cache should follow Leave No Trace guidelines to avoid trampling plants, disturbing the ground, or leaving behind any trash.

Race to More Adventure

If mountain biking, kayaking, and rappelling off tall cliffs sounds like fun to you—why not do it all in one trip? You can if you compete in an adventure race. An adventure race is like a backcountry triathlon in which competitors test their outdoor skills and overall stamina. Teams of two to five people race to complete a series of checkpoints on foot, bike, kayak, and even horseback. Unlike regular races, competitors not only need to be fast, they also need to master certain skills like rock climbing, map-reading (GPS devices often are not allowed), and knot-tying to overcome the obstacles in their path. To learn more or to search for adventure races in your area, check out the website for the United States Adventure Racing Association, at usara.com.

Giving Back to the Outdoors

The next time you encounter a series of well-cut log steps on the trail, remember that they didn't get there on their own. Most trail work is accomplished by volunteers—hikers just like you who devote an afternoon or a weekend to building and repairing the trails they enjoy the rest of the year

Groups like the Sierra Club (sierraclub.org) arrange multiple service trips every year, as does the Appalachian Mountain Club (outdoors.org) along the East Coast. Local trail conservancies and environmental groups often organize projects, too. Plus, on the first Saturday in June, the American Hiking Society (americanhiking.org) celebrates National Trails Day, an event where many outdoor organizations schedule service projects.

Hiking for a Higher Goal

Want to find a ghost town, an old mining camp, or an out-of-the-way hot spring? Have you ever hiked to a fire tower or seen a footprint made by a dinosaur 150 million years ago? All these inspiring destinations can be goals for adventurous hikes and backpacking trips. When I lived in northern New Mexico, I would hike with a guidebook to Native American civilizations in one hand and a GPS device in the other—spending many weekends combining my love of history and the outdoors. If hiking from trailhead to trailhead isn't exciting anymore, find a purpose for being outside that you can be passionate about. And, in case you always wanted to be an archaeologist, now you can thanks to the U.S. Forest Service's Passport in Time (PIT) program. PIT matches volunteers to archaeological projects at Forest Service properties across the country. The program is free, and a complete list of projects can be found at passportintime.com.

Power to the Pedal

Traveling on two wheels—instead of two feet—is just another way to explore the outdoors. People who go on bike tours love the freedom of the open road, the ability to cover 50-plus miles a day, and the incredible scenery that rolls by. Some cyclists camp every night, loading their bikes with specialized bags that hold tents, sleeping bags, and cooking gear just like a backpacker.

Others follow the "credit card" method of staying in motels or bed-and-breakfasts. No matter where you choose to sleep, you'll find that bike touring is the perfect blend of traveling and sightseeing.

 Trail Tips To find a touring bike that fits you, straddle the frame with both feet flat on the ground. The ideal bike should have 2 to 3 inches of clearance between your body and the top tube—the horizontal tube between the handlebars and the seat post.

Joining an Organized Tour

Signing up for an organized bike tour lets the experts worry about the logistics, leaving you free to enjoy the ride. You can find tour companies in the classified advertisements at the back of magazines like *Outside* and *Bicycling*. Organized tours tend to focus on the most scenic routes like the Pacific Coast Highway in California. Other popular destinations include the Southwest, New England, and overseas trips to Europe, especially in bike-crazy Holland and France.

Cycling Solo

Planning a trip by yourself will keep costs lower and gives you the freedom to explore your own route at your own pace. Before you pick a destination, however, you need to determine what kind of tour experience you want. Bike tours can range from luxurious to primitive, so as you plan your trip, consider these questions:

◊ How many miles can you comfortably ride each day?

◊ Are you interested in the most direct route or the least congested route?

◊ What are you looking for: exercise, meeting people, scenic views, exploring the country?

◊ Do you want to camp or stay in motels or B&Bs?

◊ Do you want to cook or buy food in restaurants and diners?

Once you know your touring style, your next stop should be bike touring guidebooks for your chosen destination. Like hiking guides, these books provide ideas on where to go along with important maps and logistical details. The Adventure Cycling Association sells detailed guides for many popular regional and national bike trails. These guides include information on where to find bike repair shops, water sources, hot showers, and places to sleep. You can search for routes and download maps at the Adventure Cycling Association's website, adventurecycling.org.

Gearing Up for the Road

The most important piece of equipment for this sport is your bike, especially a bike that fits you and can hold everything you plan to carry. Dedicated touring bikes sport thicker tires and longer, stronger frames than road bikes, but they aren't quite as robust as mountain bikes. This hybrid design allows touring bikes to handle bumpy roads while maintaining some of the speed advantage of narrower tires.

Traveling by Canoe and Kayak

Lewis and Clark didn't walk from St. Louis to the Pacific Ocean. When they could, they traveled by river. Floating a river in a canoe or skirting the ocean shore in a sea kayak is a relaxing and efficient way to explore the outdoors. Not only do these methods allow you to carry more gear with less effort, but sometimes, you can rest your paddle and let the current carry you along.

Where You Can Float

The first place to look for routes is a canoeing or kayaking guidebook focused on waterways in your area. These books will inform you about boat put-ins, average water levels, sections of rapids, and campsite locations. You can also research trips at *Canoe & Kayak* magazine's website, canoekayak.com. Even if you don't own a canoe or kayak, many top paddling destinations have outfitters who rent boats and provide transportation to waterways.

Safety Check If you're new to paddling, stay close to shore where the winds and waves are usually calmer and it's easier to escape a sudden storm.

Outfitting Your Boat

All the gear you store in a canoe or kayak should be either able to get wet or secured inside a waterproof bag or container. Even if you don't flip your boat, splashing water will soak anything that's not protected. Here's how to keep it all dry:

◊ Pack all your gear in waterproof "dry bags." Fewer, larger dry bags work best for canoes, while multiple, smaller bags are ideal for stuffing inside a kayak's compartments.

◊ Store valuable gear like your cell phone, car keys, and wallet in a small waterproof bag and tie it to the boat.

◊ In canoes, buckle or rope in all dry bags, trunks, and loose gear to prevent them from shifting around or floating away if you capsize.

◊ Balance loads in between the two sides of a canoe, slightly weighted toward the stern. Place the heaviest items on the bottom and keep all loads below the level of the gunwales (the upper edges of a canoe).

SUMMARY

Adding a new challenge or skill will keep your outdoor adventures fresh and exciting. Jump on a bike or into a canoe to travel beyond the trail, or become an expert in wilderness first aid, wildlife photography, or winter camping to increase your confidence and ability to engage with nature. Once you become more experienced, one of the best things you can do is introduce the world of hiking and backpacking to a child or someone who wants to learn how to do it right.

GLOSSARY

10 essentials   The classic list of safety, navigation, and survival gear—from a map to a headlamp—that hikers should bring on every outing.

A-frame tent   A simple and often inexpensive A-shaped tent with a center ridge pole and limited interior space because of sloping walls and a peaked ceiling.

anaphylactic shock   A rapid and dangerous allergic reaction to a substance, usually insect venom or food, which causes immediate swelling of body tissues (including the throat), difficulty breathing, and a sudden drop in blood pressure.

backcountry areas   Remote regions inside parks and recreation districts with rugged trails and terrain, making them an adventurous place to backpack. Backcountry areas are also sometimes described as *wilderness areas*.

backpacking   A hiking trip that lasts longer than one day and requires camping out for at least one night in a tent, cabin, or lean-to.

bail-out route   A quick and direct way to leave a trail to reach a town, road, or other known place to make contact with civilization or emergency services.

base layer   An insulating layer of clothing, usually made of polypropylene, wool, or silk, worn closest to the skin.

bathtub floor   A tent feature in which the floor material curls up several inches along the tent sides to create a durable, waterproof bond to the walls.

bear bag A durable stuff sack used to store food and other odor-emitting gear to protect it from scavenging animals. Bear bags are normally hung at least 10 to 12 feet off the ground by hoisting the bag over a sturdy tree limb with a rope system.

bear canister A hard-sided plastic or metal container used to store food in areas where bear bags are unsuitable because of precocious bears or a lack of trees.

bearing A common navigational term associated with a compass, map, or GPS. A bearing is the direction (indicated by degrees) that an object or a location is in relation to your direction of travel. Often confused with *heading*.

blaze A marking or symbol that identifies a particular trail. Blazes are often painted or nailed to tree trunks at regular intervals along a trail.

bushwhack Off-trail travel that usually involves crashing through bushes and brambles and scrambling on difficult terrain.

cairn A small pile or pyramid of rocks used to indicate a trail. Often used at higher elevations and mountain ridges where few trees exist for marking blazes.

cat hole A small hole dug at least 8 inches deep by hikers to bury their human waste underground.

cell tower triangulation A search-and-rescue technique used to calculate the location of a lost hiker using a mobile phone. Cell phone signals are bounced off three or more cell towers to give emergency responders the approximate location of the caller.

compression straps Adjustable nylon straps on a backpack that compress and stabilize the load and allow additional gear to be attached to the exterior.

contour lines Thin squiggly lines on a topographical map that indicate a specific elevation and can help hikers determine the steepness of a trail or the location of terrain features.

day-hike A hiking trip you can complete in a single day without sleeping overnight along the trail.

declination A navigation term that describes the difference in degrees for a specific location between *magnetic north* (where the magnetic needle of a compass points) and *true north* (the geographic North Pole that aligns most maps). Declination varies from place to place and must be corrected when using a map and compass together.

DEET The active chemical ingredient in the most effective insect repellents. Higher percentages of DEET provide longer-lasting protection.

denier A number that indicates the durability of pack fabrics by measuring the thickness of individual nylon threads. The higher the denier number, the thicker the fiber. Most backpacks are made with 150- to 300-denier nylon, but ultralight packs feature 100-denier or less.

dome tent A popular freestanding tent design where the poles intersect over the top to create high-arching walls and a spacious interior.

DWR The abbreviation for *durable water repellent,* a term that describes a waterproof coating applied to the exterior surface of boots, jackets, and tents to prevent rain and moisture from saturating the fabric.

exposure A hiking term that describes a hiker's vulnerability to falling at a particular spot. The more exposure a trail has, the more likely and dangerous a fall would be.

four-season gear Any hiking equipment—especially tents and sleeping bags—designed to withstand the cold temperatures, snow, and strong winds of winter conditions.

freestanding tent A shelter that can be pitched without stakes because the pole structure naturally supports the inner canopy and rainfly. A freestanding system is helpful when camping on rock slabs where stakes can't be used.

full-grain leather The thickest most genuine type of nonprocessed leather used in hiking footwear. It is also the most durable and water-resistant material for footwear.

gaiters Flexible footwear coverings made from durable and sometimes waterproof nylon and designed to block rocks, sand, and moisture from getting inside boots. Low gaiters extend from the ankle to the shin, while high gaiters end just below the knee.

gearheads A nickname for people who are fascinated with reading about, buying, using, and customizing their backpacking and camping gear.

geocaching A popular outdoor sport for hikers that requires a GPS-enabled smartphone or device and navigational clues downloaded from an app or website to locate boxes of trinkets hidden in parks and other recreation areas.

Giardia lamblia A waterborne protozoan responsible for the majority of cases of diarrhea, fatigue, and stomach cramps among hikers. *Giardia* infections, also called *beaver fever*, are acquired by drinking contaminated water.

Gore-Tex The oldest and most well-known waterproof breathable membrane used in jackets and other garments that permits the evaporation of sweat but blocks outside moisture.

gorp The acronym for *good ol' raisins and peanuts*, a common trail snack made with those ingredients, plus fruit, nuts, chocolate, and many other foods defined by personal preference.

GPS (Global Positioning System) The satellite-based navigational system that pinpoints the coordinates, usually by latitude and longitude, of a smartphone, personal locator beacon, or handheld receiver anywhere on the globe to an accuracy of between 20 and 100 feet.

gray water Leftover water used for cooking, cleaning, or washing.

guylines Ropes or cords that hold down tents and other shelters to stakes embedded in the ground.

half-dome tent A freestanding tent design that utilizes a ridge pole to create steep side walls and substantial headroom, while remaining light and durable enough for backpacking.

heading   A common navigational term associated with a compass, map, or GPS. Your heading is the direction (indicated by degrees) that you are currently moving—your direction of travel. Often confused with *bearing*.

headlamp   A compact and adjustable light that wraps around your forehead with an elastic band.

hot spot   A red and painful skin irritation caused by excessive friction that develops just prior to a blister. Most hot spots and blisters occur on the heels and toes.

kindling   Small, dry sticks with diameters less than the width of your pointer finger used to start a campfire.

Leave No Trace (LNT)   An international outdoor movement that promotes leaving as small an impact on nature as you can by removing trash, burying waste, and being respectful of wildlife.

magnetic North Pole   A location in the Canadian Arctic where the magnetic needle of a compass points to. Different from *true north*, the geographic North Pole at the top of the globe that aligns most maps. Adjusting for *declination* reconciles the difference between these two locations for navigating with a map and compass.

natural spring   A drinkable water source created when an underground stream or river reaches the Earth's surface.

nubuck   A hiking footwear material made of full-grain leather with a top layer that has been brushed to create a softer fine-grain surface more durable than suede.

polypropylene   A synthetic polyester fabric, also called *polypro,* used to make outdoor apparel like base layers, T-shirts, and shorts.

rainfly   A waterproof tent covering that repels rain and snow using polyurethane or silicone-coated nylon.

repetition (rep)   While exercising, a single lift from start to finish.

ripstop nylon A durable fabric used to make backpacks where the threads are sewn in a crosshatched pattern to prevent holes and tears from expanding.

s'mores A popular and gooey campfire snack made by placing a roasted marshmallow and several pieces of milk chocolate between two graham crackers.

scale A navigational term that determines the level of map detail by defining how a distance measured on the map compares to a corresponding distance on the actual ground. Smaller scales, like 1:24,000, indicate more detailed maps than larger scales, like 1:75,000.

scree Small stony rock fragments that slide underfoot and are often found on steep slopes and ridges at high elevations. Often located near *talus.*

section hiking When hikers divide a long route (like the Appalachian Trail) into shorter segments that they complete over a series of multiple trips.

set While exercising, a series of reps or lifts followed by a short rest.

shakedown An important practice hike undertaken prior to the main trip to check your fitness level, test your gear, and make sure everything goes smoothly.

split-grain leather A hiking footwear material made with the inner more flexible layer of leather that has been split away from the durable top layer to create a thinner hide.

stuff sack A nylon bag used to store and pack compressible gear like a sleeping bag, tent, or clothing. Stuff sacks come in multiple sizes, and some are waterproof.

suede A hiking footwear material made of split-grain leather that has been buffed to create a smooth velvety surface.

summit fever When a hiker ignores dangerous weather conditions, timing, or terrain despite serious risks to themselves or others in their group.

switchback Zigzagging paths that reduce the slope of steep trails to make them easier to climb.

talus   Large unstable rocks and boulders that are often found on steep slopes and ridges at high elevations. Often located near *scree.*

three-season hiking   Any hiking that takes place in the spring, summer, and fall—but not the winter.

thru-hiker   A backpacker in the process of hiking a long-distance footpath, such as the 2,178-mile Appalachian Trail.

tincture of benzoin   A red liquid commonly found in first aid kits that improves the adhesion of tape and bandages and acts as a mild antiseptic.

torso length   The body measurement used to size and fit backpacks. It's the distance in inches between a person's C7 vertebra bulge at the back of the neck and the top of the hip bone.

trailhead   The starting point for a trail. Trailheads are usually located near a road, campground, or parking lot, and most have specific names and provide informational signs and maps. Some trailheads require hikers to register, sign a trail log, or pay parking fees.

true north   The geographic North Pole at the top of the globe that aligns most maps. Different from the *magnetic North Pole*, the location in the Canadian Arctic where compass needles point to. Adjusting for *declination* reconciles the difference between these two locations when navigating with a map and compass.

ultralight backpacking   A popular hiking philosophy that emphasizes carrying extremely light loads, with full backpacks often weighing 20 pounds or less.

vestibule   A gear storage area for tents covered by the rainfly but outside the main part of the tent.

widowmaker   A dead branch or tree that looms above a campsite and could fall during a wind or rainstorm.

RESOURCES

Books

Auerbach, Paul S. *Medicine for the Outdoors: The Essential Guide to First Aid and Medical Emergencies, 6th ed.* New York: Saunders, 2015.

Auerbach, Paul S., Tracy A. Cushing, and N. Stuart Harris. *Auerbach's Wilderness Medicine, 7th ed.* Amsterdam: Elsevier, 2016.

Berger, Karen. *A Trailside Guide: Hiking and Backpacking.* New York: W.W. Norton & Co., 2003.

Bryson, Bill. *A Walk in the Woods: Rediscovering America on the Appalachian Trail, 2nd ed.* New York: Anchor, 2006.

Conners, Christine, and Tim Conners. *Lipsmackin' Backpackin': Lightweight Trail-tested Recipes for Backcountry Trips, 3rd ed.* Lanham, MD: Falcon Guides, 2018.

Fletcher, Colin, and Chip Rawlings. *The Complete Walker IV.* New York: Knopf, 2002.

Kirkconnell, Sarah Svien. *Freezer Bag Cooking: Trail Food Made Simple.* Morrisville, NC: Lulu.com, 2007.

Krakauer, Jon. *Into the Wild.* New York: Anchor, 2007.

———. *Into Thin Air: A Personal Account of the Mt. Everest Disaster, reprint ed.* New York: Anchor, 1999.

Ladigin, Don. *Lighten Up! A Complete Handbook for Light and Ultralight Backpacking.* Lanham, MD: Falcon Guides, 2005.

Linxweiler, Eric, and Mike Maude, editors. *Mountaineering: The Freedom of the Hills, 9th ed.* Seattle: Mountaineers Books, 2017.

Nielson, Emily, and Aimee Trudeau. *Dirty Gourmet: Food for Your Outdoor Adventures.* Griffin, GA: Skipstone, 2018.

Schimelpfenig, Tod, and Joan Safford. *NOLS Wilderness Medicine, 6th ed.* Mechanicsburg, PA: Stackpole Books, 2016.

Simpson, Joe. *Touching the Void: The True Story of One Man's Miraculous Survival, revised ed.* New York: Perennial, 2004.

Skurka, Andrew. *The Ultimate Hiker's Gear Guide: Tools and Techniques to Hit the Trail, 2nd ed.* Washington, D.C.: National Geographic, 2017.

Smith, Dave. *Backcountry Bear Basics: The Definitive Guide to Avoiding Unpleasant Encounters, 2nd ed.* Seattle: Mountaineers Books, 2006.

Townsend, Chris. *The Backpacker's Handbook, 4th ed.* New York: International Marine/Ragged Mountain Press, 2011.

Yaffe, Linda Frederick. *Backpack Gourmet: Good Hot Grub You Can Make at Home, Dehydrate, and Pack for Quick, Easy, and Healthy Eating on the Trail, 2nd ed.* Mechanicsburg, PA: Stackpole Books, 2014.

Regional/State Hiking Guides

50 Hikes Series (Countryman Press, countrymanpress.com)

100 Classic Hikes Series (Mountaineers Books, mountaineersbooks.org)

Best Hikes with Dogs (Mountaineers Books, mountaineersbooks.org)

Hiking Guides (Falcon Guides, falcon.com)

Magazines

Backpacker
backpacker.com

Backpacking Light
backpackinglight.com

Bicycling
bicycling.com

Canoe & Kayak (Adventure Sports Network)
canoekayak.com

Outside
outsideonline.com

Websites, Apps, and Trail Maps

Website	App	Find Trails	Download Offline Maps	Trail Reviews
backpacker.com/trips (*Backpacker* magazine)	ViewRanger	Free	Yes	No
alltrails.com	AllTrails	Free	Subscription	Yes
hikingproject.com	Hiking Project	Free	Yes	Yes
gaiagps.com	Gaia GPS	Free	Subscription	Yes

Hiking Partners

Adventurers Meetup
adventurers.meetup.com

Fitness Singles
fitness-singles.com

GoSporty
GoSporty.com

HikerSingles
hikersingles.com

OutdoorDuo
outdoorduo.com

Trail Organizations (State/Region)

Adirondack Mountain Club (New York)
adk.org

Appalachian Mountain Club (mid-Atlantic, New England)
outdoors.org

Colorado Mountain Club (Colorado)
cmc.org

Florida Trail Association (Florida)
floridatrail.org

Green Mountain Club (Vermont)
greenmountainclub.org

The Mountaineers (Pacific Northwest)
mountaineers.org

NY-NJ Trail Conference (New York, New Jersey)
mynjtc.org

Potomac Appalachian Trail Club (mid-Atlantic)
patc.org

Sierra Club (National)
sierraclub.org

Wasatch Mountain Club (Utah)
wasatchmountainclub.org

Gear Stores

Backcountry.com
Backcountry.com

Cabela's
cabelas.com

Campmor
Campmor.com

Eastern Mountain Sports (EMS)
EMS.com

L.L. Bean
LLBean.com

MountainGear.com
MountainGear.com

Recreational Equipment, Inc. (REI)
REI.com

Sierra Trading Post
sierratradingpost.com

Gear Review Websites

Backpacker.com/gear

BackpackGearTest.org

Outsideonline.com/outdoor-gear

Outdoorgearlab.com

Gear Review YouTube Channels

Darwin onthetrail

TheOutdoorGearReview

Topographical Maps

MyTopo.com
mytopo.com
1-877-587-9004

National Geographic Trails Illustrated
natgeomaps.com
1-800-962-1643

United States Geological Survey (USGS)
store.usgs.gov
1-888-ASK-USGS (1-888-275-8747)

Recreation Areas

Bureau of Land Management
blm.gov
202-208-3801

National Park Service
nps.gov
Interactive Map: nps.gov/findapark
202-208-6843

Parks Canada
www.pc.gc.ca
Interactive Map: pc.gc.ca/en/voyage-travel
1-888-773-8888
1-877-737-3783 (Reservations)

U.S. Forest Service
fs.usda.gov
1-800-832-1355

Campgrounds

Bureau of Land Management (BLM)
Public campgrounds
blm.gov

Campendium.com
Boondock (remote) campgrounds
campendium.com

KOA (Kampgrounds of America)
Private campgrounds
koa.com

National Park Service
Park campgrounds
nps.gov/findapark

Recreation.gov
Federal campgrounds
recreation.gov

Reserve America
Public and private campgrounds
reserveamerica.com

TheDyrt.com
Boondock (remote) campgrounds
thedyrt.com

U.S. Forest Service
fs.usda.gov
1-800-832-1355

Campground Reviews

CampgroundReviews
Private and RV campgrounds
campgroundreviews.com

Google.com
All types of campgrounds
google.com

TheDyrt.com
Tent sites and car camping
thedyrt.com

TripAdvisor
Private and public campgrounds
tripadvisor.com

EQUIPMENT CHECKLISTS

Day-Hiking

- ○ Hiking boots, trail runners, or trail shoes
- ○ Daypack
- ○ Wool or synthetic socks
- ○ Map
- ○ Compass
- ○ Cell phone
- ○ GPS with extra batteries (optional)
- ○ Headlamp with extra batteries
- ○ Water bottles or hydration bladder
- ○ Lunch and snack food
- ○ First aid kit (see detailed list later in this appendix)
- ○ Multitool/utility knife
- ○ Whistle
- ○ Signal mirror
- ○ Butane lighter or fire starter
- ○ Flammable tinder
- ○ Wool or fleece hat
- ○ Sunscreen (SPF 30+)
- ○ Bandanna
- ○ Insect repellent (at least 30 percent DEET)
- ○ Synthetic shorts or trekking pants
- ○ Synthetic T-shirt
- ○ Synthetic underwear
- ○ Rain jacket or windproof shell
- ○ Insulating fleece or long-sleeve top

Backpacking

Clothing

- ○ Hiking boots, trail runners, or trail shoes
- ○ Camp shoes or sandals
- ○ Wool or synthetic socks
- ○ Synthetic underwear
- ○ Synthetic shorts or trekking pants
- ○ Synthetic T-shirts
- ○ Rain jacket or windproof shell
- ○ Insulating fleece or long-sleeve top
- ○ Fleece or wool sweater
- ○ Wool or fleece hat
- ○ Lightweight synthetic gloves or mittens
- ○ Bandanna
- ○ Sunglasses
- ○ Gaiters (optional)
- ○ Rain pants (optional)
- ○ Insulated hiking boots (winter)
- ○ Down booties (winter)
- ○ Expedition-weight long underwear (winter)
- ○ Water-resistant synthetic or soft-shell hiking pants (winter)
- ○ Fleece pants (fall, winter)
- ○ Insulated parka or jacket (winter)
- ○ Heavyweight waterproof gloves or mittens (winter)
- ○ Balaclava (winter, optional)

Shelter

- ○ Three-season tent with rainfly and footprint
- ○ Internal or external frame backpack
- ○ Three-season down or synthetic sleeping bag (rated 40°F or lower)
- ○ Foam or inflatable sleeping pad

○ Four-season or convertible tent (winter)
○ Down or synthetic sleeping bag (in winter, rated at least 0°F)

Kitchen Gear

○ Backpacking stove (white gas or canister) and fuel
○ Jetboil-style canister stove (ultralight)
○ Cook kit (pots, pans)
○ Mess kit (plates, bowls)
○ Water bottles or hydration bladders
○ Cooking and eating utensils
○ Insulated mug
○ Butane lighter or fire starter
○ Flammable tinder
○ Water filter, purifier, or chemical treatment
○ Food
○ Snacks
○ White-gas stove and liquid fuel bottle (winter)
○ Insulated water bottle sleeves (winter)
○ Insulated hydration tube sleeve (winter)

Camp Gear

○ Multitool or knife
○ Headlamp with extra batteries
○ Map
○ Compass
○ Cell phone
○ GPS with extra batteries (optional)
○ Whistle
○ Foldable solar panel and rechargeable battery (optional)
○ Signal mirror
○ Zipper-lock plastic bags
○ Sunscreen (SPF 30+)

- ◯ Insect repellent (at least 30 percent DEET)
- ◯ Toothbrush and toothpaste
- ◯ Biodegradable soap
- ◯ Microfiber pack towel
- ◯ Duct tape (wrapped around water bottle or trekking poles)
- ◯ Gear repair kit
- ◯ Bear-bag nylon rope (50–100 feet), carabiner, and stuff sack (or bear canister)
- ◯ Toilet paper and plastic trowel
- ◯ Trekking poles (optional)
- ◯ Chemical heat packs (winter)
- ◯ Snowshoes (winter)

First Aid Kit

- ◯ Adhesive bandages: butterfly and rectangular
- ◯ Stretch bandages
- ◯ Sterile gauze pads
- ◯ Wound closure strips
- ◯ Adhesive tape
- ◯ Cotton swabs
- ◯ Painkillers (Advil, Aleve, or Motrin)
- ◯ Benadryl
- ◯ Antidiarrhea medicine (Imodium A-D)
- ◯ Tincture of benzoin
- ◯ Moleskin or Second Skin
- ◯ Antibiotic ointment
- ◯ Burn salve or aloe vera skin lotion
- ◯ Oral rehydration salts
- ◯ Sugary drink packets
- ◯ Moist towelettes or baby wipes
- ◯ Quart-sized zipper-lock plastic bags
- ◯ EpiPen (optional)
- ◯ SAM splint (optional)

INDEX